WRITERS

EXPRESS

A Handbook for
YOUNG WRITERS, THINKERS, AND LEARNERS

Written and Compiled by
Dave Kemper, Ruth Nathan, Patrick Sebranek

Illustrated by Chris Krenzke

WRITE SOURCE

GREAT SOURCE EDUCATION GROUP
a Houghton Mifflin Company
Wilmington, Massachusetts

Acknowledgements

We're grateful to many people who helped bring *Writers Express* to life. First, we must thank all the students from across the country who've contributed their writing and their ideas.

Also, thanks to some of our favorite authors and teachers who helped make *Writers Express* a reality.

Sandy Asher for *Writing Realistic Stories* and *Writing Plays*
Nancy Bond for *Writing Fantasies*
Roy Peter Clark for *Writing Newspaper Stories*
Will Hobbs for *Revising Your Writing*
Toby Fulwiler for *Writing as a Learning Tool*
Stephen Krensky for *Writing Stories from History*
Gloria Nixon-John for *Giving Speeches*
Susan Ohanian for *Writing Tall Tales*
Anne-Marie Oomen for *Writing Poems*
Marie Ponsot for *Sharing Family Stories*
Peter and Connie Roop for *Writing a Classroom Report*
Paula and Keith Stanovich for *Building Vocabulary Skills*
Lorraine Sintetos for *Writing Riddles*
Peter Stillman for *Writing for Fun*
Charles Temple for *Becoming a Better Speller* and *Writing Songs*
Toni Walters for *Using Reading Strategies*
Allan Wolf for *Performing Poems*

Another thank-you goes to our team of educators, editors, and designers: Laura Bachman, Laurie Cooper, Marguerite Cotto, Carol Elsholz, Tom Gilding, Julie Janosz, Beverly Jessen, Kathy Juntunen, Lois Krenzke, Heather Monkmeyer, Candyce Norvell, Sherry Schenning-Gordon, Ed Schuster, Linda Sivy, and Sandy Wagner.

Printed in the United States of America

International Standard Book Number: 0-669-38633-2 (hardcover) 0-669-38632-4 (softcover)

12 13 14 15 -RRDC- 01 00 99 98 97

Express Yourself!

Writers Express is divided into five major parts . . .

1 **The Process of Writing** ● Use this section to answer your questions about writing, from selecting a subject to proofreading a final draft.

2 **The Forms of Writing** ● Would you like to start a personal journal, or write a poem, or create a tall tale? Then this section is for you!

3 **The Tools of Learning** ● If your study, reading, or test-taking skills could use a little pumping up, turn to "The Tools of Learning."

4 **The Proofreader's Guide** ● Have a question about punctuation? Spelling? Capitalization? Here's where you can "Check It Out!"

5 **The Student Almanac** ● Full-color maps, a historical time line, the metric system— Writers Express is truly an all-school handbook!

Table of Contents

The Process of Writing

The Forms of Writing

The Tools of Learning

The Proofreader's Guide

The Student Almanac

The Process of Writing

Getting Started

3 All About Writing
8 One Writer's Process
12 A Basic Writing Guide
16 Writing with a Computer
18 Planning Your Portfolio

Prewriting and Drafting Guide

24 Building a File of Writing Ideas
26 Selecting a Subject
28 Starting Points for Writing
30 Collecting Details
32 Planning and Drafting Tips
34 Building a Resource of Writing Forms

Revising and Editing Guide

37 Revising Your Writing
42 Conferencing with Partners
46 Sharing Family Stories
50 Editing and Proofreading
54 Publishing Your Writing

Building Paragraphs and Essays

59 Writing Paragraphs
72 Writing Essays
78 A Writing Sampler

Improving Your Writing Skills

85 Writing Basic Sentences
90 Combining Sentences
94 Writing with Style
96 Modeling the Masters
98 Writing Terms

The Forms of Writing

Personal Writing

105 Writing in Journals
110 Writing Personal Narratives
116 Writing Friendly Letters

Subject Writing

123 Writing Newspaper Stories
132 Writing Book Reviews
138 Writing Explanations
142 Writing Business Letters
148 Writing Observation Reports

Writing Tales and Stories

153 Writing Fantasies
160 Writing Tall Tales
164 Writing Realistic Stories
170 Writing Stories from History

Writing Poems, Plays, and Songs

177 Writing Poems
188 Writing Songs
192 Writing Plays
198 Writing Riddles
202 Writing for Fun

Research Writing

207 Using the Library
216 Writing a Summary
220 Writing a Classroom Report

The Tools of Learning

Improving Your Reading
237 Using Reading Strategies
246 Reading Pictures

Improving Your Spelling and Vocabulary
255 Building Vocabulary Skills
270 Becoming a Better Speller

Improving Your Speaking and Listening
275 Giving Speeches
282 Performing Poems
288 Improving Viewing Skills
292 Improving Listening Skills

Improving Your Thinking
295 Getting Organized
300 Thinking and Writing
308 Thinking Clearly

Improving Your Learning Skills
315 Writing as a Learning Tool
318 Completing Assignments
322 Working in Groups
328 Taking Tests
336 Keeping Good Notes

Proofreader's Guide: Check It Out

Marking Punctuation

- **343** Period
- **344** Ellipsis
- **345** Comma
- **347** Semicolon, Colon
- **348** Hyphen, Dash
- **349** Apostrophe
- **350** Quotation Marks, Question Mark
- **351** Exclamation Point, Italics, Parentheses

Editing for Mechanics

- **352** Capitalization
- **355** Plurals
- **356** Numbers, Abbreviations

Checking Your Spelling

- **358** Commonly Misspelled Words

Using the Right Word

- **362** Commonly Misused Words

Understanding Sentences

- **371** Parts of a Sentence
- **372** Clauses and Phrases
- **373** Types of Sentences

Understanding Our Language

- **375** Noun
- **377** Pronoun
- **380** Verb
- **384** Adjective
- **385** Adverb
- **386** Preposition
- **387** Interjection
- **387** Conjunction

The Student Almanac

Useful Tables and Lists

391 Sign Language
392 Foreign Words
393 Animal Facts
394 The Metric System
395 American to Metric Table
396 Conversion Table
397 Additional Units of Measure
398 Planet Profiles

Using Maps

400 All About Maps
403 Maps
413 Index to Maps

Improving Math Skills

416 Solving Word Problems
420 Symbols, Numbers, and Tables
422 Computer Keyboard

History in the Making

424 U.S. Constitution
428 U.S. Presidents
430 Historical Time Line

Index

440 Your Handbook Index

Why Write?

A Note from the Editors

Not too long ago, in a not too faraway place, a bunch of friends got together during summer vacation and started a newspaper. *King's Cove* they called it, after a park in their neighborhood. Each issue was filled with the local gossip, the latest jokes, lists of stuff for sale, and the names of good books to read. Some writers added stories; others wrote poems. A few wrote basic news reports.

Why did these friends go to all of this trouble and do all of this writing? Why not just hang out and goof around? If you were to ask them, you might be surprised by their answers.

Summer Fun

First, they'd tell you writing a newspaper was fun! Yes, it was a lot of work; but in school they had a classroom newspaper, and it was just plain fun to see their ideas and names in print.

Feeling Good

Second, they would tell you it felt terrific working as a team, helping each other out. And third, they would admit that having the other kids read the newspaper gave them a feeling of pride. They were **being heard** and **feeling useful**.

Why write? This group of young writers, in talking about *King's Cove,* offered some very good answers. They wrote to have fun, to work together, and to be heard. We could not have said it better ourselves.

> 66 *Writing blows me away! Each time I write, I realize I know more than I thought. Cool ideas pop up out of nowhere.* 99
> —Chris, *King's Cove* writer

The Express Connection

We've created *Writers Express* to help make writing an important part of your life, no matter if you are completing assignments in school or working on writing projects in your own neighborhood. Many writers, teachers, and students from across the country have helped put this handbook together, and it is loaded with all kinds of great writing ideas.

Always have your copy of *Writers Express* right next to you when you write. Then turn to it for help whenever you have any questions about your work.

Once you get to know the handbook better, you will see that it is a writing guide plus much more. It contains information that will help you become a better reader, thinker, speaker, learner, and all-around student. Not bad for one little book!

> 66 Why write? Maybe we should ask, Why write and read and think and speak and learn? We hope you find many answers to either question in Writers Express—and we hope that you have a lot of fun along the way. 99
> —The Editors

The Process of Writing

Getting Started

All About Writing

One Writer's Process

A Basic Writing Guide

Writing with a Computer

Planning Your Portfolio

All About Writing

Wishful Thinking

Let's say that you plot out your next writing assignment on your special computer pad, like this:

Subject:	Class elections
Purpose:	To report on election results
Form:	News story
Audience:	Students at Pitts Elementary

Then you plug your keyboard into the pad, set it on automatic pilot, and eat a piece of pizza or read a good book while your story is being written. This would take all of the work and worry out of writing. By pressing a few buttons, your writing would come out just the way you ordered it, every time.

The Real Story

As you probably know, such a gizmo has not been invented yet. For now, and for years to come, you will have to work very closely with your writing to make sure it is done right. You, and *only you*, are in control of the words and ideas you put on paper. And this is exactly how it should be. Writing is too important to be left in the "hands" of a machine.

Points to Remember

The ideas listed below will help you understand what writing is really all about.

✔ *Writing is a natural thing to do.*

All of us have the ability to write (even without the help of a special computer pad). This is especially true when you write to learn and to explore your own thoughts and feelings.

✔ *Writing is a lot of different things, and all of them are important.*

Writing is thinking on paper. Writing is learning new things. Writing is making contact with friends and family members. Writing is dealing with bad days, and much more.

> ❝*I have found another side of myself that I've never known before. When I leave 5th grade, I'm not going to stop writing because I don't want to close up a world that I just unlocked.*❞
>
> —Heidi Bimschleger, grade 5

✔ *Writing is a process.*

Your favorite writers do a lot of planning, writing, and rewriting to produce the books and stories you like to read. That is why writing is called a process. It's very important for young writers like you to understand and use this process in your own writing. (You will learn more about the writing process on the next pages.)

✔ *Writing is a skill that must be practiced.*

Your handbook says a lot of good things about writing. But there is really only one way to learn how to write, and that is by actually putting pen or pencil to paper, or fingers to the keyboard. That's why it is important to practice all kinds of writing: journal writing, story writing, report writing, and so on. (Even writing notes to friends is good practice.)

The Steps in the Process

When we talk about the writing process, we really mean the steps a writer usually follows whenever he or she writes. We have divided the writing process into the following basic steps:

PREWRITING refers to selecting a subject, collecting details, and any other planning that goes on during a writing project.

WRITING THE FIRST DRAFT refers to the actual writing, when a writer gets all of his or her ideas on paper. (Writers often write more than one draft.)

REVISING refers to the changes a writer makes to improve his or her writing. Ideas may be added, cut, or switched around; sentences may be cut or rewritten.

EDITING & PROOFREADING refers to all of the final changes made in the revised writing. During this step, writing is checked carefully for errors.

PUBLISHING

There is one more important step in the process—publishing. Sharing your story with friends or classmates is one form of publishing; so is sending it to the school or city newspaper. You will naturally work harder at your writing if you know that it is going to be published. (**SEE** pages 54-57 for more information.)

THINK IT OVER

A writer may repeat some of these steps before a piece of writing is finished. For example, after the first draft, a writer may decide to do some more prewriting and planning.

The Writing Process in Action

These two pages provide a basic look at the writing process in action. You will find this information helpful if you have never used the writing process before or if you would like a general guide to follow when you write.

PREWRITING

Prewriting means getting ready to write. Follow these basic steps during prewriting:

- **Select** a subject that really interests you.
- **Collect** details about your subject if you don't know a lot about it.
- **Plan** what you want to say about your subject (the main idea of your writing) and how you want to say it (the form of your writing).

WRITING THE FIRST DRAFT

Once you've collected your thoughts about your subject, write the first draft of your paper.

- **Write** this draft freely, getting *all* of your ideas on paper.
- **Imagine** that you are talking to a group of friends.
- **Let** your prewriting and planning be your guide as you write.

REVISING

When you revise, you try to make improvements in your draft. Follow this basic revising plan:

- **Read** your draft two or three times.

- **Ask** at least one classmate or friend to read and react to your draft.

- **Decide** what changes need to be made.

- **Work** on improving your writing.

EDITING & PROOFREADING

When you edit and proofread, you make sure the revised version of your writing is clear and accurate. Follow this basic editing and proofreading plan:

- **Look** closely at the style of your writing. (Your words and sentences should read smoothly.)

- **Check** your writing for spelling, punctuation, and grammar errors. (Ask for help from a classmate or teacher.)

- **Write or type** a neat final draft of your writing.

- **Proofread** this draft for any additional errors.

One Writer's Process

One Step at a Time

For one of her assignments, Hillary Bachman was asked to write about her favorite teacher. Here's how she used the writing process to complete her assignment.

PREWRITING *Planning Your Way*

Selecting a Subject ● Hillary started by thinking about all of her favorite teachers, past and present. She thought of Mrs. Thompson, Mr. Schwarz, Mrs. Bolstad, and Mr. Vetter. The one teacher that really stood out was Mr. Vetter, so she decided to write about him.

Collecting Details ● She then freely listed ideas about her subject.

funny, nice, helpful, coach, two boys my age, helps students, friend, room 203, math, fun learning, answers questions, laughs, tells us jokes, we learn, sees when I'm upset, called Mr. V, . . .

WRITING THE FIRST DRAFT

Mr. Vetter was one of Hillary's current teachers, so she had no trouble writing about him. This is part of her first draft.

Hillary starts with words from her collecting list. →

She continues by writing freely about her subject. →

A Great Teacher

Funny, helpful, and friendly. What am I describing? Is it one of your classmates or your best friend? Beleive it or not, I'm describing a teacher! His name is Mr. Vetter. We call him Mr. V.

One thing that really like about him is the way he makes learning fun.

If math seams boring, he will make it fun by saying something that is so funny so you want to learn. Once I sneezed really loud in the middle of class. Right away, Mr. V. said "googolplex*." It sounded just the same as gesundheit or bless you.

Mr. V. also...

*Googolplex refers to a very large number.

REVISING *Improving the Writing*

After reviewing her first draft, Hillary tried to make her writing clearer and more complete. (The comments on the right side of her paper were made by a classmate.)

Who is

A Great Teacher *?*

Hillary changes the first line into a question.

Funny, helpful, and friendly. ~~What am I~~

describing? Is it one of ~~your~~ *my* classmates or ~~your~~ *my*

best friend? Beleive it or not, I'm describing ~~a~~ *my math*

teacher! His name is Mr. Vetter. We call him Mr. V.

One thing that really like about him is the

way he makes learning fun.   *Why is this sentence all alone?*

If math seams boring, he will make it fun by

She rewrites a wordy sentence.

saying something ~~that is~~ so funny so ~~you~~ *we* want to

learn. Once I sneezed really loud in the middle

of class. Right away, Mr. V. said "googolplex." It

sounded just the same as gesundheit or bless you.

Good example!

Mr. V. also...

EDITING & PROOFREADING

Hillary then made sure that her writing read smoothly and was free of errors. She paid special attention to spelling and punctuation. (She would check for errors one more time after writing a neat final draft of her paper.)

A Great Teacher

Who is funny, helpful, and friendly? Is it one of my classmates or my best friend? Beleive it or not, I'm describing my math teacher! His name is Mr. Vetter, but we We call him Mr. V.

One thing that I really like about him is the way he makes learning fun. If math seems seams boring, he will say something funny so we want to learn. Once I sneezed really loud in the middle of class. Right away, Mr. V. said "googolplex." It sounded just the same as gesundheit or bless you.

Mr. V. also . . .

Hillary combines two sentences for smooth reading.

A comma and capital letter are added to the dialogue.

A Basic Writing Guide

Seven Secrets to Success

1 What should I write about?

Repeat this line after me: *I will write about a subject that really interests or excites me.* Say it again. Let this point be your guide each time you start a new writing project.

> **"**Writing has never been my best friend. I always thought it was hard, but now I'm able to pick better topics that I enjoy, and I have grown to love it. **"**
>
> —Shaun McDonnell, grade 5

See what I mean? Writing about something that interests you can make all the difference! It's what writing is all about.

When you can't think of anything to write about, complete one of the selecting activities listed on pages 26-27.

2 Do I have to collect a lot of details before I write?

That depends on the type of writing you are doing. If you're writing about a personal experience (like your first sleep-over), all of the important facts and details may be very clear to you. So you're probably ready to start your first draft right away.

But let's say you decide to write a classroom report about old-time movie monsters. You would have to collect quite a bit of information about this subject before you would be ready to write.

You can start your collecting by talking to someone about your subject or by writing down what you already know about it. Then you can go on from there by reading and trying other collecting activities.

SEE pages 30-31 for basic guidelines and activities to help you collect details for your writing.

3 Should I say everything I know about my subject?

No, your writing would probably go on and on if you say *everything* about it. So you have to think of some way to keep it under control. You can decide what your readers *really* need to know about your subject, and write just that information.

In addition, you can think of a focus, or main idea, for your writing. A focus may be a special feeling that you have about a subject, or it may be a certain part of a subject that you really want to talk about. For example, in a story about your best friend, you could focus on one of his or her important personality traits, like *kindness* or *loyalty*.

SEE page 32 for more information about planning your writing.

4 How should I write my first draft?

Write your first draft freely and honestly, as if you were telling it to a group of friends. Don't worry about making mistakes or using your best penmanship. In a first draft, you can cross out words, write in the margins, draw arrows, and so on. Remember that first drafts are often called *rough drafts*.

Also, don't worry about saying too much or too little about your subject. A first draft is only your first look at a writing idea; you will make changes later. If you have planning notes or a basic outline, use it as a guide when you write.

SEE page 33 for more on writing first drafts.

5 How do I know what changes to make in my first draft?

You are the best judge of your own writing. If important details seem to be missing, add them. If a certain part doesn't sound right, fix it. But it is also very important to have at least one or two classmates review your work. They may catch some important things that you didn't see.

When you revise, look first at the main points in your writing. Make sure that they are clear and complete. Once all of these ideas are in order, then look at more specific things like word choice and spelling.

SEE pages 37-41 for more information about revising writing.

6 Do I have to find all of the spelling and grammar errors in my writing?

Let's put it this way: No one expects you to be an expert speller or a master of all of the mechanics and grammar rules. But *everyone* expects you to correct as many errors as you can before you publish or share a piece of writing. Writing that contains a lot of errors is hard to read.

Find as many errors as you can on your own. For example, you can make sure that each of your sentences begins with a capital letter and ends with a period. Then ask a classmate or your teacher to check your work. (All professional writers have editors who help them edit and proofread their work.)

SEE pages 50-53 for more information on editing and proofreading.

7 How do I know if my writing is good?

Here is a quick and simple way to evaluate your writing. If you can nod your head after at least three of these questions, you should feel good about your work.

_____ *Did you select a subject that really interests you?*

_____ *Did you think of a special way to write about this subject?*

_____ *Did you make changes in your writing until it said what you wanted it to say?*

_____ *Did you share your work during the writing process?*

SEE page 45 for a basic checklist that will help you evaluate your writing.

Writing with a Computer

Tools of the Trade

People simply can't work or play without the right tools. A family doctor couldn't carry out an examination without a stethoscope or tongue depressor (say ahhh!). A mechanic without socket wrenches and screwdrivers might as well close up shop. A spelunker, someone who explores caves, would be lost without a flashlight and hard hat.

> Until you become quick on the keyboard, the personal computer will probably be most helpful to you as a revising and editing tool.

All "Keyed Up"

One tool that many writers could not do without is the **personal computer**. Writers will tell you that a computer allows them to say a lot in a short amount of time. They will also tell you that revising and editing first drafts is very easy on the computer.

Coming On-Line

Even if you don't have your own computer, your school is (or soon will be) equipped with them. If you are just learning to use a computer, the following comments about computers and writing will be helpful.

Know Who's in Control ➤ A computer can't think for you (not yet anyway), and it can't write for you. You still have to come up with all of the words and ideas.

Know When to Use Your Computer ➤ Don't put your pencils and paper away once you start using a computer (unless you are a keyboard wizard). You may want to do your planning and first drafts on paper. Then enter or type your work on the computer. At that point, you can make revising and editing changes on the computer screen or on a neat computer printout.

Know What Your Computer Can Do ➤ Word processing programs make a computer the high-tech writing machine it is. All programs allow you to enter your writing on the computer and work with it in many different ways. You can add or cut ideas and move parts around. You can check your work for spelling errors, and so on. (**SEE** the Bright Idea below.)

Learn the Golden Rule ➤ Expect to lose one of the first few assignments you write on a computer, even if you are very careful. It happens to everyone. Remember the golden rule of the computer age: *Always make a backup copy of your work.*

Learn How to Keyboard ➤ Practice keyboarding as often as you can—before, during, and after school. The faster you get, the more you will like using a computer. (**SEE** pages 422-423 for illustrations that will help you with this skill.)

Bright IDEA

To learn how your word processing program works, enter an old story or paragraph into the computer. Then practice making changes in your writing. (When you get stuck, refer to the program manual or ask a friend or classmate for help.)

Planning Your Portfolio

Organizing Your Own Writing

All writers keep a special collection of their work in a three-ring binder, in file folders, or in some other type of organizer. A collection like this is called a **personal portfolio**. My portfolio is in a three-ring binder, but I think of it more as a treasure chest— probably because all of the writing it contains is very special to me.

One Writer's Portfolio

I've divided my portfolio into four sections: *new ideas, important drafts, writing just for me,* and *finished writing.* You can learn more about the different sections in my personal portfolio on the next page.

> 66 *Your portfolio represents your work as a writer. The pieces you include in it should say something about your personal talents and your writing process.* 99
> —Anne-Marie Oomen

Personal Portfolio Model

Notice that my portfolio is basically organized according to the steps in the writing process.

New Ideas ● In this part of my portfolio, I collect interesting thoughts and descriptions scribbled on notebook paper, dinner napkins, and so on. I go to this section whenever I need ideas for writing.

Important Drafts ● This section includes writing projects that are almost finished. In one case, I may need to talk to someone about the writing. In another case, I may just need to get away from the writing for a while.

Writing Just for Me ● The writing in this section has great personal value to me, but I will never try to publish any of it. Included here are personal letters and special pages from my journal. Sometimes ideas for new writing projects come to mind as I reread this section.

Finished Writing ● I've taken all of these pieces through the entire writing process. They are as good as I can make them. Some of this work has already been published, and some of it I am still trying to get into print.

New Ideas

Important Drafts

Just for Me

Finished Writing

Bright IDEA

You might want to divide your personal portfolio according to the different types of writing you like to do: *poems, stories, plays,* and *letters.* Or you might want to divide it by different audiences: *personal and private, family, friends,* and so on. It's your choice.

Preparing a Classroom Portfolio

If you do a lot of writing in your class, your teacher may ask you to put together a portfolio of your work at the end of the grading period. For a basic introduction to the classroom portfolio, read the next two pages.

What is a classroom writing portfolio?

A classroom portfolio is a collection of the best writing you choose to turn in for evaluation. It will also contain basic self-evaluation sheets related to your writing, and maybe a few other things. (Your teacher will provide you with the self-evaluation sheets.)

How is a classroom portfolio different from a basic writing folder?

A writing folder contains all of your in-class writing, from old assignments to the latest story you are working on. A portfolio, on the other hand, contains only your best efforts.

Why would your teacher ask you to put together a portfolio?

Your teacher knows that a classroom portfolio makes the writing process much more real and meaningful for you. You are, after all, going to be judged on the writing *you* decide to include in your portfolio.

❝*I used to think of writing as my most dreaded fear. Now it's what I look forward to . . . When I look over my work, I feel honored that I wrote it.*❞

—Kristen Tomlinson, grade 5

What will you include?

Your teacher will make it very clear what your portfolio should contain. He or she will tell you how many pieces to include, what types of writing you can choose from, and when your portfolio must be ready.

What is the most important thing to remember about a writing portfolio?

A writing portfolio is the story of your writing experiences. If you put forth your best efforts, your portfolio will be a success.

Planning Tips

Be Prepared ● It's up to you to understand *all* of the requirements for your portfolio, including what it should contain and what it should look like. (Teachers usually provide special portfolio folders, but you might be able to design your own.)

Stay Organized ● Never, ever lose any of the drafts for writing you are going to include in your portfolio. (We will personally give you six lashes with a wet noodle for each draft you lose.)

Keep on Schedule ● Don't wait to the last minute to complete your writing or other parts of your portfolio. (Remember that it takes time to produce your best efforts.)

Ask for Help ● When you have questions about anything, ask your teacher and classmates for help. (Don't be bashful with something as important as a writing portfolio.)

Do Your Best Work ● All of your work should be neat and in the right place when you turn in your portfolio. (Try to make a good first impression.)

Prewriting and Drafting Guide

Building a File of Writing Ideas

Selecting a Subject

Starting Points for Writing

Collecting Details

Planning and Drafting Tips

Building a Resource of Writing Forms

Prewriting and Drafting Guide

This section contains guide-lines, lists, and suggestions for getting ready to write. We hope they help!

BUILDING A FILE OF Writing IDEAS

Most writers are interesting people. They know a lot about all of the different things going on around them. And they try to remember and save as many details from their experiences as they can, knowing that these ideas can be used in their own writing. You can begin to save ideas, just like your favorite authors do, by completing some of the activities listed below. Have fun!

Think and act like a writer!

Always keep your eyes and ears open for interesting sights and sounds. On the way to school, you might see two crazy squirrels dashing up and down a tree, as if they were running a shuttle race. In class, you might hear someone whisper, "What's the answer to number five?" Later at home, you might daydream about being famous someday. Without too much trouble, you could probably think of a story to write, using any one of these ideas.

Helpful Hint Reserve a section in a notebook or journal where you can list some of these sights and sounds.

Keep track of your experiences!

Start a "This Is My Life" list and keep adding to it throughout the school year. Here's what you might include:

- People I'll Never Forget
- Animals I'll Never Forget
- Important Places Near and Far
- Favorite Books and Movies
- Special Skills and Talents
- Unforgettable Moments
- Biggest Blunders
- Important Beliefs
- Prized Possessions
- Wild Ideas

Make new discoveries!   Get involved in many different experiences. Join teams, visit different places, help people out, and have fun with friends. The more you do, the more you know.

Read a lot!   Read books, magazines, newspapers, and whatever else you like. Jot down any names, descriptions, or ideas that jump off the page as you read. These jottings may give you ideas for your own writing.

Write a lot!   Explore your thoughts and feelings in a personal journal or diary, and you will always have a good supply of writing ideas. (**SEE** pages 106-108 for more information.)

Draw a life map!   Start your life map with your birth and work right up to the present. Choose the experiences you want to picture along the way. This idea comes from two writers named Dan Kirby and Tom Liner. (See the model below.)

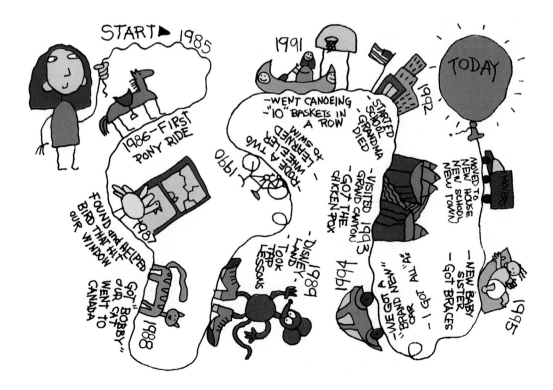

Let's say you've been asked to write about a memorable experience. You say to yourself, "No problem. I'll write about . . ." But then no ideas come to mind. What should you do?

First, see what your handbook has to say about your writing assignment. (Tips for selecting a subject are provided for many forms in "The Forms of Writing" section.) Then check your journal or writer's notebook for ideas. If you still need help, you can talk about the assignment with your classmates, or try one or more of the activities listed here.

Activities for Selecting a Subject

Clustering ■ Begin a cluster by writing an important word related to your assignment. Then list related words and ideas around it. Circle and connect new words as shown in the model.

Note: After 2 or 3 minutes of clustering, a writing idea or two may begin to take shape. (Try free writing about one of these ideas.)

Free Writing ■ Write freely for 3 to 5 minutes. *Do not stop and think during this time; just write.* Begin free writing with an idea related to your assignment. As you write, one or two subjects may come to mind. (*SEE* pages 28-29 for ideas for free writing.)

Listing ■ Freely list any ideas that pop into your head when you think of your assignment. You and a classmate can help each other think of possible subjects by listing or brainstorming together.

Sentence Completion ■ Complete a sentence starter in as many ways as you can. Make sure that your sentence starter relates to your assignment. Here are six samples:

> I remember when . . .   I really get mad when . . .
>
> One place I like . . .   I just learned . . .
>
> I wonder how . . .   School is . . .

Review the Basics of Life Checklist ■ Many of the things we need to lead a full life fall into the basic categories or groups listed below.

agriculture	faith	love
animals	family	machines
art/music	food	money
books	freedom	plants
clothing	friends	science/technology
community	health	work/play
education	housing	
energy	laws	
environment		
exercise		

MINI LESSON   Here's how you can use this checklist to think of possible subjects:

1. Choose one of the categories or groups. *(food)*

2. Decide how this category relates to your assignment. *(memorable experience)*

3. List possible subjects. *(your most memorable meal, a kitchen disaster, and so on)*

Starting Points

FOR WRITING

When you need a subject or starting point for a writing assignment, look at the prompts and topics on the next two pages for ideas.

Writing Prompts

The following prompts will get you thinking about possible subjects for writing. For example, think of the many ways you could complete this phrase: "The first time I . . . ." You will find this page of prompts especially helpful when you are writing about a personal experience.

Best and Worst

My best day
My worst moment
My biggest accomplishment
My saddest experience

It could only happen to me!

It sounds unbelievable, but . . .
I felt so foolish.
I looked everywhere for . . .

What if . . . and Why?

What if animals could talk?
What if I had three wishes?
Why is it important to win?
Why do we have to go so fast?

Quotations

"Be yourself. Who else is better qualified?"
"Following the crowd can lead nowhere."
"Everyone needs a place to hang out."

First and Last

The first time I . . .
My last visit with . . .
My first goal
The last place I want to go

I Was Just Thinking

I believe in . . .
I worry about . . .
Things that make me angry

School Days

I never worked so hard.
I'd like you to meet . . .
Where did I put my
   assignment!

"More is not always better."
"We all make mistakes."
"Take life one day at a time."

Writing Topics

As you can see, the following topics are organized according to the four basic reasons for writing. They will be especially helpful when you need ideas for a specific kind of writing (descriptions, explanations, narratives, and persuasive paragraphs).

Describing

People: a relative, a teacher, a classmate, a neighbor, someone who bugs you, someone you spend time with, someone you wish you were like

Places: your room, a garage, a basement, an attic, a rooftop, the alley, the gym, the library, a barn, a lake, a river, a yard, a park, the zoo, a museum

Objects or things: a poster, a stuffed animal, a video game, a book, a drawing, a junk drawer, a photograph, a letter, a pet, a souvenir, a model, a key, a dream

Explaining

How to . . . make a taco, care for a pet, impress a teacher, earn extra money, get in shape, be a friend, stop hiccups, run a race, saddle a horse, teach . . . , choose . . . , build . . . , fix . . . , grow . . . , save . . . , find . . .

The causes of . . . rust, acid rain, friendship, hurricanes, happiness

Kinds of . . . music, commercials, clouds, heroes, cars, pain, groups, restaurants, fun, streets, stores, books

The definition of . . . love, learning, a good time, friendship, a team, equality, a teacher, courage

Persuading

school rules, homework, smoking in public places, shoplifting, carrying guns, air bags, something that needs improving, something that's unfair, something everyone should see or do, something worth supporting

Narrating (Sharing)

getting caught, getting lost, getting together, making a mistake, being surprised, making the news, learning to _____ , being scared, winning

Try writing freely about one of the prompts or topics related to your assignment. As you write, you may discover a number of possible writing ideas.

You really have three basic ways to collect facts and details about a subject. You can . . .

✔ talk to someone about it,

✔ read and learn about it yourself,

✔ and try one or more of the following collecting activities.

Free Writing ■ Let's say your subject for a writing assignment is the first time you slept over at a friend's house. If you write freely about this time, you will see how many details you really remember about it. *Don't stop and think for this type of writing; just keep the ideas flowing.* (Sometimes your free writing will be so good that you can use it as your first draft.)

To give your free writing a special twist, write to a specific audience: a group of preschoolers, your parents, a student from another country, etc.

Bright IDEA

5 W's of Writing ■ Answer the 5 W's—*Who? What? When? Where?* and *Why?*—to collect basic information about your subject. (Add *How?* to the list for even more details.)

Clustering ■ Use the subject of your writing as the nucleus word for a cluster. Then list, circle, and connect words related to your subject. (**SEE** page 26 for a model.)

Subject Talk ■ Make up a dialogue in which two people (real or imaginary) talk about your subject. Keep the conversation going as long as you can.

Focused Thinking ■ To think carefully about a subject, write freely about it in two or three of the following ways:

☐ *Describe it.* What do you see, hear, feel, smell, taste?

☐ *Compare it.* What is it like? What is it different from?

☐ *Apply it.* What can you do with it? How can you use it?

☐ *Break it down.* What parts does it have? How do they work?

☐ *Evaluate it.* What are its strengths and weaknesses?

Crazy Questions ■ To help you see your subject in creative ways, make up some crazy questions about it, and then try to answer them. Some sample questions follow:

Writing About a Person

What type of clothing is this person like?

Which city or place should this person never visit?

Writing About a Place

What does this place like to do?

What song does it like?

Writing About an Object

What does this object do on weekends?

What does it look like upside down?

Writing to Explain a Process

Where does this process like to shop?

What sport is it like?

Writing About an Experience (a Narrative)

What movie is this experience like?

What colors does it call to mind?

Collection Sheet ■ Use a collection sheet or gathering grid to help you keep track of the facts and details you collect. (**SEE** pages 173 and 226 for examples.)

PLANNING AND Drafting Tips

All successful sports teams start out with a game plan. This plan keeps them organized and focused as the game starts. A game plan (a writing plan) can help you do the same thing when you start a first draft. Here's one way you might draw up your plan.

Developing a Writing Plan

The First Step ➤ Start with these five important points:

> **Subject:** *Who or what are you writing about?*
>
> **Purpose:** *Why are you writing? (To explain? To describe?)*
>
> **Form/Organization:** *What form will you use (poem, paragraph, etc.)?*
>
> **Audience:** *Who are your readers?*
>
> **Voice:** *How will your writing sound (serious, funny, etc.)?*

A Sample Plan ➤ Let's say I plotted out the following assignment:

> **Subject:** My best friend, Roy
>
> **Purpose:** To describe why I like him
>
> **Form/Organization:** Letter
>
> **Audience:** Classmates and Roy
>
> **Voice:** Friendly

The Next Step ➤ Next, I would decide on the type of ideas I want to include. I could, for example, write about the funny things Roy does, or the different things we like to do together.

At this point, I would be well prepared to write. I would know who I was writing about, how I wanted my writing to look, and what I wanted to say. (If something in my plan didn't work out, I could always change part of it.)

Writing a First Draft

Remember that your first draft is your first look at your writing, so it doesn't have to be (and shouldn't be) perfect. Don't stop and think and worry. Just write freely. All you need to do is get your main ideas on paper.

Be Prepared ● It is always easier to write a first draft when you know a lot of facts and details about your subject, and you have a basic plan to follow.

Be Willing to Work ● Write your draft while all of your collecting and planning are still fresh in your mind.

Be Open-minded ● If some new ideas pop into your mind as you write, don't be afraid to include them in your writing.

Be Honest ● Let the real you come through in your writing. This is your paper, so make it sound like you!

You may want to talk about your ideas with a classmate or friend before you actually begin to write. Sharing your thoughts can help you test them out before you write them down. Talking can also help you write more freely and naturally.

Plan the Opening Sentences

Sometimes it helps to plan exactly what you want to say in the opening sentences before you dive into your first draft. Make sure your first lines sound interesting. But also make sure that they state your true feelings about your subject.

You may want to start your writing in one of the following ways:

■ Begin with a surprising fact or quote.

■ Start with a question.

■ Open with some dialogue.

■ Share a brief story about the subject.

■ Introduce some of the main points you plan to cover.

Helpful Hint   **SEE** "Writing a Lead" on page 130 for more ideas and examples.

Have you ever written and designed a storybook? Have you ever created your own bumper sticker or written your own book of riddles? Just thinking about all of the forms of writing available to you might help you to write.

Advertisements
Autobiographies
Biographies
Book Reviews
Bumper Stickers
Cartoons, Comic Strips
Descriptions
Dialogues
Dictionaries
Directions (how-to)
Editorials
Family Parables
Instructional Manuals
Interviews
Jokes
Journals, Diaries
Letters

Myths
Narratives
Newspaper Writing
Pamphlets
Photo Captions
Plays
Poems
Proposals
Radio Plays
Recipes
Reports
Requests
Reviews
Riddles
Slogans
Songs
Tall Tales
Time Lines

Other Forms You Might Try

Anecdote ● a little story used to make a point

Aphorism ● a short, wise saying

Bio-poem ● a poem about someone's life

Case Study ● a story of one person who represents a larger group

Character Sketch ● a description of a real person

Commentary ● a personal opinion about the state of the world

Dramatic Monologue ● a one-way conversation in which someone tells a lot about him- or herself

E-mail (electronic mail) ● a message sent between two people using computers

News Release ● an explanation of a coming event using the 5 W's

Observation Report ● writing that records sights, sounds, and other sensory details

Oral History ● writing down tape-recorded or filmed conversation about an earlier time period

Parody ● a funny imitation of a serious piece of writing

Pet Peeve ● a personal feeling about something that bugs you

Petition ● a formal request addressed to someone in power

Profile ● a detailed report about a person

Time Capsule ● writing that captures a particular time period

Travelogue ● writing that describes travel pictures (slides, video, film)

THINK IT OVER

You can learn a lot about writing by experimenting with many of these forms. For example, by writing photo captions, you may learn something that will help you write more effective descriptive paragraphs.

Revising and Editing Guide

Revising Your Writing

Conferencing with Partners

Sharing Family Stories

Editing and Proofreading

Publishing Your Writing

Revising Your Writing

Improving Your First Draft

If you say something silly or stupid, there is not much you can do about it. What's said is said. On the other hand, when you write something that sounds kind of dumb, you can always change it. You can, in fact, change it again and again until it says exactly what you want it to say. That's what makes writing so powerful.

Making changes, or *revising*, is the subject of this chapter. You will learn how to turn your first drafts into more complete and creative pieces of writing. Remember that all of your favorite authors spend a lot of time revising their first drafts. It's important that you do the same in your own work.

❝ Writing a story takes time and energy, but it feels really good when it's done. **❞**
—Lauren Brydon, student

What Does It Mean to Revise?

Improve the Ideas ● When you revise a first draft, you make sure that all of the important points about your subject are made. You also make sure that your readers can understand all of your ideas.

Wait with Spelling and Mechanics ● Don't spend a lot of time looking for specific errors in your sentences. First, get all of your main ideas in shape.

How Do You Get Started?

Take a Break ● The first step is easy. Slip your first draft into a folder and forget about it. You need to get away from your writing for a while before you try to change it.

Read and Share ● When you come back to your first draft, read it two or three times. Try reading it out loud. Also have one or two classmates read and react to your draft. Listen carefully to their comments.

What Should You Look For?

Look for the Strong Parts ● Always find one or two things you like in your draft. You may like the dialogue in one part of your writing and a descriptive sentence in another part. Put a star next to these parts. It's good for the spirit.

Look for the Weak Parts ● You must also look for parts that need work. Important details may be missing in one part of your writing, or your sentences may sound confusing in another part. (The checklist on the next page will help you review your work.)

Revising Checklist

Use the following checklist as a guide when you review and revise a first draft.

_____ *Did I focus on a certain part of my subject, instead of trying to say everything about it?*

_____ *Do I need to add any information?*
- ✔ Do I need to add a topic sentence, or a sentence that states the main idea of my writing?
- ✔ Do I need to add any important details?
- ✔ Do I need to add a closing or concluding sentence?

_____ *Do I need to cut any information?*
- ✔ Did I include any details that don't support my main idea?
- ✔ Have I repeated myself in any parts?
- ✔ Have I said too much about a certain idea?

_____ *Do I need to rewrite any parts?*
- ✔ Are there ideas or sentences that are unclear or confusing?
- ✔ Did I do too much telling and not enough showing? (**SEE** the next page.)
- ✔ Could I improve my explanation in a certain part?

_____ *Do I need to reorder any parts of my writing?*
- ✔ Do any ideas or details seem to be out of place?
- ✔ Did I place my most important point in the best spot?
- ✔ Did I follow an effective method of organization? (**SEE** page 68.)

Show Don't Tell

If you do a lot of telling in your first draft, try turning it into writing that shows. If readers can't *see* and *hear* and *touch* and *taste* and *feel* what you've written, it just won't come to life for them. Here's the basic rule:

Use your five senses as you write, and show your readers what you mean.

One Writer in Action

Here's how author Will Hobbs explains writing that shows.

Let's say I almost drowned last summer, and I'm trying to tell a reader what it was like: "I was drowning. It was really bad. I thought I was going to die. I was really scared . . ." Now, does the reader feel what it was like? The answer is no. Did I tell, or did I show? I told. I didn't use the five senses.

Don't Use "Telling" Words ■ I try not to use words that tell, like "scared" or "angry." When Cloyd is walking out on a high ledge in my novel *Bearstone*, I didn't want to tell the readers he was scared. I tried to show them instead.

Use "Showing" Words ■ ***"The shape of the rock had forced his body weight out over the thin air, and he was in bad trouble. Stretched tight, the tendons above his heels began to quiver, then to tremble. His strength deserted him in a rush. He paused to rest, but his legs began to shake violently."***

More Revising Tips

Check for Details

"I went to my first basketball game. It was fun."

These two sentences don't say much, do they? We don't know who went to the game, who played, who won, and so on. In other words, a lot of details are missing. Always make sure that you have included enough details in your writing.

Include a Beginning, Middle, and Ending

Your writing should be clear and complete from start to finish. That means it should contain an effective beginning, middle, and ending.

Beginning: Make sure your opening lines grab your readers' attention and tell them something about your subject:

"Listen everybody. Let's keep our buses clean!"

Middle: Stick to the point! All of the ideas in the middle, or body, of your writing should support or explain your subject.

Ending: Add a closing idea to stress the importance of your subject and to keep your reader thinking about it:

"I've seen enough ABC gum, paper wads, and old Kleenex to last me a long time. I hope you have, too."

Add a Title

Once you have all of your main ideas in place, think of a title for your writing. List a number of possible choices, and select the best one. A good title should hook your readers into your writing:

Four Quarters of Fun sounds better than *My First Game.*

Have Garbage Will Travel sounds better than *Bus Litter.*

 You may have to revise your writing two or three times before all of your ideas are clear and complete.

Conferencing with Partners

Sharing and Learning

Writers spend a lot of time thinking and writing by themselves. But sooner or later they need an audience, someone to listen to what they've written. Do you ever nudge your neighbor at school and say, "Hey, Josh, listen to this"? Or at home, do you ever ask your mom or dad to react to something you are writing? If you do, you are acting like a real author.

Getting Started

This chapter is all about working in writing groups and helping one another become better listeners, thinkers, and writers.

Anytime writers share ideas about their writing, they are having a conference. You can conference in pairs or in small groups, in school or at home, with classmates or with your teacher, with friends or with family members.

Counting on Your Friends

All good writers (like you!) know they need to find someone who will listen to their writing and help them make it better. Fifth graders in room 18 at Wixom Elementary in Wixom, Michigan, gave these reasons for talking with their classmates in writing conferences:

Conference partners help writers . . .

- think about all of the ideas in their writing,
- discover new ideas to add to their writing,
- and learn new skills (like writing dialogue).

A good conference partner . . .

- makes you feel comfortable,
- helps you stay on track (so you don't talk too much about recess),
- shows an interest in your subject,
- listens carefully,
- and gives you straight answers.

❝When I conferenced, I became friends with more people. I felt wonderful because I knew some of me was in their writing. ❞
—Damian Broccoli, grade 5

Helping One Another

Conference partners can help you throughout the writing process. Their advice is especially important once you complete a first draft. They can help you identify the parts that work well in your writing, as well as the parts that need work.

They can also help you when you are ready to edit and proofread your work. Good conference partners will catch the spelling or grammar errors that you miss. Finally, they can react to the final draft of your writing. This is the most exciting (and perhaps the scariest) part of the writing process.

Conference Guidelines

During a conference, authors read their drafts to partners who listen and respond. Listed below are tips for conference partners.

Suggestions for Authors:

- Come prepared with a piece of writing you really care about.
- Tell your partner about your interest in this writing.
- Point out any problems you're having.
- Read your work out loud. (Speak clearly and don't rush.)
- Pay attention to what your partner tells you is working or not working in your draft. (His or her questions and suggestions will help you improve your writing.)
- Don't take suggestions personally. Your partner is just trying to help.

Suggestions for Listeners:

- Listen carefully (and take notes) so you can make good observations. (**SEE** "Good Listener Checklist," page 293.)
- Begin your response with positive comments. ("I like the way . . .")
- Ask questions if you are confused about something or want to know more. ("What do you mean when you say . . .?")
- Make suggestions in a helpful way. (Don't say, "Your writing is boring." Try something like, "Many of your sentences begin in the same way.")
- And always be kind and polite. Writers work hard!

THINK IT OVER

Conference partners should praise a classmate when they like something in his or her writing, but they should really mean it. Writing conferences should not be popularity contests.

Response Sheets

How can you help an author remember all of your comments and suggestions? You can write them down on a response sheet. Your teacher may already have response sheets for you to complete. If not, it is easy enough to make up your own. Here are two ideas.

Memorable

On the top half of a sheet of paper, write the word "Memorable." List the things you really like about a piece of writing under this word.

More

Halfway down this sheet, write the word "More." List one or two suggestions or questions you may have under this word.

Checklist

Organization:

✔ Does the writing have a beginning, a middle, and an end?
✔ Are all of the ideas arranged in the best order?

Details:

✔ Do all of the details support the subject (topic sentence)?
✔ Are enough details and examples included?

Style:

✔ Is the writing easy to follow?
✔ Does the writing contain interesting or descriptive words and ideas?

Mechanics:

✔ Is the writing accurate (free of careless spelling and punctuation errors)?
✔ Is the writing neatly presented?

Sharing Family Stories

Tell Me Again

Sharing stories can be a very powerful learning tool. Each time you listen to one of your classmate's stories, and tell him or her what interests you about it, you are helping your classmate and yourself grow as writers. Writing and sharing go hand in hand. **We write to share; we share to write better.**

Writing and Learning

As you learn how to write family stories in this chapter, you will also be provided with guidelines for sharing your work. (You will also use some of the conferencing tips included in the last chapter.) The experience you gain here will make it that much easier for you to share your work in the future.

You can also expect to have a lot of fun. Sharing family stories is a very enjoyable thing to do.

> " Everybody has heard family stories . . . The fun of hearing about my grandfather's life taught me to listen with pleasure. "
> — Marie Ponsot

Finding Family Parables

In all my years of school, I've never studied a subject called "My Grandpa." But I know him better than the multiplication table. I've visited him at work. I've watched him at his hobby, making fine things out of wood. I especially remember the maple boxes and building blocks he used to make. And best of all, I've heard him talk.

What happened around us usually reminded Grandpa of something, and then he'd tell us a story about it. I loved that. Today I call these stories **family parables.**

The Older, the Better

Everybody has heard family parables. Older folks often tell really good ones—the ones that have been told most often, for the longest time. Just think, many grandparents were alive 50 years ago. When they talk about *their* grandparents, they are telling stories that might be 100 years old. But don't forget your parents and aunts and uncles; they, too, have a lot of good family stories to share.

Student Model

Student writer Charles Vodak will never forget the following family story. It has been told to him time and time again. (As you can see, some family stories can be very short.)

My mom always tells me this story when we're at my grandmother's house.

When my mom was a little girl, she had to share a room with my Aunt Ann. My mom's side of the room was clean, but my aunt's side was always a mess. One day my aunt cleaned her closet, and she found some kittens in there. And guess what? They didn't even have a cat!

Writing a Family Story

Lots of family parables are about times of change or about trying something new. Such stories sleep in our memories till a word or an experience calls them to mind. They haunt a happy part of our thoughts. It's a part we can't always get at directly. But stories will come to us, once we search them out.

PREWRITING *Planning Your Writing*

Select a Subject ● Begin your subject search by telling a brief family story to a friend or classmate. Listen to one of hers or his. Tell another. Listen again. As you do, you'll get a feel for one or two stories that you might like to write about.

Helpful Hint   If you are working by yourself, complete this sentence starter: "I remember the story of . . ." Then continue listing ideas until you hit upon a subject.

WRITING THE FIRST DRAFT

Start Writing ● Once you select a favorite family parable, the next step is to write it down from memory. I like to begin my writing with a one-sentence introduction. For instance, I'll write, "This is a story my grandmother told during a thunderstorm." Then I start the actual story in a new paragraph.

Keep It Going ● There are no rules about how long or how short a family parable should be. That will depend on how it was told to you, and how you remember it.

Now, stop reading, choose a favorite story from your list, and begin to write your parable.

REVISING *Improving Your Writing*

Share Your Writing ● Read your first draft aloud to a small group of classmates. Make sure to read loudly enough and slowly enough for everyone to hear your words.

After the reading, members of your group should take turns telling you what they liked about your parable. Listen carefully, so you can do more of these things the next time you write.

Now listen to other members of your group read their stories. Share your ideas about each story. (The more often you respond to someone's writing, the better writer you will become.)

Review Your First Draft ● After the sharing session is over, review your first draft on your own. Then consider any changes you would like to make in your work.

EDITING & PROOFREADING

Edit Carefully ● Make sure your parable reads smoothly and clearly from start to finish. Also check for spelling, punctuation, and grammar errors. A family story should be treated with a great deal of respect, so edit it carefully.

Proofread Your Final Draft ● Type or write a neat final copy of your work. Then check it one last time for any periods or capital letters you may have missed.

MINI LESSON You should also practice making written observations about shared stories. Follow these steps:

❑ Ask one author to read his or her story aloud.

❑ Write about what you remember. An easy way to practice this kind of writing is to begin with "It interests me that . . ." and then add whatever you like to complete the sentence. List as many "interests" as you can.

❑ Share your written observations about this story as a group.

❑ Take turns listening, observing, and responding to the stories.

Editing and Proofreading

Polishing Your Writing

This chapter deals with editing and proofreading, the step in the writing process when you get your writing ready to share or publish. Remember that editing and proofreading becomes important *after* you have changed, or revised, any of the main ideas in your first draft.

Make Every Word Count!

The guidelines in this chapter will help you check your writing for style and correctness. All of your sentences and words should read smoothly, and they should be free of careless errors. In other words, this chapter will help you make every word count in your work.

H·m·m·m···

Writers EXPRESS

Thesaurus

Dictionary

❝I think about what I write, and put great care into picking the words I use. ❞
—Catherine Ferrante, student

Checking Your Sentences

Combine Short Sentences ● If you use too many short sentences one after another, your writing may sound choppy. You can correct this problem by combining some of your sentences.

Four short sentences:

> *The dog followed Mary.*
> *It followed her for half a mile.*
> *It stayed very close behind her.*
> *She forced herself to stay calm.*

■ **Two Longer, Smoother Sentences:**

> *The dog followed Mary for half a mile. It stayed very close behind her, but she forced herself to stay calm.*

Change Your Sentence Beginnings ● If too many of your sentences begin in the same way, your writing may sound dull and lifeless. You can correct this problem by changing the way you start some of your sentences.

Three sentences beginning with the subject *I*:

> *I slowly ate the cooked carrots. I washed them down with milk to cover the taste. I tried to hide some of them when my mom wasn't looking.*

How to Change Sentence Beginnings

■ **Start with a Modifier:**
> *Slowly, I ate the cooked carrots.*

■ **Start with a Phrase:**
> *To cover the taste, I washed them down with milk.*

■ **Start with a Clause:**

> *When my mom wasn't looking, I tried to hide some of them.*

Correct Sentence Errors ● There are three basic types of errors you should look for in your writing: *sentence fragments, run-on sentences,* and *rambling sentences.* (**SEE** page 87.)

Checking for Word Choice

Use Powerful Verbs ● As writer Will Hobbs says, "Verbs power sentences, making them fly or jump or sink or swim." They help make your ideas come alive for your readers. Here are two sentences from *Bearstone* by Will Hobbs. The powerful verbs (in bold type) give an effective picture of the action.

> The big fish **flip-flopped** against Cloyd's leg. He **nudged** it back into the water with his foot, then **leaped** across the Rincon stream.

Use Specific Nouns ● Some nouns like *car, fruit, store, flowers,* and *candy* are general and give readers a fuzzy picture. Other nouns like **Dodge Shadow, kiwi, K-Mart, tulips,** and **Snickers** are specific and give readers a much clearer picture. Always try to use specific nouns in your writing.

Choose Colorful Modifiers ● Effective adjectives and adverbs can add color to your writing.

■ **Using Adjectives:**

She wandered into the **deep** *shade of the* **giant** *cottonwoods.* (The adjectives make the picture clearer.)

■ **Using Adverbs:**

Rover ran **wildly** *after Rachael. She headed* **directly** *for the back door.* (The adverbs add to the action.)

Modifiers are very important to use, but be careful not to *overuse* them. Too many adjectives and adverbs can make your writing sound unnatural.

Select the Right Word ● Make sure that the words you use in your writing are correct. For example, it's easy to confuse words that sound the same—*there, their,* and *they're; know* and *no.* (**SEE** pages 362-369 for a list of words that are often confused.)

Editing and Proofreading Checklist

Use this checklist as a guide when you edit your writing. Also use it when you are ready to proofread your final draft.

Sentence Structure

✔ Did I write clear and complete sentences?
✔ Did I write sentences of different lengths?
✔ Did I begin my sentences in different ways?

Punctuation

✔ Does each sentence end with an end punctuation mark?
✔ Did I use commas in a series (*Larry, Moe, and Curly*)?
✔ Did I place commas before connecting words (*and, but, or*) in compound sentences?
✔ Did I punctuate dialogue correctly? (**SEE** pages 346 and 350 for help.)

Capitalization

✔ Did I start all my sentences with a capital letter?
✔ Did I capitalize nouns that name specific people, places, and things?

Usage

✔ Did I use powerful verbs, specific nouns, and colorful modifiers?
✔ Did I use the correct word (*to, too,* or *two; your* or *you're*)? (**SEE** pages 362-369 for help.)

Spelling

✔ Did I check for spelling? Did I use the spell checker on my computer? (**SEE** pages 270-273 for help.)

Publishing Your Writing

The Final Step

Publishing is a very important part of the writing process. It makes all of your planning, drafting, and revising worth the effort. And it also gets other people to listen to your ideas.

Publishing can take many forms. Reading a finished story to your classmates is a form of publishing—so is selecting a poem for your classroom portfolio. If your classmates and teacher really like your writing, you might want to explore some of the following ways to publish it.

Mail It!

Greeting cards

Letters to public figures

Requests for information

Thank-you letters to field-trip guides, bus drivers, etc.

Letters that complain about or praise a product or service

Letters to pen pals in other schools, cultures, or countries

Notes to parents about school activities

Perform It!

Plays for school and community audiences
> **Puppet shows**

Radio shows over the school public address system
> **Talking books for the visually impaired**

Taped interviews for a class project
> **New words for familiar music**

Presentations at PTA or school board meetings
> **Introductions of guests at assemblies**

Videotaped documentaries for local TV stations

Print It!

- All-school or classroom collections
- *Stories just for veterinarian clinics, doctors' offices, or other waiting rooms*
- Manuals on how to do certain things
- *School-survival guides for younger students*
- Programs for school productions
- *Newspaper reports of class trips or projects*
- School handbook updates
- *Kid's-eye-view brochures for local travel agency or chamber of commerce*

Submit It!

There are many magazines published every month that feature student writing. Write to one that you think might publish your work. Ask your teacher for help. Also ask your teacher or librarian for a list of contests you can send your writing to.

Magazines That Publish Student Work

Owl

Topics: Environment/Science/Nature

Forms: Letters, drawings, poetry, short short stories

Address: *Owl*, Editor
179 John St., Suite 500
Toronto, Ontario
CANADA M5T 3G5

Daybreak Star

Topics: Native American Life

Forms: Essays, fiction, poems, true stories

Address: Unified Indians of All Tribes Foundation
1945 Yale Place East
Seattle, WA 98102

Skipping Stones

Topics: Multicultural/Nature

Forms: Fiction, songs, games, true stories, poems, essays

Address: *Skipping Stones*, Editor
P.O. Box 3939
Eugene, OR 97403

Creative Kids

Topics: Writing

Forms: Book reviews, essays, fiction, crafts/hobbies, riddles, poems, true stories

Address: Prufrock Press,
Submission Editor
P.O. Box 8813
Waco, TX 76714

Highlights for Children

Topics: General

Forms: Fiction, poems, true stories, letters to the editor

Address: Children's Mail
803 Church Street
Honesdale, PA 18431

Stone Soup

Topics: Writing/Art

Forms: Stories, poems

Address: *Stone Soup*, Editor
P.O. Box 83
Santa Cruz, CA 95063

(You must include a self-addressed stamped envelope.)

❝It feels wonderful to be an author of a real story. I like to publish my writing because it is like making my ideas come alive!❞

—Stephen Greenberg, grade 5

Bind It!

To make or bind your own book for publication, follow these six basic steps. Make sure to add your own personal touches as you put your book together.

1 Stack in order the pages to be bound and add extra pages for titles, etc.

2 Staple or sew the pages together.

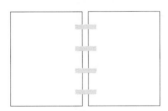

3 Cut two pieces of cardboard 1/4 inch larger than the page size. Tape them together.

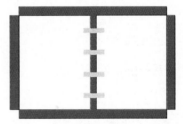

4 Place the cardboard on the cover material (contact paper or glue-on wallpaper). Turn the edges of the cover material over the cardboard.

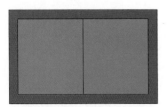

5 Attach construction paper or contact paper to the inside of the book cover.

6 Fasten the bound pages of the book into the cover with tape.

Building Paragraphs and Essays

Writing Paragraphs

Writing Essays

A Writing Sampler

Writing Paragraphs

What Is a Paragraph?

A paragraph is a group of sentences that tells about one subject or idea. Each sentence in a paragraph must give information about the topic. And the sentences must be in the right order, so your readers can understand the information.

A good paragraph presents a complete and interesting picture. The specific subject is stated in one sentence—usually the topic sentence. All of the facts and details in the rest of the sentences add to the readers' understanding of the subject. In other words, all of the parts work together.

In this chapter, paragraphs are explained, the different parts are named, and the basic types are identified. Step-by-step tips for writing good paragraphs are also given.

The Basic Parts of a Paragraph

You can think of a paragraph as a train. The **topic sentence** is the train's engine. It's the main idea that all the other sentences are connected to. The sentences in the **body** of the paragraph are the boxcars. They carry the paragraph's "cargo"—facts, figures, examples. The **closing sentence** is the caboose. It doesn't carry cargo; it just sums up what went before.

The Topic Sentence ● A paragraph begins with a *topic sentence*: a sentence that tells the reader what the paragraph is about. A topic sentence has two main parts—a specific subject and a focus.

The subject: The **subject** of a topic sentence has to be specific or small enough to explain in one paragraph. You couldn't write a paragraph on "the history of baseball." It would be too long! But you could write a paragraph on "yesterday's softball game." That subject is more specific!

The focus: You need more than a subject to write a topic sentence. You also need a **focus**. A focus is usually a feeling or an attitude about the subject. It lets the reader know what you're going to say about the subject.

MINI LESSON   Here is a simple **formula** that makes it easy to write good topic sentences. Use it whenever you have to write a paragraph.

> **Subject** (Who? or What?)
> + **Feeling/Focus** (What about it?)
> ──────────────────────────
> = **Topic Sentence**

Sample Topic Sentence

In yesterday's softball game (specific subject), *the fourth grade pounded the fifth grade* (focus).

The Body ● The middle of the paragraph is called the *body*. It includes the sentences between the topic sentence and the closing sentence. These sentences must give the reader all the information needed to understand the topic. Below are sentences that could follow the topic sentence in a paragraph about "yesterday's softball game."

Sample Body

When the fourth grade batted, Tim started off with a double. Jamie batted next and hit a home run. The fifth grade scored two runs in the third inning to tie the score. After Sarah hit a grand slam for the fourth grade in the next inning, the fifth grade never scored again.

The Closing Sentence ● A paragraph ends with a *closing sentence*. This sentence may sum up the information in the paragraph, or tell what it means. Below is a sample closing sentence that could be used after the "Sample Body" above.

Sample Closing Sentence

Thanks to Sarah's grand slam, the fourth grade won by four runs.

 If you put the *Sample Topic Sentence, Sample Body,* and *Sample Closing Sentence* together, you'll have a **Sample Paragraph!**

In yesterday's softball game, the fourth grade pounded the fifth grade. When the fourth grade batted, Tim started off with a double. Jamie batted next and hit a home run. The fifth grade scored two runs in the third inning to tie the score. After Sarah hit a grand slam for the fourth grade in the next inning, the fifth grade never scored again. Thanks to Sarah's grand slam, the fourth grade won by four runs.

Types of Paragraphs

There are four kinds of paragraphs you can write.

■ To describe something, write a **descriptive** paragraph.

■ To tell a story, write a **narrative** paragraph.

■ To express your opinion, write a **persuasive** paragraph.

■ To explain something, write an **expository** paragraph.

Descriptive Paragraph

A **descriptive** paragraph describes a person, a place, a thing, or an idea. When you write a descriptive paragraph, you should use words that help your readers see, hear, smell, taste, and feel what you are describing. You should tell your readers what colors things are, how big things are, what things sound like, etc. Your readers should feel as if they are right there with you.

Model Descriptive Paragraph

You can tell a lot about Evan by looking at his face. The first thing you notice are his big brown eyes that always seem so shiny and alert. You wouldn't notice his pug nose except that it seems to be running all of the time. Like many little boys, he wipes it with his sleeve rather than a Kleenex. His mouth seems to have two basic positions. He smiles when he's got trouble on his mind, or he clenches his mouth shut when he doesn't want to do something, like eat his lunch. Evan's tongue, which he likes to stick out, is usually orange from his favorite fruit drink. Whenever someone tries to clean his mouth or chin, he squirms and turns away. Evan likes his face just the way it is.

Narrative Paragraph

In a **narrative** paragraph, you tell a story by sharing the details of an experience. A narrative paragraph should pull your readers into the story and keep them wondering what will happen next. It's important to include a lot of colorful details to make the experience come alive.

Model Narrative Paragraph

Evan leaves a trail of trouble even when he isn't trying. The last time I baby-sat for him, we were painting pictures at the kitchen table. Evan painted a couple of monster faces, and then decided he wanted to do something else. He even offered to help clean up, which surprised me a little. He was carrying the bowl full of dirty water from our paint brushes when disaster struck. He tripped right in front of the sink in the utility room and the dirty water went flying. I did my best to clean up the mess while Evan had a snack. As I worked, I reminded myself never to let Evan help again.

Bright
IDEA

To make sure you have included all the important details in your narrative paragraph, ask the following questions: *Who? What? When? Where? Why? How?*

Persuasive Paragraph

A **persuasive** paragraph gives the writer's opinion on the topic and tries to get the reader to agree with it. When you write a persuasive paragraph, you should give facts and examples to back up your opinion. Otherwise, you won't *persuade,* or convince, your reader that your opinion is the right one.

Model Persuasive Paragraph

Anyone who baby-sits for Evan should receive an extra bonus. For one thing, you have to put up with Evan's screaming. He likes to sneak up behind you and scream in your ear. He's very good at scaring just about anyone with this move. For another thing, you never get a chance to rest for even a minute. Evan likes to keep things active by teasing the cat, locking himself in his room, overloading the circuits, falling off his bike, and so on. And finally, you have to clean up after him. There is always spilled milk to wipe up in the kitchen and dumped toys to pick up in every other room. For conditions like these, the regular hourly rate is not enough!

Helpful Hint   Read your paragraph out loud so that you can listen for missing information. Also turn to page 309 in your handbook for more on using facts and opinions in your writing.

Expository Paragraph

The main purpose of an **expository** paragraph is to give information about a topic. It may explain ideas, give directions, or show how to do something. An expository paragraph uses transition words (such as *first, second,* and *most importantly* in the model below). These words help guide the reader through the explanation.

Model Expository Paragraph

Always be prepared when you baby-sit for Evan. First, make sure to bring a flashlight in case of a blackout. Evan likes to overload the circuits. Second, bring a few first-aid supplies like cotton balls and Band-Aids. Evan will get at least two or three scratches or cuts while you are there, and sometimes their first-aid kit is low on materials. You can also use the cotton balls to plug your ears if Evan starts screaming. Most importantly, have a phone number where you can contact Evan's mother. No matter how prepared you are, you can't baby-sit for Evan all by yourself. You will need to call his mother at least once for help or advice.

TAKE NOTE Sometimes it's helpful to list the facts or examples you are going to include in your paragraph. That way, you can put your supporting ideas into the best possible order before you begin.

Sample Listing

Topic Sentence: *Always be prepared when you baby-sit for Evan.*

- ✔ *Bring a flashlight*
- ✔ *Bring first-aid supplies*
- ✔ *Have a phone number to contact his mother*

Writing the Paragraph

1 **Plan your paragraph.** To begin planning your paragraph, you can ask yourself the following questions:

Subject: *Who or what will I write about?*

Purpose: *What feeling about my subject will I focus on?*

Audience: *Who will be reading my paragraph?*

Form: *What kind of paragraph will work best?*

2 **Gather information.** Once you've answered these questions, you are ready to begin gathering details for your paragraph. This chart will help you decide what information you need to collect.

For a . . .	you'll need . . .
descriptive paragraph	lots of details about how things look, sound, smell, feel, etc.
narrative paragraph	details about an experience you want to share: how it began, what problems occurred, how it ended
persuasive paragraph	facts, figures, and examples to back up your opinion
expository paragraph	facts to explain the thing or process you're writing about

3 **Put the information in order.** The topic sentence is first. Next comes the body—the sentences that tell about the topic sentence. At the end is the closing sentence that sums up the paragraph, or tells what it means. (**SEE** pages 60-61.)

4 **Check your work.** Read your paragraph. Imagine that you are reading it for the first time. Does it tell everything you need to know to understand the topic sentence? Is it interesting and clear?

Details in a Paragraph

Details are an important part of any paragraph. They are the facts and examples that bring the paragraph to life.

Personal Details

Most of the details you use in your paragraphs will be personal details—things you know from your own experience. Here are the different kinds of personal details you can use:

Details from Your Senses ● These details come from the world around you and are picked up by your five senses. They are things that you see, hear, smell, taste, and touch. You will need a lot of these when writing a descriptive paragraph.

Details from Your Memory ● These details come from memories of things you've done and experienced. In an expository paragraph, such details will help you to explain how to do something. In descriptive and narrative writing, they will help you to bring the past to life.

Details from Your Imagination ● These details come from inside your mind and deal with your hopes, wishes, and wonders. *What if Evan were a teacher?* Thoughts like this one can make narrative paragraphs interesting and fun.

Details from Other Sources

When you write a paragraph, first think about what you already know about the subject. Then add details from other sources:

- Ask people who may have the answers you need—teachers, parents, neighbors, friends.
- Ask an expert on the subject. For example, if you are writing a paragraph about the flu that's going around, talk to a doctor or a nurse.
- Check newspapers, magazines, and books. Check the ones you have at home and the ones in your library.

Putting Things in Order

The sentences in the body of a paragraph must be organized so that the reader can follow the information from one sentence to the next.

Time order. It is easy to understand things that are explained in the order in which they happened. You may use words like *first*, *second*, *next*, and *finally*.

> **When** the fourth grade batted, Tim started off with a double. Jamie batted **next** and hit a home run. The fifth grade scored two runs in the third inning to tie the score. **After** Sarah hit a grand slam for the fourth grade in the next inning, the fifth grade never scored again.

Place order. When things are described in the order in which they are located, the description usually goes from left to right or from top to bottom. Place order can work well when you are writing a descriptive or an expository paragraph. Use words and phrases like *above*, *below*, *to the left of*, and *in front of* to guide your reader.

> **Looking at** the infield from home plate, the batter sees the third baseman on her far left. **To the right** of the third baseman is the shortstop. **To the right** of him is the second baseman, and **to the right** of her is the first baseman.

Order of importance. News stories are often organized this way. They tell the most important news first. Persuasive or expository paragraphs are also organized in this way, with the most important detail coming first *or* last.

> Very early this morning, an adult male ostrich escaped from the zoo. He was found about half a mile north of the zoo running along Adams Boulevard. Zoo officials say the ostrich was safely back in captivity within 15 minutes of his escape.

Transition or Linking Words

Words which can be used to show location:

above	around	between	inside	outside
across	behind	by	into	over
against	below	down	near	throughout
along	beneath	in back of	off	to the right
among	beside	in front of	on top of	under

Words which can be used to show time:

about	during	until	yesterday	finally
after	first	meanwhile	next	then
at	second	today	soon	as soon as
before	third	tomorrow	later	when

Words which can be used to compare two things:

in the same way	likewise	as
similarly	like	also

Words which can be used to contrast things (show differences):

but	otherwise	on the other hand	although
yet	however	still	even though

Words which can be used to emphasize a point:

again	for this reason	in fact

Words which can be used to add information:

again	and	for instance	as well
also	besides	next	along with
another	for example	finally	

Words which can be used to conclude or summarize:

as a result	finally	in conclusion
therefore	last	in summary

Finding Paragraphs

You know how easy it is to go on and on when you have something important to say to one of your friends. "Guess what I did . . ." Well, the same thing can happen when you are writing about something that means a lot to you. You may start out writing a simple paragraph and end up filling a whole page or two with great ideas.

Keeping Your Ideas Together

When your writing does go on and on, make sure it is organized into paragraphs before you share it. Otherwise, your readers may have trouble following your ideas. The guidelines that follow will help you find the paragraphs in your writing so that it is ready to be enjoyed.

> *When I thought about my message, it became important for my readers to understand it.*
>
> —Erik Olsen, student

How You Do It

To find the paragraphs in longer pieces of writing, repeat these three steps—*Label, Name, Find*—until you come to the end of your work.

1. Label: Put a paragraph sign (⁊) before the first word in your paper.

2. Name: Identify the first main idea in your writing.

3. Find: Locate the first sentence that is **not** about this idea.

* * * * * *

1. Label: Put a paragraph (⁊) sign before this sentence (#3 above).

2. Name: Identify the main idea of this paragraph.

3. Find: Locate the first sentence that is **not** about this idea.

* * * * * *

1. Label: *Repeat the process until you are done.*

Sample Writing

Here is part of an autobiography by student writer Elizabeth Hartfield. As you can see, it is not divided into paragraphs. (We took them out so you can see how the three-step process works.)

My name is Elizabeth Frances Hartfield. I'm going to tell you about my life starting with the day something exciting and sad happened. What happened was that I moved from my home in Springfield to a house in West Chester. I was nervous and scared. I didn't think that I would make a lot of friends, but I did. Since I moved to West Chester, I have gone to three different schools. The first one I went to was Saints Simon and Jude. I went there for first and second grade. I went to Sacred Heart Academy in Bryn Mawr for third grade, and now I go to Villa Maria Academy. I am now in fourth grade. I like to draw a lot. On April 25, 1993, I won an award for a piece of artwork that I did. My favorite activities besides art are reading and dancing . . .

Following the Steps

Finding the paragraphs in this autobiography is easy if you follow the three-step process.

1. Label: Put a paragraph sign (¶) next to the first word.
      ¶ My name is . . .

2. Name: Identify the main idea of the first paragraph.
      Moving to West Chester

3. Find: Locate the first sentence that is **not** about this idea.
      Since I moved to . . .

                    * * * * * *

1. Label: Put a paragraph sign before this sentence.
      ¶ Since I moved to . . .

2. Name: Identify the main idea of this paragraph.
      Different schools I've attended

3. Find: Locate the first sentence that is **not** about this idea.
      (See if you can find the last paragraph!)

Writing Essays

Think Before You Write!

Even if you've never written an essay before, you've probably thought out many of them. For example, if you've just read something interesting —maybe about saving trees—and decide to tell someone about it, you are "thinking" an essay. Or, if you're trying to figure out why you are such good friends with someone, you are also thinking an essay.

Facts and Feelings

An essay is a form of factual writing that is more than one paragraph in length. Some essays are informational and sound like basic classroom reports. Other essays are freely written and include a lot of personal feelings. Most essays fall somewhere in between. They present a lot of good information about a specific subject, plus some of the writer's personal feelings.

The guidelines and model in this chapter will help you write a very basic informational essay—maybe your first essay ever! Good luck, and remember to think before you write.

What an Essay Can Do

There are three basic reasons to write essays: *to present information, to share a strong opinion,* and *to make everyone think.*

➤ Present Information

If you want to present important facts and details about a subject, you can write an *informational essay.* In this type of writing, your goal is to inform your readers about something new or important. (An informational essay is like a classroom report, only shorter and not as detailed.)

Subject Ideas: **Reasons for Recycling Newspapers**

Introducing a New Computer Game

➤ Share a Strong Opinion

If you want to share an opinion about something going on in your school or community, you can write a *persuasive essay.* In this type of essay, your goal is to convince your readers to agree with your way of thinking. It's important that your opinion is supported by believable facts and details.

Subject Ideas: **Keeping the Buses Cleaner**

Why a Computer Club Is Needed

TAKE NOTE

The most common type of persuasive essay is the letter to the editor. (**SEE** page 131 for an example. Also, see pages 308-311 for other helpful information.)

➤ Make Everyone Think

If you want to share your thoughts about a fun or serious subject related to your personal life, you can write a *personal essay.* Your goal is to entertain your readers, or to express your feelings about your subject.

Subject Ideas: **Fashion Trends with My Friends**

Living with Allergies

Writing an Informational Essay

Writing an essay is no trouble at all if you know the **ins and outs** of the process.

PREWRITING *Getting Started*

To begin planning, answer three basic questions:

Subject ● Who or what am I writing about? (Make sure that your subject really interests you and that you already know something about it.)

Audience ● Who will be reading my essay? (Are you writing for your classmates, for another group of students, or for someone else?)

Voice ● How do I want my writing to sound? (Do you want to sound serious, funny, or somewhere in between?)

PREWRITING *Collecting and Organizing*

Next, decide on the type of information you plan to include:

Explore ● Write down all that you know about your subject.

Focus ● Review your writing, and decide what part of your subject you would like to cover. (For example, if your subject is recycling newspapers, you might focus on the ways it helps the environment.)

Collect ● Gather more information about your subject if you feel that you need to know more about it.

Organize ● Decide what details you are going to include in your essay and how they will be organized. (**SEE** page 77 for help.)

WRITING THE FIRST DRAFT

When you are writing an essay, remember that each part—the beginning, the middle, and the ending—plays a special role:

Beginning ● Your first paragraph should say something interesting or surprising about your subject to get your readers' attention. It should also name the specific part of the subject that your essay will cover.

Middle ● The middle should include all of the ideas (facts, figures, examples) that support the subject. This information must be clearly organized. (This part may be more than one paragraph.)

Ending ● The final paragraph summarizes the main points covered in the essay. It should also remind readers why the subject is important, or help them remember it better.

REVISING & EDITING

The following checklist will help you improve your first draft:

✔ Have I written a title that helps identify my subject?

✔ Have I introduced my subject in an effective way?

✔ Have I included enough facts and details to support my subject? Are they clearly stated?

✔ Will readers understand why my subject is important or interesting?

✔ Do I like the sound of my words and sentences? Have I checked for errors?

Model Essay

The following informational essay deals with a very important subject, recycling. As you will see, all of the ideas are clearly stated and organized.

Beginning
A personal story introduces the subject.

Middle
Basic facts support the subject.

Ending
The main points are summarized.

Why My Family Recycles Newspapers

In my family, we recycle our newspapers. My sister talked my parents into it after she studied recycling in school. I learned from her that old newspapers can be made into usable paper again. I also learned how recycling newspapers helps the environment.

There are three basic benefits when old paper is recycled. First, recycling saves trees. As more and more paper is recycled, fewer trees have to be used to make paper. Second, recycling saves energy. It takes less energy to recycle paper than to start the papermaking process by cutting down trees. Third, recycling old paper is cleaner than making paper in the old way. This means recycling causes less pollution.

It's easy to recycle old newspapers. We just put them in paper bags and drop them off at the recycling center every Saturday. It's worth the little time it takes because we are saving trees and energy and helping keep our air cleaner. Have you started recycling yet?

The question at the end of this essay will help readers remember the subject by encouraging them to start recycling, too.

Organizing Your Essay

To help you organize the supporting facts and details in your essay, try *listing, clustering,* or *outlining*.

Listing ● For some essays, you can simply list the supporting details in the order you want to write about them.

- Recycling saves trees.
- Recycling saves energy.
- Recycling causes less pollution.

Clustering/Webbing ● When you have a lot of information, you may want to try a cluster or web. (**SEE** pages 26 and 222-223.)

Outlining ● Or, you may want to organize your ideas in an outline. An outline helps you arrange information from general to specific. A *topic outline* contains only words and phrases. (See the sample below.) You can also write a *sentence outline* if you want to add more detail.

Sample Topic Outline

Help for Blind People

I. Help with reading and learning   ← Main Idea
   A. Braille
   B. Talking books   ← Examples
   C. Enlarged-print books
      1. Each letter enlarged by special machine
      2. Readers feel large letters   ← Supporting Details
II. Help for moving about
   A. Special walking cane
   B. Trained dog
   C. Sonar device

YOU DON'T SAY

In an outline, everything comes in pairs. If you have a *I,* you must have a *II*. If you have an *A,* you must have a *B,* and so on.

A Writing Sampler

Making Contact

All of the different *people, places, events,* and *objects* in your life have something special to offer you and your readers—if you take the time to write about them. You will see what I mean when you read the personal narratives and essays on the next five pages. They do more than just retell what happened to the writers. They show that the writers have carefully thought about their experiences and formed new ideas about them.

Learning About Yourself

Writing about your personal experiences will help you practice storytelling. Part of becoming a good writer is being able to tell a good story. It will also help you understand that writing is much more than putting a few words on paper. You will learn that writing can be a very meaningful way to share, and even celebrate, special parts of your life.

> **"**Writing from experiences is easy because I know all the details. Once I start, I can't stop. **"**
> —Mike Franzago, student

Writing About a Special Person

Writing about another person is a very important form of writing. It is sometimes called biographical writing. A *biography* is the story of another person's life.

Selecting a Subject ● Write about someone you know well, or someone you would like to know well.

Collecting Details ● *List* details that describe your subject. *Remember* important things he or she has done. *Compare* your subject to other people. Who is he or she most like? *Ask* others about your subject, and *explain* why your subject is important.

Student Model

Adam Garelick had a lot to say about his father in this story. His writing includes a lot of examples and real feelings.

Beginning
The writer introduces the subject.

Middle
One main activity is described.

Ending
Real feelings are expressed.

Someone Who Cares

My dad is very special because he does so many things with me. He helps me with my homework, and if I ask him to take me somewhere, he'll do it. He even gives me confidence when I am having trouble with baseball.

My dad and I do so much together. Last summer, we took a trip across the country. We got to talk to each other a great deal. My dad told me about the time he was in the middle of nowhere and ran out of gas. After that story, I watched the gas gauge every other minute! He said he had made the same trip when he was 23 years old with his best friend. Now, it was him and me.

I wish everyone could have a companion like my dad. We all need an ally, or friend, in our lives; because if we have problems or need to express our feelings, we need a responsible person to turn to. I have my dad.

Writing About a Special Place

Writing about a place is part descriptive writing and part narrative writing. You need to include details that describe your subject, but you also need to tell a good story about it.

Selecting a Subject ● Write about a place that has played an important role in your life. It can be a big place like a house you used to live in, or a small place like a certain tree in a yard.

Collecting Details ● If possible, *visit* this place, and *jot down* what you see, hear, smell, and feel. *Remember* personal experiences related to it. *Compare* your subject to other places. And *explain* what you like or dislike about it.

Student Model

In this sample, Terra Wilcoxson remembers a special tree. She uses a lot of descriptive words and similes in her writing.

Beginning
The writer remembers the tree.

Middle
The writer's feelings change.

Ending
Sadness is expressed.

It Was Tall and Mighty

Even though it lay on its side, it somehow seemed tall and mighty, like a friendly bear protecting me. When I climbed across it, nothing existed beyond the short range of the tree. My pudgy little hands could grasp branches that stuck out like spikes. I'd lift myself up and scamper across the trunk, afraid of plunging into the ditch of leaves below. When I finally reached the end, a sense of accomplishment and pride came over me.

Day after day passed, and I slowly drifted away, until my tree seemed to move into another dimension, isolated. Now it no longer stands tall or mighty. It just hangs there, like an old toy, forgotten.

Sometimes, I glance out the window at the weeping tree. It reminds me of all the hours I've spent climbing the bear it used to be.

Writing About an Event

When writing about an event, make the action come alive for your readers, but don't try to say everything about your subject. It's better to focus on one exciting part of it. (**SEE** 110-115 for a related form of writing.)

Selecting a Subject ● Write about any recent event, or an event you plan to attend. For example, you may have attended a sporting event or a concert, watched a parade, and so on.

Collecting Details ● *Write down* all of the details related to your subject. Include sights, sounds, and smells. Also try to answer the 5 W's (*who? what? when? where?* and *why?*) related to it. Then *decide* why this event is worth sharing.

Student Model

In this personal story, Michelle Diamond recalls the time she met her tennis idol. She makes this event sound very exciting.

Beginning
The writer wonders about meeting her idol.

Middle
The main activity is described.

Ending
The writer feels closer to her subject.

The Unforgettable Autograph

I couldn't imagine really getting her autograph. What would it be like? I felt faint. She is my idol because at 14 she plays tennis so well. As she gets older, she will surely get even better.

While I was walking toward the practice courts, in my head I was hoping I would at least see her play. I was sure my sister was thinking the same thing. Then, suddenly, there she was, Jennifer Capriati, wearing her tennis jacket and listening to headphones. My sister and I ran over to her as fast as horses to a finish line. I stared at her with butterflies in my stomach. She actually signed my paper, and I felt like nothing else mattered.

Later, while I was watching her play, it might have been my imagination, but I thought she winked at me!

Writing About a Special Object

When you write about an object, think of an interesting story to tell about it, a story that will help your readers know why this object is special to you. This is more important than describing the object in great detail.

Selecting a Subject ● Write about an object that you know well. You may have a special stuffed animal, a favorite baseball glove, a lucky charm, or a useful gadget of some type.

Collecting Details ● *List* details that describe the size, shape, and smell of your subject. *Remember* interesting stories related to the object. *Ask* yourself if your feelings about your subject have remained the same or have changed over time.

Student Model

Michele Dreiding shares her feelings about an object that once played an important role in her life.

I'm Growing Up

Beginning
The writer gives background information.

Middle
The story about the flashlight is told.

Ending
The ending ties into the title: "I'm Growing Up."

When I was little, I was scared of the dark. I thought monsters or ghosts would come out and yell "Boo!"

Finally, I got a flashlight, and that worked like a charm. It lit up my room a little so I could sleep better. Through the years, I enjoyed having my flashlight right next to my bed.

Now I am older, and I don't need it anymore. I no longer have a fear of the dark. Every time I take my flashlight out of the socket, my mom puts it back in again. I want to say, "Stop, Mom! I am growing up. I am not a baby anymore. You have to understand that I like the dark."

I know she is only trying to help, but . . .

Writing About the Condition of Things

Some personal essays or stories are about the way things are, or about the *condition of things*. An essay about having allergies or about being too tall would fall into this category. In this type of writing, you share your feelings about a certain part of your life.

Selecting a Subject ● Write about some part of your life that makes you angry, happy, sad, or proud. You might write about wearing glasses, sharing a bedroom, or watching TV.

Collecting Details ● *Write down* all of your thoughts about your subject. If possible, *list* details that help answer *who? what? when? where?* and *why?* about the condition. Then *think* of the different ways this condition has affected your life.

Student Model

In this essay, Christopher FitzSimons asks himself why he has to have allergies. A lot of honest feelings are expressed.

Why?

Beginning
The writer asks questions about his condition.

Rachel has one problem—me. Wait. It's not me. It's my allergies! So why do I feel so guilty? Why do I think I'm shattering someone's dreams when my allergies are out of control? How come I feel like I've stabbed my sister in the heart when I can't stop my eyes from watering, tingling, itching?

Middle
The questions continue.

Most of all, why do my allergies start right when everything is going so well, like when my family is about to buy a pet, or when we're playing with a kitten, or even when I'm watching my favorite TV show and I'm snuggled up in a warm, furry blanket.

Ending
The final lines are filled with emotion.

I feel empty, like there's nothing inside of me, no love or compassion. I want to be in control, but I can't do anything about it.

Rachel can't get a cat because of me . . . me . . . ME!

Improving Your Writing Skills

Writing Basic Sentences

Combining Sentences

Writing with Style

Modeling the Masters

Writing Terms

Writing Basic Sentences

Keeping Your Ideas Under Control

Let's say the tracking on Joe's VCR goes bonkers right in the middle of a good video. He tries everything, but the picture keeps jumping up and down like it has a bad case of hiccups. Finally, he gives up and turns off the machine.

Your readers may end up doing the same thing if your sentences seem out of control. If they can't follow your ideas, they will simply give up on your writing. That is why it is so important to use complete sentences. The guidelines in this chapter will help you write clear, correct sentences so that all of your ideas will be easy to follow.

Always check your writing for sentence errors. This may be your most important job when you edit and proofread your work.

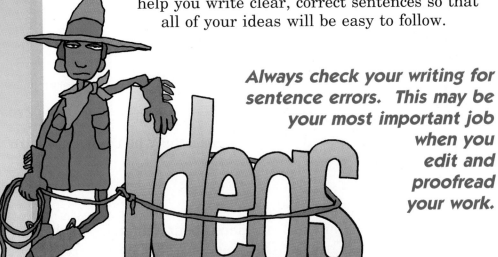

SENTENCE REVIEW

Sentences are not hard to figure out. They are groups of words that express complete thoughts. You already know a sentence when you hear one because your mind is tuned in to complete thoughts. ***Your job as a writer is to listen carefully and write complete sentences.***

The Basic Parts of a Sentence

All sentences have two basic parts—the subject and the verb.

Subject ● The subject usually tells us who or what is doing something.

JOE watched his favorite video.

Verb ● A verb expresses action or links the subject to another part of the sentence. (The verb is sometimes called the **predicate**.)

Joe WATCHED his favorite video. (action)

He IS nuts about adventure movies. (linking)

Additional Words ● Most sentences also contain additional words that describe or complete the thought.

Joe watched HIS FAVORITE VIDEO.

Compound Subjects and Verbs ● A sentence may include more than one subject or more than one verb.

His MOM and BROTHER were in the kitchen. (two subjects)

Then the tracking WENT bonkers and RUINED Joe's fun. (two verbs)

Compound Sentence ● Two sentences may be connected with *and, but,* or *or.*

Later, Joe's mom fixed the tracking, AND he watched the video.

 **TAKE NOTE** You can find more about sentences in the "Check It Out" section. (**SEE** pages 370-373.)

SENTENCE ERRORS

Sentence Fragments ● A **sentence fragment** is a group of words which does not express a complete thought. It is missing important information.

Sentence Fragment: *Thinks she is so cool.* (The subject is missing.)

Corrected Sentence: *Martha thinks she is so cool.*

Sentence Fragment: *Not cool to me.* (The subject and verb are both missing.)

Corrected Sentence: *She is not cool to me.*

Run-On Sentences ● A **run-on sentence** occurs when two sentences are joined without punctuation or a connecting word.

Run-On Sentence: *I thought the lopsided game would never end the score just kept getting worse and worse.* (Punctuation is needed.)

Corrected Sentences: *I thought the lopsided game would never end. The score just kept getting worse and worse.* (Punctuation has been added.)

Corrected Sentence: *I thought the lopsided game would never end, and the score just kept getting worse and worse.* (Punctuation and the connecting word *and* have been added.)

Rambling Sentences ● A **rambling sentence** happens when you put too many little sentences together with the word *and*.

Rambling Sentence: *I went skating down at the pond and three kids from my school were there and we fell on our fannies again and again and we laughed so much our stomachs hurt!* (Too many *and*'s are used.)

Corrected Sentences: *I went skating down at the pond, and three kids from my school were there. We fell on our fannies again and again. We laughed so much our stomachs hurt!*

SENTENCE AGREEMENT

Make sure the parts of your sentence "agree" with one another. If you use a singular subject, use a singular verb; if you use a plural subject, use a plural verb. (Your subject and verb will then be in *agreement*.) The examples below will show you how this works.

One Subject ● In most basic sentences, you have one subject at the beginning of a sentence followed by the verb. Since they are often right next to each other, it is easy to check for subject/verb agreement.

> *Amy wants* **to go bowling.** (*Amy* and *wants* agree because they are both singular.)

> *Her parents want* **to go bowling, too.** (*Parents* and *want* agree because they are both plural.)

Compound Subjects Connected by AND ● If a sentence contains a compound subject connected by *and*, it needs a plural verb.

> *Harry and Earl spend* **most of their time teasing girls.**

> *Sarah and Jesse sing* **like squawking chickens.**

Compound Subjects Connected by OR ● If a sentence contains a compound subject connected by *or*, the verb must agree with the subject nearer to it.

> *Either the cat or the dog wakes* **me up each morning.**
> (A singular verb is needed because *dog* is singular.)

> *Anna or her brothers feed* **the pets each evening.**
> (A plural verb is needed because *brothers* is plural.)

THINK IT OVER

Sometimes the subject will not come at the beginning of the sentence. This will happen in questions and sentences beginning with the word *there*. Check these types of sentences very carefully for subject/verb agreement.

SENTENCE PROBLEMS

Check your sentences for these problems:

Double Subjects ● Avoid
sentences in which a pronoun is
used immediately after the subject.
The result is usually a double subject.

> **Double Subject:** *Some cats they eat all the time.* (The pronoun *they* should be omitted.)

> *Corrected Sentence:* *Some cats eat all the time.*

Pronoun/Antecedent Agreement ● Make sure that the
pronouns in your sentences agree with the words they replace.
(These words are called antecedents.)

> **Agreement Problem:** *If my brother and his friend each eat three Big Macs, he will really be stuffed.* (The pronoun *he* is singular. The words it replaces—*my brother and his friend*—are plural.)

> *Corrected Sentence:* *If my brother and his friend each eat three Big Macs, they will really be stuffed.* (Now the pronoun and the words it replaces agree; they are both plural.)

Double Negatives ● Do not use two negative words, like
never and *no* or *not* and *no*, in the same sentence.

> **Double Negative:** *Never give no one a note in class.*

> *Corrected Sentence:* *Never give anyone a note in class.*

> **Double Negative:** *I didn't have no mistakes in my paragraph.*

> *Corrected Sentence:* *I didn't have any mistakes in my paragraph.*

Confusing OF for HAVE ● Do not use *of* in a sentence when
you really mean *have*. (When *have* is said quickly, it sometimes
sounds like *of*.)

> **Incorrect Usage:** *We should of won the game.*

> *Corrected Sentence:* *We should have won the game.*

Combining Sentences

One Plus One Equals One

Sentence combining is making one smoother, more detailed sentence out of two or more shorter sentences. For instance, take a look at the following sentences:

> *My dog loves to run fast.*
> *He loves to jump fences.*
> *He loves to chase rabbits.*

These three sentences are fine, but see what happens when they are combined. All of the ideas flow more smoothly.

> *My dog loves to run fast, jump fences, and chase rabbits.*

The guidelines in this chapter will help you learn how to combine sentences. Learning this skill will help you write with more style.

Sentence combining will come in handy when you are checking your writing for sentences that don't read smoothly.

Combining with a Key Word or Series

Use a Key Word ● Ideas from short sentences can be combined by moving a key word from one sentence to the other. This key word may be an adjective or an adverb.

Short sentences: *Kelly's necklace broke. It was beaded.*

■ *Combined sentence with an* **ADJECTIVE:**
   *Kelly's **beaded** necklace broke.*

Short sentences: *I am going to start my book report. I'll start it tomorrow.*

■ *Combined sentence with an* **ADVERB:**
   ***Tomorrow** I am going to start my book report.*

Use a Series of Words ● Ideas from short sentences can be combined into one sentence using a series of words or phrases.

Short sentences: *The gym teacher is strict. The gym teacher is organized. The gym teacher is fair.*

■ *Combined sentence with a* **SERIES OF WORDS:**
   *The gym teacher is **strict**, **organized**, and **fair**.*

 All of the words or phrases you use in a series should be *parallel*—stated in the same way. Otherwise, your sentences will sound like they are out of balance. (Look at the example below.)

Awkward series: *The dog was friendly, playful, and he was pretty smart, too.*

■ *Corrected sentence:*
   The dog was friendly, playful, and smart.

Note: This sentence is now correct because all the words in the series—friendly, playful, smart—are single-word adjectives. They are parallel.

Combining with Phrases

Use Phrases ● Ideas
from short sentences
can be combined into
one sentence using
prepositional or
appositive phrases.
(***SEE*** pages 386 and 346.)

Short sentences: *Our cat curls up.*
 *He curls up on top
 of my homework.*

■ *Combined sentence with a* **PREPOSITIONAL PHRASE:**
 Our cat curls up on top of my homework.

Short sentences: *Mrs. Keller makes the best cookies on the block.*
 Mrs. Keller is our next-door neighbor.

■ *Combined sentence with an* **APPOSITIVE PHRASE:**
 Mrs. Keller, **our next-door neighbor***, makes the best cookies on the
 block.*

Use Compound Subjects and Compound Verbs ●

A compound subject includes two or more subjects in one sentence.
A compound verb includes two or more verbs in one sentence.

Two short sentences: *Tom danced around the room.*
 Mary danced around the room, too.

■ *Combined sentence with a* **COMPOUND SUBJECT:**
 Tom and Mary danced around the room.

Two short sentences: *John slipped on the ice.*
 He fell on his rear end.

■ *Combined sentence with a* **COMPOUND VERB:**
 John slipped on the ice and fell on his rear end.

Combining with Longer Sentences

Use Compound Sentences ● A compound sentence is made up of two or more simple sentences joined together. The conjunctions *and, but, or, nor, for, so,* and *yet* are used to connect the simple sentences. (Place a comma before the conjunction.)

Two simple sentences: *My puppy has hair hanging over her eyes.*
She looks just like a dust mop.

■ *Combined sentence with* **AND:**
My puppy has hair hanging over her eyes, **and** *she looks just like a dust mop.*

Two simple sentences: *Our dog likes to eat shoes.*
He won't touch my brother's smelly slippers.

■ *Combined sentence with* **BUT:**
Our dog likes to eat shoes, **but** *he won't touch my brother's smelly slippers.*

Use Complex Sentences ● A complex sentence is made up of two ideas connected by words called subordinate conjunctions (*after, when, since, because, before,* etc.) and relative pronouns (*who, whose, which,* and *that*).

Two short sentences: *My best friend shares his lunch with me.*
He doesn't like what his dad packs.

■ *Combined sentence with* **BECAUSE:**
My best friend shares his lunch with me **because** *he doesn't like what his dad packs.*

Two short sentences: *Very cold weather closed school for a day.*
The cold weather came down from northern Canada.

■ *Combined sentence with* **WHICH:**
Very cold weather, **which** *came down from northern Canada, closed school for a day.*

Learning by Doing

Style comes in many shapes and sizes. You may like to perform a certain stunt that gets you and your skateboard high off the ground. That's part of your own special style. You may like pepperoni on your pizza. That's also part of your style. You may like to wear your hair cut short or long or half-and-half. That's your style, too. What's *in style* for you depends on your own interests and tastes.

The Way You Write

As a young writer, you have your own special way of expressing your thoughts and feelings on paper. This is your writing style, and it will develop naturally as you write more and more. However, you can help your writing style along if you follow our suggestions in this chapter.

> **❝Writing isn't just words on paper anymore. It's me. ❞**
> —Meredith Dempsey, student

Developing a Sense of Style

Your writing style will grow strong and healthy if you follow the advice listed below.

➤ **Practice often.** Keep a daily journal. This is the best way to develop your writing style.

➤ **Try different forms.** Write poems and riddles; write news stories and personal stories. Each form of writing has something special to offer you.

➤ **Write about ideas that are important to you.** If you write about subjects that really interest you, your writing style will have a better chance of developing.

➤ **Please yourself.** If you don't feel good about your writing, try again. Make it sound like the real you.

➤ **See how other writers do it.** When you read, look for sentences that read smoothly or contain eye-catching words. Write some of these sentences down. Then see if you can write your own sentences in the same way.

➤ **Write with details.** Writing without details is like baking cookies without flour. One of the most important ingredients is missing. Use details that help readers see, hear, smell, taste, and feel your subject. Also use similes (like the sentence about cookies) and metaphors.

➤ **Know when your writing doesn't work.** Watch for sentences that all sound the same as well as sentences that sound boring or lifeless. Then try to fix these!

MINI LESSON This activity will help you write sentences with style. List five or six sentences from your writing (your best or your worst). Then try to change each sentence so it sounds better. You might change the order of the words in one sentence and use a different descriptive word in another one.

Modeling the Masters

Follow the Leaders

Beginning artists learn a lot about art by studying the work of famous painters. In the same way, you can learn a lot about writing by studying the work of your favorite authors. When you come across sentences or short passages that you especially like, practice building sentences of your own that follow an author's pattern of writing. This process is sometimes called "modeling." Here are some guidelines you can use for doing your own modeling.

Guidelines for Modeling

- **Find** a sentence (or short passage) that you especially like.
- **Select** a subject for your copychange.
- **Follow** the pattern of your model sentences as you write about your subject.
- **Build** your sentence one small section at a time.
- **Review** your work, and change any parts that seem confusing or unclear.

One Writer's Experience

Modeling Roald Dahl

Kate has enjoyed Roald Dahl's stories for a long time, so every once in a while she tries to write like him. Here is one sentence from Dahl's book *Danny the Champion of the World*:

> **Grown-ups are complicated creatures, full of quirks and secrets.**

Here's Kate's sentence, modeling Roald Dahl's sentence:

Cats are complex beasts, going from lazy to crazy in no time.

Kate might have written, "Some cats can be really nutty. They can go from being couch potatoes to crazy blurs of fur in no time." While this is fine, her modeling has taught her that she can create powerful ideas with fewer words. She has discovered a new pattern of writing.

Modeling Will Hobbs

Later, Kate tried modeling a longer sentence from Will Hobbs's book *The Big Wander*. (This sentence describes the spooky sound made by a band of coyotes.)

> **It wasn't but a second until the barks became yips and the yipping shifted into quavering sirens climbing higher and higher in pitch, as maybe a half-dozen coyotes harmonized like a band of lunatics and brought the hair rising on the back of his neck.**

Kate especially liked the sound of this sentence. She also liked the descriptive language it contained (*quavering sirens* and *coyotes harmonized like a band of lunatics*). Here's her sentence: (Notice that she is still thinking about her cat!)

It wasn't but a minute until her paws became claws and the claws grew into slashing weapons, as a howling nightmare filled her head like a pack of mad dogs and made the fur on her back stand straight up on end.

Writing Terms

This list contains words used to describe different parts of the writing process. It also includes certain writing devices, or special ways of stating an idea.

Anecdote ● A brief story used to make a point. The story of young Abe Lincoln walking more than two miles to return several pennies to a customer is an anecdote which shows how honest Abe was.

Arrangement ● The way details are organized in writing. (**SEE** page 68 for more information.)

Audience ● Those people who read or hear what you have written.

Body ● The main part of the writing that comes between the opening and closing ideas. The body of a piece of writing contains the specific details that support or develop the main idea.

Brainstorming ● Collecting ideas in groups by freely sharing all of the different possibilities.

Cliche ● A familiar word or phrase which has been used so much that it is no longer a good way of saying something, such as *good as gold* or *bright as the sun*.

Closing/Concluding sentence ● The sentence which sums up the main point being made in a paragraph.

Composition ● Writing in which all the ideas work together to form a finished product.

Conferencing ● Working and sharing in writing groups.

Description ● Writing which paints a picture of a person, a place, a thing, or an idea using specific details.

Details ● The specific facts, examples, and words used in a piece of writing to support or explain the main idea.

Diction ● A writer's choice of words. In a story about everyday life, a writer may use very informal, everyday language. For a business letter, a writer will use more formal or proper language.

Editing ● Checking your writing to make sure the words and sentences are strong and smooth reading. Editing also means checking for spelling, grammar, and mechanics errors.

Exaggeration ● Words that stretch the truth. Exaggeration is used in tall tales: *The mosquito is so big it needs a runway to land.*

Exposition ● Writing which explains, such as a report or research paper. (Also called expository writing.)

Figure of speech ● A special way of writing to create an effective word picture. A figure of speech usually involves making a comparison of some type. (**SEE** *simile, metaphor,* and *personification.*)

First draft ● The first complete writing about a subject.

Focus/Main idea ● Concentrating on a specific part of a subject. When writing about a favorite person, you could focus on his or her sense of humor.

Form ● The shape of writing—a poem, an essay, a novel, a play, and so on. (**SEE** pages 34-35 for a complete list.)

Free writing ● Writing freely and rapidly to discover new ideas.

Generalization ● A statement which gives the general meaning rather than the specific details of a subject. "Writing helps you learn" is a generalization. (**SEE** *topic sentence.*)

Grammar ● The rules and guidelines of a language, which are used when you want to be correct in your writing and speaking.

Irony ● Using a word or phrase to mean the exact opposite of its normal meaning: Having the flu is *so much fun,* don't you think?

Journal ● A daily record of thoughts, feelings, and ideas.

Limiting the subject ● Narrowing a general writing subject to a more specific writing idea: *Pets—dogs—Labradors—older Labs—caring for older Labs.*

Metaphor ● A figure of speech that compares two different things without using a word of comparison such as *like* or *as:* *The streetlight was my security guard.*

Modifier ● A word, or group of words, which describes another word or idea. (**SEE** "Adjectives" and "Adverbs" on pages 384-385.)

Narration ● Writing which tells a story or recalls an experience.

Objective ● Writing which includes facts, with no opinions or personal feelings.

Parallelism ● The repeating of phrases or sentences that are written in the same way: Josie *scratched her head, bit her nails,* and *shrugged her shoulders.*

Personal narrative ● Writing which tells a story from the writer's life.

Personification ● A figure of speech in which an idea, object, or animal is given qualities of a person: *The rock refused to move.*

Persuasion ● Writing which is meant to change the way a reader thinks or acts.

Prewriting ● Planning a writing project. *Selecting a subject* and *collecting details* are prewriting activities.

Process ● A way of doing something which involves several steps; the writing process includes prewriting, writing the first draft, revising, editing and proofreading, and publishing.

Proofreading ● Checking a final draft for spelling, grammar, and mechanics errors.

Prose ● Regular writing in sentences and paragraphs.

Pun ● A word or phrase used in a way that gives it a funny twist: That story about rabbits is a real *hare raiser.*

Purpose ● The main reason a person has for writing.

Revising ● Changing a first draft to improve it.

Sarcasm ● Praise that actually means the opposite, and is meant to put someone down: That's *just great!*

Sensory details ● Details which help us to see, feel, smell, taste, and hear a subject.

Simile ● A figure of speech that makes a comparison using either *like* or *as*: *A gentle summer wind feels like a soft cotton sheet.*

Slang ● Special words and phrases used by friends when they are talking to each other. "Chill out" is a slang term.

Style ● A writer's choice of words, phrases, and sentences.

Subjective ● Writing which includes personal feelings.

Supporting details ● The details used to develop a subject or bring a story to life.

Theme ● The central idea or message in a piece of writing.

Topic ● The specific subject of a piece of writing.

Topic sentence ● The sentence which contains the main idea of a paragraph. (**SEE** pages 60-61.)

Transitions ● Words which help tie ideas together. (**SEE** page 69.)

Voice ● The way a writer expresses ideas. Writing that sounds believable is often written in an honest, natural voice.

The Forms of Writing

Personal Writing

Writing in Journals

Writing Personal Narratives

Writing Friendly Letters

Writing in Journals

Your Very Bad Day

Your old friend Bobbi Jones told everyone that your socks didn't match. Your mother packed you a cheese sandwich and two carrot sticks for the third day in a row. You never got a chance to bat during gym class. And on the way home from school, you left your favorite folder on the bus. Repeat after me: "It was a terrible, horrible, no-good, very bad day!"

How should you deal with a day like this? You could head straight for the Oreo cookies in the kitchen, "chill out" in front of the TV, or give your pillow a couple of body slams. But what happens when you can't look at another Oreo or watch another rerun? Your "very bad day" will still be there.

Here's what I would do: After a couple of cookies, I would get out my personal journal and write about all of the things that happened. Writing helps me sort out my thoughts. It helps keep me in control. It helps make bad days not seem so bad. And I almost always feel better when I'm done.

Why Should You Write In a Personal Journal?

There are many reasons to write in a journal. You can . . .

✔ **make notes of interesting things you see and hear,**
✔ **collect ideas for stories, poems, and reports,**
✔ **practice writing on your own,**
✔ **deal with your bad days,**
✔ **and relive all of your good times.**

Here's how to get started . . .

1 **Gather the right tools.** All you need is a notebook and some pens or pencils (or a computer).

2 **Find a special time and place to write.** Get up early in the morning and write while it is quiet in your house. Write at a regular time during school. Or plop down on your bed right after dinner and see how that works.

3 **Write every day.** Write freely, exploring your thoughts and feelings as they come to mind. Don't worry about what you say or how you say it. Just keep writing for as long as you can (at least 5-10 minutes at a time).

4 **Write about those things that are important to you.** Write about something that is bothering you or something you want to remember. Write about what you did last weekend or something silly you saw. Write about one thing and then later go on to something else.

5 **Keep track of your writing.** Put the date on the top of the page each time you write. Read through your journal writings from time to time. Underline ideas you find interesting or surprising and ideas that you would like to write more about in the future.

A Closer Look at Journal Writing

Journal writing works best when you can *reflect* or really think about your experiences and learn from them. When you can do this, your writing becomes more exciting—and full of surprises.

➤ *Reflect*

Thinking and writing in the following ways will help you explore and reflect upon your experiences.

Ask questions: As you write, ask yourself some questions: *"What was fun or interesting about this experience?" "How do I feel about it now?"* Or simply ask yourself *why?* at different points in your writing, and try to discover some answers.

Wonder: Also think about what you have learned from an experience. *Compare* it to others you've had. *Wonder* what you could have done differently, or *predict* what the experience will mean to you in the future.

Read the model journal writing on page 108, and you will see that this student was writing and thinking (reflecting) about his father.

➤ *Push Yourself*

If you push yourself in your writing, you are sure to make some interesting discoveries.

Keep it going: When you start a new journal writing, pick up right where you left off in your last entry. When you find an idea that surprises you, try to say more about it. When you think that you have said all that you can about a certain subject, keep going for at least a few more lines.

Make connections: And if you want a challenge, try to make connections between ideas that seem really different. You can also make connections to events in the news, movies, songs, and so on.

Kinds of Journals

If you enjoy exploring your thoughts in a personal journal, you might also enjoy writing in one of the special journals listed below.

Dialogue Journal ● In a dialogue journal, you and a friend, parent, or teacher write to each other about experiences you've had, books you've read, or ideas you wonder about. (**SEE** the sample on the next page.)

Diary ● A diary is a personal record of daily events as they happened. (You keep track of personal things in a diary.)

Learning Log ● In a learning log or class journal, you write about subjects like math and science to help you understand them better. (**SEE** pages 338-339 for more information.)

Response Journal ● Do you ever have strong feelings about the stories and books you read? You can write about these feelings in a response journal. (**SEE** page 137 for a list of writing ideas.)

A Special-Event Journal ● You may want to write about your experiences while participating in a sport, while preparing for a new member in the family, or while doing a special project.

Sample Journal Writing

In the first sample, a student thinks and writes about his father and the army.

Oct. 26

I never imagined growing up without a father. He could have died in the Vietnam War. I never thought of it that way. I'm sure my mother did. The subject never comes up at home. But I think about my dad's military service a lot.

I wonder what I would do if I was in the army. Lt. Craven, it has a nice ring to it. Jogging 20 miles, 50 push-ups, and cheap food.

Just watching war movies I know what my father went through. I'm glad he's home, and everyone's happy . . .

Dialogue Journal

In this second sample, a student and teacher carry on a conversation about a book.

Feb. 3

Dear Susan,

That part in <u>Mrs. Frankweiler</u> where the kids are hiding in the bathroom made me think of the time I hid from my mom in K-Mart. I didn't want to go home, so I hid behind the shower curtains. She was so mad! I thought of this because my heart was beating really fast whenever Mom got close to me, like the kids' hearts in the book. (Hey, when does your heart beat fast?)

Sincerely,
Mrs. N

Dear Mrs. N,

Thanks for your letter. You hid from your mother? That's funny. My heart beats fast (1) when we have spelling bees, (2) when I'm reading my book to the class, and (3) when you call on me to answer a math problem and I'm not sure where we are! (I have to number my problems!)

Your friend,
Susan

Writing Personal Narratives

The Stories of Your Life

Have you ever wished you could be the main character in a story? Well, guess what? You already are. You're the main character in the story of your life. A true story about yourself is sometimes called a **personal narrative**.

A personal narrative is a story about a personal memory. But it's not about any old memory. It's about a time so important you don't ever want to forget it.

> 66 *It's not easy to travel back into your memory and gather details. But it's worth it. They help your reader understand what happened. And they help you remember the very important chapters in the story of your life.* 99
> —Sandy Asher

First Thoughts

Think about the different chapters (or experiences) in the story of your life. Some of them might make you laugh; some might make you shudder. Then again, maybe some of them make you feel angry or happy or sad or excited. Any experience that has caused you to feel a strong emotion is a good subject for a personal narrative.

Model Personal Narrative

Here's a true story about me and my family. When it happened, I felt scared, sad, and then happy. (I'm sure you have plenty of your own exciting stories to share.)

THE GREAT GERBIL ESCAPE

When my daughter Emily was nine years old, she had a pair of gerbils named Farrah and Festus. One day, Festus escaped from our bathtub!

It sounds silly to have gerbils in your tub, but it's not. The sides are too high to jump over and too slick to climb. We plugged the drain. We put in toys and sunflower seeds. The gerbils could exercise and play safely.

But one day, I accidentally left a fuzzy blue bath mat over the edge of the tub. When Emily and I came back, Festus was gone. He'd grabbed the mat and climbed out!

The only place he could have gone was down the heat vent in the wall. We knelt beside the vent. We could hear him! "Scritch-scratch. Scritch-scratch." We lowered a rope into the vent, but he didn't climb out. We stuffed in a towel, but he didn't climb that either.

And when we pulled the towel out, there was no more "Scritch-scratch." Oh, no! I thought. We've pushed him down the vent into the furnace. We've baked our gerbil!

Emily was heartbroken. I felt terrible. We put Farrah back in the cage and went downstairs. Then I noticed another heat vent in the hall, right below the one upstairs in the bathroom. And sure enough, we could hear Festus again: "Scritch-scratch. Scritch-scratch!"

Finally, Emily remembered that gerbils love to explore boxes. We took all the tissues out of a small tissue box. Emily lowered the box into the vent as far as her arm could reach. Then Festus climbed aboard and rode to safety in his own private elevator. And that's how the Great Gerbil Escape became the Great Gerbil Rescue!

The story is organized according to time (describing what happens first, second, third, and so on).

Each new action adds suspense and interest to the story.

Gathering Story Ideas

You can start gathering ideas for personal narratives by writing in a daily diary or journal, or by making lists of personal experiences. A good way to find ideas is to ask yourself the following types of questions:

■ Who are the important people in your life?

Family members? Friends? Classmates? Neighbors? Think about the times you've shared with each one. What do you remember best? What would you just as soon forget?

■ Where have you been?

Every place you visit is an adventure, whether it's the doctor's office, the principal's office, or Disneyland. Think of the biggest place you've been, and the smallest. Think of comfortable places, and places that cause you to squirm. Think of special meeting places from your past.

■ What do you like to do?

Do you enjoy drawing or cooking or caring for animals? Do you like to play ball or just hang out? Do you like to talk on the phone or read at night when you're supposed to be asleep?

■ What do you *not* like to do?

Study? Clean your room? Babysit? Get up early? There are a lot of ways to answer this question, aren't there? And a lot of strong feelings involved, too. Isn't it nice to know that even the *worst* times you can remember are at least good for story ideas?

If you don't know **where** you're going, you'll probably end up **somewhere** else.

Writing a Personal Narrative

PREWRITING *Planning Your Way*

Select a Subject ● Choosing a subject for a personal narrative should be easy. You're looking for a memorable experience that happened over a short period of time. (**SEE** "Gathering Story Ideas" on the previous page for help.)

Collect Your Thoughts ● If the experience you select seems really clear in your mind, go right to your first draft. Write it all out as best you can. If you're a little fuzzy about all of the details, try doing a cluster or making a list.

YOU DON'T SSSSSSAY   As soon as you can answer the 5 W's—*Who? What? When? Where?* and *Why?*—about the experience, you're probably ready to write.

WRITING THE FIRST DRAFT

Start at the Beginning ● Put yourself at the beginning of the experience ("There I stood" or "As I entered the room") and continue to add details as they come to mind. Don't worry about saying everything. You can fill in any gaps later when you revise.

REVISING *Improving Your Writing*

Review Your Work ● Look over your first draft. Have you left out any important details, or put things in the wrong order? Ask a classmate to review your writing as well. Then make the necessary changes in your story. (**SEE** "Striking It Rich in Your Story" on page 114 for helpful writing reminders.)

EDITING & PROOFREADING

Check for Careless Errors ● Make sure that your writing makes sense and reads smoothly. Then write a neat, error-free final draft and proofread it.

Striking It Rich in Your Story

Here are some special reminders to help you develop your personal narrative:

Add Physical Details ● Take another look at my gerbil story. Can you see what I saw? There are two gerbils in the tub, with its high, slick sides. There's the fuzzy blue bath mat and the heat vent in the wall. It's important that you help your readers see the details that matter. You do this by adding important facts and by leaving out facts that are less important to your story.

Add Sounds, Tastes, Smells, and Textures ● Sounds make readers feel as if they were there, living the adventure with you. I emphasize one important sound in my story: "Scritch-scratch!" What about taste, smell, and touch? Did I include all of those in my gerbil tale? Only touch. I mentioned that the tub was slick and the bath mat was fuzzy. Taste and smell weren't important in my story, but they might be in yours.

Add Dialogue ● Dialogue always makes a story seem real. Here's how I might have started my story with dialogue:

> *"Mom, look!" Emily shouted. "Festus is gone!"*
>
> *"Gone?" I asked, rushing into the bathroom after her. "What do you mean?"*

Add Thoughts and Feelings ● What helped you understand my thoughts and feelings in "The Great Gerbil Escape"? Comments like "Oh, no!" and "I felt terrible" surely helped. A narrative without the writer's thoughts and feelings would not have that special personal touch that can make this type of writing so much fun to read.

TAKE NOTE Write the way you feel. If your subject makes you laugh, try to make your readers laugh. Or, if your subject makes you feel sad or excited, try to make your readers feel the same way.

Student Model

In this model narrative, Jessica Gilbert recalls a motorcycle ride that taught her an important lesson.

When I Got Burned on My Dad's Motorcycle

As I was going outside, I was happy because I was going to ride on my dad's motorcycle. It was always fun.

"Come on. Get up," said my dad cheerfully.

"Okay," I answered. But just as I was getting onto the seat, I burnt myself on one of the accelerator pipes!

"Ow!" I yelled as I started to cry.

"Are you all right?" asked my mom.

"No," I answered.

"Come here," said my mom. "Let's take a look at that burn. It's really bad. I don't think she should go for a ride on the motorcycle."

I felt really glad that my mom had said that.

"Aw, come on. It won't hurt her anymore than she's already hurtin'," said my dad. I started to get really angry. I mean, I was only five years old. I hurt! Why should I have to ride the motorcycle?

Then he picked me up and set me on the seat of the motorcycle.

"Dad, I don't wanna go!" I said, still crying.

"Nonsense. Now stop crying," said my dad. And we took off.

I have to admit that during the ride, I started to laugh. My burn hardly hurt anymore. I was still sniffling a little when we got back, but it had been a fun ride.

I'm really glad my dad made me get on the motorcycle. If he hadn't, I probably never would have gotten on it again. From that day on, I knew I would never give up after I got hurt. I would just get back up and try it again.

Dialogue makes the story seem real.

The writer shares her thoughts and feelings with the reader.

Writing Friendly Letters

Keeping in Touch

Do you ever run to the mailbox to see if anything is addressed to you? Everyone enjoys receiving mail, especially letters. Letters from friends make friendships stronger. Letters from relatives make you feel closer. The best way to make sure you receive a letter is to send one.

Parts of a Friendly Letter

Friendly letters have five parts: the *heading*, the *salutation*, the *body*, the *closing*, and the *signature*.

➤ The **heading** includes your address and the date. Write it in the upper right-hand corner.

➤ The **salutation** or greeting usually begins with the word *Dear* and is followed by the name of the person who will receive the letter. Place a comma after the name. Write a salutation at the left-hand margin, two lines below the heading.

➤ The **body** of the letter contains your thoughts and ideas. Begin writing on the second line after the salutation. Keep the paragraphs short for easy reading.

➤ Write the **closing** two lines below the body of your letter. Capitalize only the first word and follow it with a comma. Put your **signature** under the closing.

Model Friendly Letter

Tracy introduced herself in this letter to her new pen pal, Grace.

Heading

123 Wixom Road
Wixom, MI 48386
January 8, 1994

Salutation   Dear Grace,

My name is Tracy, and I am your new pen pal. I'm in the fifth grade at Wixom Elementary School in Wixom, Michigan.

I'll start by telling you about some of my hobbies. I am taking keyboard lessons because I got a keyboard for Christmas, and I think it will be fun. I'm not very good, yet, but I can play two songs. Have you ever played a keyboard?

Another hobby of mine is horseback riding. Have you ever been horseback riding? When my dad was 15, besides school, he worked at a horse ranch. I think that is neat.

Body

I really like to draw, paint, and read stories. I also love to read mystery books and fiction books. My favorite mystery series is Nancy Drew. Do you like to read?

I have three people in my family: my mom, my dad, and me. My mom is in advertising, and my dad is in sales. I also have ten pets: seven fish, two parakeets, and a dog. My dog's name is Hershey. My family and I named her that because she's all brown, like a Hershey's chocolate bar. My two birds, Sammy and Tweedy, are green, blue, yellow, and black. Tweedy bites, and because of that, it's really hard to train her. Sammy is trained and can ride on my shoulder in the house.

As you probably have noticed, I love animals. I want to work with animals when I grow up, especially with whales. What do you want to be when you grow up?

Closing

Sincerely,

Signature

Tracy Randlett

P.S. Write back soon!

Writing a Friendly Letter

PREWRITING *Planning Your Letter*

Choose a Friend ● This part is easy! Write to someone who wrote to you, someone you haven't seen in a long time, or a special person you want to talk to in a letter. Maybe you'd like to have a pen pal as Tracy did.

Gather Ideas ● List all of the ideas you want to include in your letter. Gather all the details you will need to make each idea clear. Here are some ideas to get you started:

- Share a good story.
- Tell what's been on your mind.
- Describe something you like to do.
- Tell about the latest book you've read.
- Share a favorite poem, or write one of your own.
- Provide a few questions for your friend to answer.

WRITING

Get Started ● Begin by telling all about one of the ideas on your list. Any one will do! Tracy started by telling all about her hobbies and the things she likes to do. Then she told about her family and pets.

Write Back ● If you are writing back to a friend, you can start by answering the questions he or she may have asked. Then add the new information about yourself.

THINK IT OVER Writing a friendly letter gives you a chance to think about your own life. In this way, you benefit from writing a letter as much as the person who receives it.

REVISING *Improving Your Letter*

Try to make your letter easy to read and entertaining. Read the sentences over to be sure they make sense. Remember to start a new paragraph each time you switch to a new story or idea.

EDITING & PROOFREADING

Check your letter for spelling, punctuation, and capitalization. Also check the form of your letter, especially if you are writing to someone who is not a close friend or relative. Then neatly write or type a final copy if you need to. A correctly written letter will make a good first impression.

P.S. If you have already finished your letter and then remember something you forgot to say, add a P.S. (postscript) at the bottom under your signature.

Address the Envelope

Address the envelope clearly and correctly so it is sure to reach its destination. Also make sure to fold your letter so that it fits neatly into the envelope. (**SEE** page 146.)

```
Miss Tracy Randlett                              USA
123 Wixom Rd.                                     ¢
Wixom, MI   48386



              Miss Grace Jackson
              682 State St.
              Springfield, IL    62704
```

Writing Social Notes

Sometimes you will need to write a special kind of friendly letter—a thank-you note or an invitation. These are often called **social notes**.

Parts of Social Notes

A social note begins with a **salutation** (*Dear _____ ,*). The middle of your note, the **body**, is usually one or two paragraphs. The paragraphs are short and to the point. "Your friend" or "Love" are common **closings**. Don't forget to sign your note with your **signature**.

Invitations ➤ When you are inviting someone to come to a party or special event, you'll need to write an **invitation**. Be sure to include these items:

- **What:**   a party, a celebration
- **When:**   the date and time
- **Where:**   the place and address
- **Who:**   who the party is for
- **Why:**   birthday, bar mitzvah, going away

Ask for an answer in your letter if you want to know whether or not the person will be coming to your event. You can also add R.S.V.P. and your telephone number in the lower left-hand corner.

Thank-You Notes ➤ When writing a *thank-you note*, be specific. If you are thanking someone for something special he or she did, explain why it was important to you. If you are thanking someone for a gift, tell why you like it and how you are using it.

Bright IDEA

You can make your own customized notes and invitations with rubber stamps, watercolors, colored markers, stickers, special lettering, etc. Be creative!

Sample Invitation

Dear Josh,

    My tenth birthday is coming up, and my dad said I could have a party. He's going to take us to the zoo, and the director said we could go on a scavenger hunt.

    The party will be on my birthday, April 29th. You can be dropped off at 12:30 and picked up at 4:00 p.m.

    My address is 3200 North Main Street. Bring a raincoat if it looks like rain. Please call me to let me know if you can come.

Anna
R.S.V.P. 639-2231

Sample Thank-You Note

THANK YOU
THANK YOU
THANK YOU
THANK YOU
THANK YOU
THANK YOU
THANK YOU
THANK YOU
THANK YOU
THANK YOU
THANK YOU
THANK YOU
THANK YOU

Dear Josh,

    Thanks for coming to my party. The book and paper-making kit you gave me are great. I started reading 50 Simple Things Kids Can Do to Save the Earth, and I'm already working on some of the ideas.

    I started collecting junk mail to use for the paper-making kit. I'll show you how my first paper turns out. Thank you very much for the presents. I really like them.

                Your friend,
                Anna

Subject Writing

Writing Newspaper Stories

Writing Book Reviews

Writing Explanations

Writing Business Letters

Writing Observation Reports

Writing Newspaper Stories

Look!
Up in the Sky!
It's a Reporter!

How would you like to be Superman for a day? Would you like to zoom through the sky? Leap over tall buildings? Discover secrets with your X-ray vision?

You may remember that Superman, when he wasn't flying around in his long underwear, had a real job. As Clark Kent, he worked as a newspaper reporter.

Real-Life Reporters

Some reporters think that writing stories about important events and memorable people is more interesting than being a comic-book hero. As you read this chapter, maybe you'll see why.

> 66 *Starting today, you can be a reporter in your own classroom, school, and community. All you need is a little curiosity, an interest in people, and, of course, a reporter's notebook! With a little energy and creativity, you can even produce your own newspaper.* 99
> —Roy Peter Clark

The Parts of a Reporter

Interviewing

Many wonderful stories result from interviews. During an interview, the reporter asks people questions about their experiences. The result can be a dramatic and funny adventure, like this one:

JAWS!
By Karin Fraser

One day last summer during school vacation, a boy named Billy Shannon was at the Don CeSar Beach. He was swimming in the Gulf of Mexico. He was swimming near the deep water markers, and he felt something rubbery slide against his leg and saw a fin.

He called "Help!" about four or five times. A few people went out of the water. The movie <u>Jaws</u> flashed through his mind. The lifeguard went to him in a jet-ski. He pointed out that they were dolphins.

Billy swam back to the shore. He went to the pool where his parents were. He was quite embarrassed. He told them the story, and they thought it was funny. His brother made fun of him, and Billy punched him in the jaw.

Tips for Interviewing

✔ Prepare a list of questions beforehand.

✔ Start with a question from your list, but then try to make the interview seem like a *real* conversation.

✔ Listen carefully, write quickly.

✔ When you take notes, politely say, "I want to write that down." The person will stop so you can write.

✔ Ask the person to spell any names you're unsure of.

✔ Remember that **the meaning is more important than the exact words**.

Finding News Stories

A news story tells readers about an important or unusual event. The more important the event, the more interesting the news. An old joke says that when a dog bites a man, it is not news. But when a man bites a dog, that's news!

The headlines below show the difference between news that is news, and news that is not news.

News:

Daily Chronicle
Class Makes Flying Saucer

Not News:

Daily Chronicle
Saucer Breaks in Cafeteria

News:

Daily Chronicle
Flu Hits Jones School

Not News:

Daily Chronicle
Student Gets Headache

News:

Daily Chronicle
Artists Receive Awards

Not News:

Daily Chronicle
Art Teacher Draws in Class

MINI LESSON   Newspaper stories are about real events, not make-believe ones. Make a list of interesting things that have recently happened at your school. Put stars next to the ones that you think would make good news stories.

Three Types of Stories

Here is a list of stories written by students in St. Petersburg, Florida. They decided to name their classroom newspaper the *Cougar Chronicle*, after the school mascot. The newspaper's motto is "If a fifth-grader needs to know it, we print it." You will notice that these stories are listed under three general story types: news stories, human interest stories, and opinion letters to the editor.

News Stories

- A power outage kills fish in the fifth-grade aquarium.
- Swimmer Nicole Haislett, who lives nearby, wins a Gold Medal in the Olympics.

Human Interest Stories

- What is it like to see a baby being born?
- Who is the fastest reader in third grade?
- Our math teacher plays in a rock band.
- Your friend mistakes a dolphin for a shark. (**SEE** "Jaws!" on page 125.)

Opinion Letters to the Editor

- There should be a greater variety of nutritious foods in the school cafeteria.
- We should have more time for reading and more books available in our classroom.
- People should not give pets as gifts because the pets are often abandoned.

A good reporter sees the world as a storehouse of story ideas. Look around, be curious, read, and ask questions. You'll discover stories everywhere—in your classroom, school, and community—enough to fill up the pages of any classroom newspaper.

Daily Chronicle

❶Lakewood Girls Win Soccer Championship!

❷ by Anna Flanagan

The girls of Lakewood High School made history yesterday. They became the first West Florida team to win a state soccer championship. They beat Rockledge High by a score of 1-0.

❹ "The girls played great," said Coach Bill Carter. "I'll always remember this team. In my eyes they were all stars."

❺ Ever since Susan James broke the team record by scoring five goals against Central, no one could stop Lakewood. Susan and her teammates, Darcy Smith and Colleen Kelly, played such good defense that only one goal was scored against them in their last three games.

They have set a new record for their high school, ending the season with a record of 7 wins and 0 losses.

❻ Coach Carter smiled as he said, "Eight members of our soccer team will return next year. I am ready for the season to start right now."

Parts of a Newspaper Story

❶ The **Headline** is a title that tells the story in bold type:
Lakewood Girls Win Soccer Championship!

❷ The **Byline** gives the writer credit for the story.

❸ The **Lead** tells the reader the most important news:
"The girls of Lakewood High School made history yesterday. They became the first West Florida team to win a state soccer championship. They beat Rockledge High by a score of 1-0."

❹ A good **Quote** gives life to a story:
"The girls played great," said Coach Bill Carter. "I'll always remember this team."

❺ The **Body** of the story answers questions for the reader:
- Who played well?
- How many games has the team won this season?

❻ The **Ending** gives the reader something to remember:
"Eight members of our soccer team will return next year. I am ready for the season to start right now."

Writing a News Story

PREWRITING *Planning Your Writing*

Select a Subject ● Write about a *newsworthy* subject—something important, interesting, or unusual that your readers will want to read about.

Collect Details ● You can do this by interviewing people, making eyewitness observations, and so on. A good starting point is to ask the 5 W's and H—*Who? What? Where? When? Why?* and *How?* (Try to include enough information to answer any questions your readers may have.)

WRITING THE FIRST DRAFT

Write the Lead or First Paragraph ● Begin with the most important or interesting detail. If at all possible, put a person in the lead paragraph—for example, a baker spinning a pizza crust, or a lifeguard hearing a shout for help. (**SEE** page 130.)

Write the Main Part of Your Story ● Remember that the most important information is usually stated early in basic news stories. Try to leave your readers with something to think about in the ending.

REVISING *Improving Your Writing*

Review Your Work ● Make sure you have included all of the important facts and details in your story. Also make sure your information is correct and in the best possible order.

EDITING & PROOFREADING

Check for Careless Errors ● Pay careful attention to the spelling of names! Have your teacher or a classmate review your work as well. Write the final copy of your story.

Writing a Lead

The beginning of a newspaper story is called a **lead** because it leads the reader into the rest of the story. The lead can be a short sentence or a paragraph. When it is well written, the lead pulls the reader into the story, and prepares the reader for what comes next.

Remember Karin Fraser's lead for the story "Jaws!"? She begins the story with a bit of danger, so the reader will want to find out if Billy Shannon is going to be the victim of a shark attack.

Student Models

Here are some leads written by student reporters. Read them and then imagine what the rest of the story will be about:

I rode six hours in a little yellow Datsun, but it was worth it. I finally got to see the greatest concert in years.

Picture in your mind the most beautiful sunset you've ever seen, the one sunset that you'll remember forever.

Everybody was in uniform, out on the field, and ready for the final game of the season.

Tommy Walton is "The World's Greatest Singing Hot-Dog Salesman," a 58-year-old man with the heart and soul of a teenager.

Lead Sampler

The samples listed here will help you write leads for human interest stories.

- **Question Lead:** *Have you ever watched a true hot-dog lover in action?*

- **Suspense Lead:** *Should she hold the pickle relish or mustard? Tanya Robinson couldn't decide.*

- **Surprise Lead:** *A dog with the works is worth the indigestion.*

Writing a Letter to the Editor

As a citizen of the United States, you have many rights and freedoms. Americans benefit from freedom of religion, freedom of expression, and freedom of the press. One way to practice your freedom is to write a letter to the editor of a newspaper.

BUDDY SNIDER
1715 PALM ST
ST PETERSBURG FL 33712

LETTERS TO THE EDITOR
THE COUGAR CHRONICLE
BOX 1101
ST PETERSBURG FL 33712

1715 Palm St.
St. Petersburg, FL 3
October 15, 1993

Editor
The Cougar Chronicle
Box 1101
St. Petersburg, FL 33712

Dear Editor:

During the last six years that I have been going to Bay Point Elementary School, the lunches have been getting smaller, and the prices have been getting bigger! I have noticed that the little mustard and ketchup containers have taken one whole space on the tray that used to be filled with a vegetable or something else.

We are also getting smaller main courses. When I get home from school, I eat a lot; and sometimes my mom has to tell me to stop.

Maybe it is because I'm getting older and I eat more, but I think that the school lunches are getting smaller.

Yours truly,

Buddy Snider
Buddy Snider

◀ **Here is a student's letter:**

Good newspapers will publish letters written by young people. They know that young writers have strongly felt beliefs and that their opinions are important.

Writing Book Reviews

Sharing Your Views

The students in one elementary classroom in Troy, Michigan, really enjoy sharing their thoughts and feelings in book reviews. Their classroom is loaded with books to choose from. And after reading each other's reviews, the students always know which books they want to read next.

In a book review you share your understanding of and opinion about a book you have read.

Becoming an Expert

The students also enjoy this form of writing because it gives them a chance to write about subjects that really interest them. For example, two students named Devon and Christa are both crazy about sports. When they read good sports stories, they *want* to write about them. And when other students want to read sports stories, they turn to Devon and Christa (and their reviews) for suggestions.

Model Book Review

In the following model, student writer Hilary Ormond reviews the book *The True Confessions of Charlotte Doyle* by Avi. Each paragraph in this model answers one of three basic questions: *What is the book about? What is the book's theme or message? What do I like about this book?*

The True Confessions of Charlotte Doyle

What is the book about?

<u>The True Confessions of Charlotte Doyle</u> is about a wealthy thirteen-year-old girl named Charlotte. In 1832, Charlotte is supposed to sail from England to Rhode Island with two other families, but the families never show up. Charlotte decides to sail with the crew alone. She becomes good friends with the captain, until the captain kills two of the crewmen for being traitors. Charlotte then decides to join the crew and becomes "Mr. Doyle" in the logbook. During a storm, the first mate, Hollybrass, is killed with her knife!

What is the book's theme or message?

I think Avi, the author, wanted to tell his readers that even people like Charlotte who are very shy can become strong and brave. She had to make many hard choices. I think he also wanted readers to understand that accusations aren't always true.

What do I like about this book?

I liked the book because Avi made all the characters seem real. It was well written and full of imagination and suspense. I wanted to know what would become of Charlotte Doyle, so I read into the night to get my answer.

Readers don't have to know everything that happens in your book, or all of your reasons for liking it. Try to say enough so they can decide if they want to read it themselves.

Writing a Book Review

PREWRITING *Planning Your Review*

Select a Subject ● The type of book you review is really up to you. It could be a mystery, or an adventure story, or maybe a new book about your favorite sports figure. Just make sure that you enjoyed the book, or that you have strong feelings about it.

Collect Your Thoughts ● Your book review should answer three basic questions: *What is the book about? What do I like about the book? What is the book's theme or message?* (The "Collection Sheet" on the next page will help you gather information.)

WRITING THE FIRST DRAFT

Include the Right Stuff ● The first paragraph in your review should give the name and author of your book, and also answer the "What is the book about?" question. The other two questions should be answered in separate paragraphs.

REVISING *Improving Your Writing*

Make It Clear ● Carefully review your first draft, checking for ideas that seem unclear or out of order. Also make sure that no paragraph says too much or too little. Saying too much can sometimes be a problem, especially in the first paragraph.

EDITING & PROOFREADING

Check It Out ● Make sure your review reads clearly from start to finish. Also check for spelling and punctuation errors. (Remember that titles should be underlined.) Then write a neat final draft and proofread it.

Collection Sheet

The ideas listed below will help you form answers for the three basic review questions. (Notice that there are separate ideas for fiction and nonfiction books.)

1. **What is the book about?**

    Fiction: *What events happen in the story?* (A book review should highlight a few events rather than give the whole story away.)

    Nonfiction: *What is the basic subject of this book? Is there one part of the book that seems really important?*

2. **What do I like about the book?**

    Fiction: *Does the book start in an exciting or interesting way? Does the book contain a lot of action or suspense? Does the main character show courage or strength? Does the book end in a surprising way?*

    Nonfiction: *Does the book contain interesting information? Is the information easy to follow? Does the book contain colorful illustrations?*

3. **What is the book's theme?**

    Fiction: *What message about life is the author trying to make?* (Here is a sample message: It's not easy to stand up for your rights.) *How do you know that this is the message?*

    Nonfiction: *Why do you think the author wrote this book? What basic information or message does the author want to share?*

YOU DON'T SSSSSAY

As you collect your ideas, you can write possible answers to each question on separate index cards.

A Review with a Special Focus

Another way to write a book review is to give it a special focus. Writer Heather Monkmeyer feels that *The True Confessions of Charlotte Doyle* is a very suspenseful book. As you will see, this feeling of suspense ties all of her ideas together. It is the focus of her review.

The first paragraph tells what the "focus" of the review is.

Three suspenseful events are highlighted.

In the closing, the writer invites others to read this book.

The True Confessions of Charlotte Doyle

"Not every thirteen-year-old girl is accused of murder, brought to trial, and found guilty. But I was such a girl. . . ." That is the opening line of <u>The True Confessions of Charlotte Doyle</u> by Avi. From the first line to the final paragraph, Avi creates suspense by telling just enough to make readers ask questions that need good answers.

In the first chapters, Avi creates suspense by setting up strange circumstances. As Charlotte boards the ship that will take her to America, she learns that she is the only passenger. That really made me begin to wonder.

Sometimes Avi creates suspense by the things Charlotte does. She tries to stop the captain from killing an innocent man and slashes the captain's face in the process. What will the captain do to her?

Avi packs in a double helping of suspense when the cruel captain sentences Charlotte to be hanged for a murder she did not commit, while at the same time, the crew turns against her.

If you like tales of danger, mystery, and suspense wrapped into a story about courage, <u>The True Confessions of Charlotte Doyle</u> will keep you reading far into the night.

Writing in a Reader Response Journal

A **reader response journal** is a notebook or journal in which you write freely about the books you read. In one writing, you may write about why you think the main character acts in a certain way. In a second writing, you may try to guess what will happen next in the story. In still another writing, you may relate some part of the story to your own life. The choice is yours.

How to Respond

A response journal is very much like any other type of personal journal. You turn to it whenever you feel like writing about something you have read. The point is to make discoveries for yourself, so write as openly and honestly as you can. *Some of the ideas in your journal will help you write book reviews.*

Ideas for Responding

For novels and other longer books, try to write in your journal at least four or five times. The following ideas will help you write responses at different points in your reading.

First Feelings ● What did you like about the opening chapter or two? How do you feel about the characters?

On Your Way ● Are the events in the reading clear to you? How do you feel about the characters and story now? What do you think will happen next?

The Second Half ● What seems important now? What questions or concerns do you have? Does the book keep your interest? Why or why not?

Summing Up ● How do you feel about the ending? How has the main character changed? How have you changed? What do you like most or least about this book and why?

Here are some more ideas to try: Carry on a conversation with a character, express your feelings in a poem, draw a picture, or try adding to or changing the story.

Writing Explanations

Recipe for a Baseball Card Collection
by James Lambert

First, place the autographed Mickey Mantle rookie card in a 3" x 6" plastic pallet. Then, neatly arrange your complete set of Upper Deck cards with the Juan Gonzalez card on top. Next, make sure that the Cal Ripken card is separated from the other cards (otherwise, you'll never find it). Finally, place all of these hot cards on a shelf to cool, and check them from time to time.

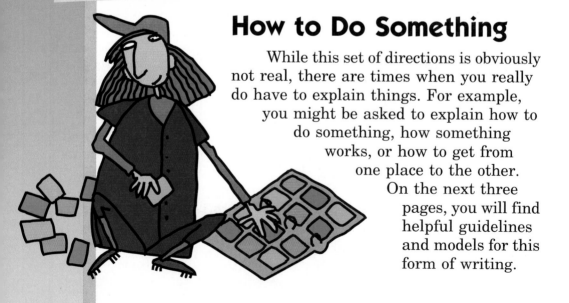

How to Do Something

While this set of directions is obviously not real, there are times when you really do have to explain things. For example, you might be asked to explain how to do something, how something works, or how to get from one place to the other. On the next three pages, you will find helpful guidelines and models for this form of writing.

Writing an Explanation

| PREWRITING | *Planning Your Writing*

Select a Subject ● Think of something you know how to do or make, or some skill you are interested in learning about. You may be skilled at shooting free throws, making pancakes, or *eating* pancakes. Or you may be interested in exploring caves, buying a guitar, or starting a fan club.

List the Steps ● List the steps involved in completing your skill. Or learn as much as you can about a new skill through reading, observing, interviewing, and participating.

WRITING THE FIRST DRAFT

Explain It Clearly ● Explain how to carry out your skill from start to finish. Start your explanation with a topic sentence that identifies the subject.

Helpful
Hint
Use linking words like *first, second, next,* and *then* to help readers move from one step to the next.

| REVISING | *Improving Your Writing*

Test It Out ● Carefully reread your first draft, making sure the directions are clear and complete. If possible, have someone else try to do what you've explained by following your directions. This will help you see if you have missed any important points.

EDITING & PROOFREADING

Check It Out ● Make sure that the revised draft of your writing reads smoothly and is free of careless errors. Proofread the final copy before sharing it.

Student Models

How to Make Something ● Here are the steps to a real recipe, stated very carefully and clearly.

My Favorite Food
by Kimberly Tso

This is how my grandma makes fried bread. First she puts some flour in a bowl. She puts baking soda and salt with the flour. She gets some warm water. She puts in a little bit of water at a time while mixing the flour to make a dough. She kneads the dough to make it soft. Then she covers it with a cloth. She lets it set for 5 minutes. She puts a pan on the stove with grease in it. She waits until the grease gets hot. By that time the dough is ready. Then she starts making fried bread. She fries pieces of bread until they are golden brown, and they taste really good.

How Something Works ● The following model explains how the digestive system works.

Digestion
by Lauren A. Kitchell

The digestive system is really a cycle. It starts as soon as you put food in your mouth. The food gets chewed up by the teeth. Then the salivary glands make a digestive juice called saliva. The saliva covers the chewed-up food, and the food goes down the esophagus or throat to the stomach. In the stomach the food gets churned up and covered with some more digestive juices. After the stomach does its job, the liver and pancreas add digestive juices for use in the small intestine. From the small intestine the digested food passes into the bloodstream. The wastes of the digested food go into the large intestine. In the large intestine the waste is stored and then finally goes out of the body.

How to Get Someplace ● In the following model, Hillary Bachman provides directions for the driver of a stretch limo that took Hillary and her friends on a special birthday ride.

Birthday Ride

For my birthday ride, I want to go from my house to Chi-Chi's restaurant in La Crosse following this route. First, drive north four blocks until you reach Montgomery Street. Then take a left. Continue past the senior high and take the second left after you pass the school. This road will take you in a big loop back to where you first turned. After you pass the senior high again, turn right and drive past Lawrence Lawson Elementary School. Then take the second left. Drive until you reach Water Street and take a right. This will take you through downtown and past Tim's house (please honk) right after you pass the Morrow Home. Turn right when you come to the A & W. This highway (16) will take us directly to Chi-Chi's. Thank you!

How to Create a Feeling ● You can also use your imagination with explanations that create a feeling or a mood.

Recipe for a Cozy Winter Day

1 snow-filled evergreen forest
1 small one-room log cabin
4 good friends who know lots of songs
1 blazing fireplace
4 mugs of hot chocolate
1 plate of chocolate chip cookies
4 marshmallows

Directions: Take small one-room log cabin. Place it in the middle of a snow-filled evergreen forest. Fill the cabin with four good friends in front of a blazing fireplace. Serve each friend a mug of hot chocolate. Put one marshmallow into each mug. Pass around one plate piled high with chocolate chip cookies. Mix in singing voices, and your cozy winter day will be complete.

Writing Business Letters

When You Mean Business

A **business letter** is different from a letter you write to an aunt in another city or to a pen pal in another country. It looks and sounds more business-like and focuses on only one subject.

You may write a business letter for different reasons:

- **when you need information** (*a letter of request*),

- **when you have a problem with something you ordered** (*a letter of complaint*),

- **or when you have a problem with a situation in your city or school** (*a letter to an editor or official*).

But no matter what type of business letter you write, you should follow the guidelines given in this chapter. Your letters will bring better results if you do them right. Pay special attention to the sample letter on page 145.

Types of Business Letters

There are three types of business letters described below: **a letter of request**, **a letter of complaint**, and **a letter to an editor or official**.

Letter of Request ●
You want to go to Yellowstone National Park on your vacation next summer, but you need to convince the rest of the family. You decide to write a letter of request asking for information. Here are some guidelines you could use. (**SEE** the model on page 145.)

✔ Explain why you are writing.

✔ Ask any questions you have.

✔ Describe what you would like to receive (and when).

✔ Thank them for their help.

Letter of Complaint ●
You ordered a pair of high-tops and received two left shoes. How will you get the shoes exchanged or ask for your money back? You could write a letter of complaint.

✔ Describe the product.

✔ Describe the problem and possible causes.

✔ Explain how you have tried to solve the problem.

✔ End with what you would like the reader (or company) to do.

Letter to an Editor or Official ●
The traffic on your street makes it dangerous for children. How will you get the city to do something about the situation? You could write a letter to your local newspaper, or to a public official. (**SEE** page 131 for a model.)

✔ Describe the situation.

✔ Tell what you think about the situation.

✔ If you have ideas for improvement or change, explain them.

✔ Support your ideas with facts and examples.

✔ End by asking that the situation be changed.

Parts of a Business Letter

Heading ● The **heading** includes the sender's address and date. Write the heading about an inch from the top of the page at the left-hand margin.

Inside Address ● The **inside address** includes the name and address of the person or company you are writing to. Place it at the left-hand margin, four to seven spaces below the heading. If the person has a special title such as park ranger, add it after his or her name. (Use a comma first.)

Mr. David Shore, Park Ranger

Salutation ● The **salutation** is a greeting, a way of saying hello. Write it on the second line below the inside address. Always use a colon at the end of the salutation.

➤ If you know the person's name, write:

Dear Mr. Shore:

➤ If you don't know the person's name, write:

Dear Park Ranger:

Dear Sir or Madam:

Dear Yellowstone Park:

Greetings:

Body ● The **body** is the main part of the letter. Begin this part two lines below the salutation. Double-space between each paragraph. Do not indent. Keep the information brief and simple so the reader clearly understands what you are asking for or explaining.

Closing ● Place the **closing** at the left-hand margin, two spaces below the body. Use **Very truly**, **Yours truly**, or **Sincerely** for a business letter closing. Capitalize the first word but not the others. Always place a comma after the closing.

Signature ● End your letter by signing your name beneath the closing. If you are typing your letter, skip four lines and type your full name. Then write your **signature** between the closing and your typed name.

Sample Business Letter

Heading

4824 Park Street
Richland Center, WI 53581
January 1, 1994

**Inside
Address**

Mr. David Shore, Park Ranger
Yellowstone National Park
Box 168
Yellowstone National Park, WY 82190

Salutation

Dear Mr. Shore:

We're having a contest in my family to see
who can plan the best summer vacation. I
want to convince everyone that a trip to
Yellowstone National Park would be better
than going to New York City or even to
Disneyland for a week. This is not going to
be easy!

Body

I would appreciate any help you could give
me. I am most interested in some up-to-date
brochures of the park with photos and maps.
I will also need information on where we can
stay and what we can do there.

Thank you for your help. Maybe I'll see you
next summer.

Closing

Sincerely,

Luke Johnson

Signature

Luke Johnson

Folding Your Letter

When you finish your letter, fold it in three parts.

Like this: ■ Fold bottom one-third up.
                ■ Next, fold top one-third down.
                ■ Crease the folds firmly.
                ■ Insert into envelope.

Or like this: ■ Fold letter in half.
                ■ Next, fold into thirds.
                ■ Crease folds firmly.
                ■ Insert into envelope.

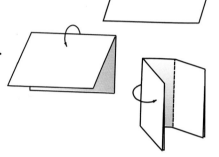

Sending Your Letter

Address the Envelope

● Place the full name and complete address of the person to whom the letter is being sent slightly to the left of the middle of the envelope.

● Place your return address in the upper left-hand corner of the envelope and the stamp in the upper right-hand corner.

MR LUKE JOHNSON
4824 PARK ST
RICHLAND CENTER WI 53581

MR DAVID SHORE
PARK RANGER
YELLOWSTONE NATIONAL PARK
BOX 168
YELLOWSTONE NATIONAL PARK WY 82190

When addressing your envelope, the post office prefers that you use all capital letters, no punctuation, and the two-letter abbreviations for states. (**SEE** page 357 for a list of abbreviations.)

Writing a Business Letter

PREWRITING *Planning Your Letter*

✔ Check your handbook for the requirements for the different types of business letters: **Letter of Request**, **Letter to an Editor or Official**, **Letter of Complaint**.

✔ Gather all of the details and facts you need.

✔ Organize your ideas for your writing.

WRITING THE FIRST DRAFT

✔ Write naturally, but keep the style somewhat formal.

✔ Explain your main points clearly.

✔ Write short paragraphs.

REVISING *Improving Your Writing*

✔ Make sure you have included the necessary facts and details.

✔ Make sure you have written honestly and sincerely.

✔ Make sure your letter is easy to read.

EDITING & PROOFREADING

✔ Make sure you proofread for punctuation, capitalization, and grammar errors. (Pay special attention to the heading, inside address, and salutation.)

✔ Make sure you've included all the necessary "parts" of a business letter. (**SEE** page 144.)

✔ Make sure your letter is neatly written or typed.

✔ Center the letter and keep the margins even.

✔ Use only one side of the paper.

Writing Observation Reports

I hear kids shouting. There is a strange scent in the air. There is a faint breeze. It is 9:35 Saturday morning, and the playground is filling up with kids. Cars keep whizzing past. Suddenly a rollerblader zooms by . . .

Using Your Senses

You have just read part of an observation report. The subject is a playground where the writer observes different *sights, sounds, smells,* and *physical feelings.* In other words, all of the writer's senses are focused on his subject. In an observation report, there is no need to get involved in any action. You simply select a location and look, listen, and learn.

Writing an Observation Report

PREWRITING *Planning Your Writing*

Select a Location ● Observe a room in your school, a street corner, a bus or subway car, a small store, an entrance to a mall, a kitchen. The choice is yours.

Observe and Write ● In a notebook, write down what you see, hear, smell, and feel at this location. If there is a lot of activity, take quick notes so you don't miss anything. (Spend at least 15 minutes at this location.)

 **YOU DON'T SSSSSSAY**

You may find a camcorder helpful for collecting, but check with your teacher before you do any recording.

WRITING THE FIRST DRAFT

Prepare Your Report ● You can write your observation report in two different ways.

1 You can share all of the details in the order that you listed them. In this way, your report will flow from one sight or sound to another. This is how the model at the beginning of the chapter is written.

2 You can organize your observations around a main idea just as you would in a descriptive paragraph. (See the model on the next page.)

REVISING & EDITING *Improving Your Writing*

Decide What Changes Need to Be Made ● Review your first draft once to make sure that it contains all of the important observations (sights and sounds). Review it a second time to check for sentence, spelling, and punctuation errors. Make all of the needed changes; then proofread the final draft of your report.

Model Observation Report

The main idea in this model paragraph is stated in the first sentence. All of the observations that follow relate to this idea.

The Big Chill
by Todd Michael

As we wait for the Christmas parade, everyone looks cold. My little brother sits on my mom's lap, trying to hide from the wind. The little boy and girl sitting next to my mom have snowsuits on, plus they have a green blanket wrapped around them. Two or three different times they say, "Mom, can we pleeease have some hot chocolate?" The man standing behind us says, "I'm from Charlotte, and I'm not used to the cold." I hear another voice say, "Just wait until it starts to snow." Five boys next to me are playing tackle tag to keep warm. They all wear colorful ski jackets and ear warmers. The road in front of us looks drab and gray under the streetlight. One family on the other curb is wrapped inside a big blue quilt. Just then a siren sounds. The parade is finally about to begin.

THINK IT OVER

Always try to show rather than tell in your writing. A *showing* sentence like "My little brother sits on my mom's lap, trying to hide from the wind" says much more than a *telling* sentence like "It was windy." (**SEE** "Show Don't Tell" on page 40 for more examples.)

Science Observation Report

In your science class, you may be asked to write an observation report on an experiment or project. For one of his science projects, Emery Sanford observed how mold grows on different kinds of bread. Part of his final report follows.

Observing Mold on Bread

PROCEDURE: On October 27, I brought my bread to school. I had four different kinds of bread: Clausen's white bread, Roman Meal bread, French bread, and pita bread. I put each piece of bread in a sandwich bag and waited a few days for the mold to grow.

OBSERVATIONS: The Clausen's bread started growing mold first. The mold was green and white. Before this, I had never seen anything other than green mold on bread. This was the first thing I learned about mold. . . .

The Roman Meal started by getting little white speckles on it. In four days there was mold on the bread. It got green, white, and yellow mold at first. Now I had found yellow mold. I had seen two new colors that I had never seen before. . . .

The French bread got stale very quickly. It got very hard and then it started getting moldy. The mold grew on the inside of the bread, not on the outside like the others.

The pita didn't grow mold at all, probably because it is made from whole wheat and oat bran. It did get hard. That's something I didn't know, that pita bread can get stale, but not moldy.

CONCLUSIONS: I learned a lot of things during this observation. I learned that there are different colored molds, why the bread shrinks (which took some thinking), how mold grows, what mold looks like under a microscope, and how it forms. And most important, I learned what kind of bread to buy if you want it to last: either pita or Roman Meal.

Writing Tales and Stories

Writing Fantasies

Writing Tall Tales

Writing Realistic Stories

Writing Stories from History

Writing Fantasies

Inventing Impossible Things

Do you ever daydream? Have you ever had an imaginary friend? Have you ever made believe you could fly, or wished you were an explorer? Have you ever invented your own private world, or pretended to be one of the characters in your favorite book? If so, you've been using your imagination, and when you do that, *anything* can happen—even impossible things.

Animals That Talk?

Anytime you write stories, you use your imagination. In one special kind of story, you get to make up all the rules yourself. It's called *fantasy*, the type of story where even a spider can save a pig. So let's begin by reading a fantasy story by a student writer.

> 66 **When you write a story, you can imagine it any way you want, just as long as your readers believe you.** 99
> — Nancy Bond

Student Model

In this story, a girl named Penny and her barnyard friends try to figure out why Montgomery the cat is acting so strangely.

MONTGOMERY MEWS MYSTERIOUSLY
by Katie Ambrogi

The setting is described in the opening paragraph.

There was a dusty barn made of old gray wood. The nails marked their age with signs of permanent rust. An old silo stood next to the barn. It looked queer and was every bit as old as the barn.

Just then, Penny appeared in front of the barn. The animals looked up at her in surprise. Penny never came into the barnyard at this time of day!

"I insist on a barnyard meeting, now!" declared Penny.

Sandy the pig stopped rolling in the mud. Mr. Winkle, otherwise known as Perry the rooster, stopped stalking the barnyard. Freedom the dog stopped lapping up week-old water. Oxford, the biggest ox you've ever seen, let out a great big bellow from the barn.

Then the characters and their problem are identified.

Baanie the sheep said to Penny, "What's the matter?"

"Yeah, what's wrong?" chorused all the animals.

"Have any of you seen Montgomery?" Penny inquired.

"No," chorused the animals.

"Well, neither have I, and I'm beginning to worry. She's hardly ever around," said Penny.

"Well," began Oxford, who was always a close observer, "Montgomery looked different today in a way I can't put my finger on, but she was very nice to Sandy. That's a sure sign that something is wrong."

"Mr. Winkle, do you think we should pry into the cat's business?" Freedom asked.

Sandy, who was listening to the conversation, stepped in and said, "No . . . but there could be something wrong with Montgomery. Not that I really care."

"Okay," began Oxford, "here's the deal. Winkle, you are the chief administrator of the spy office. We will run around, watch Montgomery closely, and report our messages to the office."

"What about me?" asked Penny.

"Penny, you record everything the spies report," Mr. Winkle said.

Just then, Montgomery slid into the barn. "Why is everyone staring at me like that? I'm fine." Montgomery quickly turned around and made her way out of the barn.

Hours later, they still had no clue to what was wrong with Montgomery. Sandy sat at her desk and tapped her fingers. Mr. Winkle fluffed up his feathers and started to twiddle his thumbs. Penny jotted down reports, but nothing was good enough to lead them to an answer.

Then the barnyard door swung open a crack. Montgomery slid through it. Six pairs of eyes traveled to the door. "You know," Montgomery began, "I guess I should have told you." The animals listened in suspense.

"You know how cats love privacy," Montgomery started again. Just then, two kittens timidly stepped in. "They were born three weeks ago," Montgomery said, her voice full of pride. She introduced the kittens. "The little one I call Mouse . . . "

So, somewhere in a barn in Vermont, there are six happy barnyard adults, two happy kittens, and one happy girl.

The characters decide how they will deal with their problem.

After hours of suspense, the problem is solved.

One Writer's Process

When I write a fantasy, I want to make my readers *believe* my story. I want them to think it could happen, just the way I've imagined it. I want them willing to pretend with me. Here's how I usually get started on my stories.

➤ Keep a Writer's Notebook

Ideas can come from anywhere at any time. I find it helps to write them down before I forget them. I can't use everything I put in my notebook, but sometimes just writing down a word or two can start a story growing in my imagination. I write down anything that interests me: funny names, unusual objects, silly thoughts. Then when I need an idea, I can look back and see what I've got.

➤ Ask Questions

When I write a story, I ask myself lots of questions about what's going on. I'll show you what I mean. Almost everyone's imagined what it would be like to fly like a bird. Suppose we want to write a story about a girl who can really do it. To me, the most interesting thing is not so much that she can fly. I want to know how she does it and what it feels like.

➤ Make Choices

The first thing we have to do is get the girl into the air. But how? Have you ever seen a Canada goose take off from a pond or a riverbank? Maybe *that's* how she does it, by running faster and faster and flapping her arms.

Maybe she flies by concentrating on feeling light. Or perhaps she has to think of nothing at all. Remember Peter Pan? He told Wendy, John, and Michael to "think lovely thoughts, and up you go!" That's another way. Have you got other ideas?

➤ Ask More Questions

Let's go a little further. Now our girl is in the air, however we decided to get her there. Let's ask some more questions. How does it feel? Does she ride the wind like a kite? Or does she have to keep flapping her arms like a bird? When she's up in the sky, what do the clouds feel like? Are they wet and cold, or soft and warm like down comforters? Maybe they're sticky, like cotton candy.

➤ Start the Story

To describe this girl in action and build some excitement into my story, I might write something like this:

> Cynthia had no warning. One minute there she was, floating on soft pillows of warm air. Her wings were stretched wide while she admired her neighborhood. Here and there among the trees a swimming pool glinted at her, a miniature car winked in the sun, and tiny people followed sidewalks, never thinking to look up to see Cynthia Bean gliding over their heads.
>
> Suddenly she blinked. It was all gone: the sun, the warmth, the houses on her block. Gray blankness filled her eyes. In a blind panic, she curled into a ball, hugging her wings tight around her, and dropped like a stone out through the bottom of the cloud . . .

Why was Cynthia falling? What will happen to her? How could this action lead to other exciting events? I would try to answer these questions as I wrote the rest of my fantasy.

THINK IT OVER

Can you think of someone else who might fly into a story? How about a young boy who suddenly finds himself floating in air on his way home from school? Why is he floating? What will he do about it?

Writing a Fantasy

PREWRITING *Planning Your Story*

Invent Characters ● Fantasy characters can be real people, talking animals, dragons, unicorns, or creatures you invent yourself. (Think of a main character and maybe one or two others.)

What are your characters' names? What do they look like? What do they like to do? Write about them and find out.

Choose a Problem to Solve ● In a fantasy, the main character's problem may be finding out why a cat is acting strangely, searching for a treasure, finding the way back home, and so on. (The way your main character solves his or her problem is the plot, the main part of your story.)

Find a Setting ● Fantasy can take place anywhere or anytime—in your neighborhood or a magical place. (Describe the setting so that your readers can see it in their minds.)

WRITING THE FIRST DRAFT

Get Started ● Begin your story by introducing the main character or setting. Or begin with something happening like two characters arguing, a narrow escape, an explosion, and so on. This action should lead to the main problem in the story.

Keep It Going ● As you continue, try to make the main character's life more and more difficult because of the problem. Include lots of dialogue. This will keep your readers interested.

Stop When You Get to the End ● The end of the story comes when the problem is solved. That sounds obvious, but sometimes writers go on to explain what their stories are about and end up writing too much.

REVISING   *Improving Your Writing*

Let It Sit ● After you've written your story, let it sit for a while. Then, when you read it again, try pretending someone else wrote it, and see what you think. You'll never be able to fool yourself totally, but you'll be able to see it a little more clearly.

Make It Believable ● Remember that your story should be imaginary *and* believable. Ask, "Do my characters act in a way that fits the story? Do the actions make sense in my setting?"

Share Your First Draft ● Listen carefully to the questions your friends ask after reading or listening to your story. This can be hard to do, but when you write a story for other people, you want them to understand it. One of your friends may be confused by something you have said in the introduction. Another friend may think that a part of your story isn't believable.

 If you're not sure about your story's ending, try removing the last sentence or paragraph. See if the story seems complete without it.

EDITING & PROOFREADING

Edit ● Take a close look at the specific words and sentences in your story once you have made all of the major changes. Have you picked the best words to describe the setting, characters, and action? Are your sentences interesting and clear? Have you used enough dialogue and punctuated it correctly?

Proofread ● Also make sure to proofread the final draft of your story before you share it.

 Writing fantasies can be fun, but reading them can be even more enjoyable. Have you read these popular fantasies?
- *A String in the Harp* by Nancy Bond
- *Flat Stanley* by Jeff Brown
- *A Wrinkle in Time* by Madeleine L'Engle

Writing Tall Tales

Ride That Mosquito!

Throughout history, **tall tales** have been told by people struggling to survive. These tales contain extraordinary heroes and heroines who can defeat anything and anybody. And they are filled with humor and exaggeration:

Daniel Boone told of smacking a mosquito with the flat of his hatchet "to calm it down a bit." Then he put a saddle on that mosquito and rode it.

People still enjoy inventing tall tales. When you use language like "she was so mean" or "he was so strong," you are well on your way to inventing a tall tale.

> **For tall tales, ordinary, run-of-the-mill, polite little lies won't do, no siree. Tall tales need lies so big and exaggerated that they make you laugh out loud and beg for more.**
> —Susan Ohanian

Model Tall Tale

In the following tall tale, Big Bob is faced with a big problem: he has to catch a runaway state!

Big Bob is described using exaggeration.

The hero has a powerful force to overcome.

He uses his strength and craftiness to tame Texas.

BIG BOB AND THE MISSING STATE
by Christopher Meyer

Dear Bob,

Knowing you are as fast as lightning with a lasso, I thought you might be able to complete this mission. Last night the chains broke loose and Texas ran away. We need you to catch it and bring it back. Good luck.

Mr. President

Texas was the fastest state in the world, but that didn't worry Bob. The next morning Bob got up, got dressed, got out his biggest lasso, which could wrap around the moon, got on his horse, and off he went to catch Texas. He rode through Utah, Nevada, Colorado, and California, but he didn't find Texas. Then one day while he was riding through Mexico, he heard a distant rumble. He started riding that way. Sure enough, when he got there, he found Texas running full speed away from him. He got off his horse and threw his lasso as hard as he could until it was out of sight. Then he lay down for the night.

The next morning he got up and ate breakfast. All of a sudden his lasso pulled tight and he knew he had lassoed Texas. He pulled and pulled and dragged it back to its place and chained it down tight so it wouldn't get away again.

Writing a Tall Tale

PREWRITING *Planning Your Story*

You can build your own tall tales by following these guidelines:

Choose a Hero or Heroine ● Remember that these heroes are always strong, brave, and smart. Use exaggeration when you describe this person. Your hero or heroine may be

. . . as strong as the Sahara Desert is dry.

. . . as smart as a city full of brain surgeons.

Create a Powerful Foe ● Think of a powerful foe or force that your hero must tame. This foe may be

. . . an outlaw so mean he could scare an entire army.

. . . a winter so cold that even the antifreeze freezes.

. . . a mosquito so big it needs a runway to land.

Show the Cleverness of Your Hero ● To tame or escape the powerful foe, your hero or heroine may be able to

. . . outsnarl and outsnort a grizzly bear.

. . . wrap a lasso around a runaway state.

A Tall Cast of Characters

Knowing something about four famous tall-tale heroes may help you plan your own story:

● *Sally Ann Thunder Ann Whirlwind Crockett uses her bowie knife as a toothpick and skins a bear faster than an alligator swallows a fish.*

● *Mighty medicine man Glooskap squeezes a water monster whose warts are as big as mountains until the monster becomes a mere bullfrog.*

● *Pecos Bill ties rattlesnakes together and invents the clothesline.*

● *Old Sally Cato crawls into the belly of the giant Billy Bally Bully and shakes out clouds of dust to make the giant wheeze and sneeze.*

WRITING YOUR STORY

Tall tales are meant to be fun and entertaining. So remember to include a lot of exaggeration and humor in your writing. If you use dialogue, have the main character say things that are funny or clever, and have other characters say things that sound a little silly or simple. (More writing tips are provided below.)

Think of yourself as an old-time storyteller with a group of eager listeners around you. Your job is to tell them a good story.

Start Out Creatively ● Introduce the main character in a creative way. (In the model, Big Bob is introduced in a letter written by the president.) Also introduce the foe your hero will be up against. Remember to exaggerate!

Keep It Going ● Have your main character set out to tame the foe. Try not to make things too easy for your hero. He or she may have to do some searching, fighting, building, waiting, and so on.

End Your Story ● In a tall tale, the main character almost always wins in the end. Will your hero win because of her or his strength, craftiness, or a combination of the two? Will there be any surprises at the end of your story?

Reading different types of tall tales will give you new ideas for your own writing. Here are three titles to consider:

- *Sally Ann Thunder Ann Whirlwind Crockett* by Caron Lee Cohen
- *How Glooskap Outwits the Ice Giant and Other Tales of the Maritime Indians* by Howard Norman
- *Cut From the Same Cloth: American Women of Myth, Legend, and Tall Tale* by Robert San Souci

Writing Realistic Stories

Amanda Comes to Life

Amanda Lowe is 11 years old. She attends Peabody Elementary School in Philadelphia. Her long red hair curls wildly, like fire flaming out of control. She is the shortest student in sixth grade.

Amanda hates being short. And she wishes she could be brave enough to tell everyone to stop treating her like somebody's kid sister. But what would happen if she did? Amanda isn't sure she wants to find out.

What are realistic stories?

Ideas for realistic stories often come from a writer's own experiences or interests. But the finished products are more fiction (made-up) than fact.

What I have just described is an idea for a **realistic story**. The main character in a realistic story may remind you of someone you know. For instance, you may know someone like Amanda. Her problem (being too short) may sound very believable. But a realistic story has not actually happened. It only *seems* real.

Student Model

In Lorraine Kenny's story, Keith and Matt have a real problem—just like Amanda—which they solve in a clever, humorous way.

THE VACATION

The main characters are introduced in the opening paragraph.

Keith and Matt lived with their Uncle Mark since the accident, which for both boys was as far back as they could remember. Mark was very good to his nephews. The boys' model train set was spread out all over the living room floor during Christmas vacation, and they were pestering Mark to buy them some bridges for the tracks. At last Mark could stand no more.

"Listen!" Mark said. "I've bought a lot of new parts for that train set already. And I am tired of tripping over those tracks every time I want to cross the room! Clean this place up!"

"Spoilsport!" murmured Keith, as he began to pick up the tracks.

The dialogue makes the story seem more real.

"You guys need a quiet hobby. How about painting or reading?" said Mark. Fifteen minutes later he was surprised when the boys asked to go out.

"I don't know if I want to do this!" moaned Keith as he and Matt walked down the street, toward the library.

Mark was astonished to see them come back with a pile of very big books! But he was also happy. "Maybe things will finally be quiet around here."

The trip to the library builds suspense into the story.

Matt and Keith hurried to their room, and all was silent for a very long time. "I've got to see what those two are up to!" Mark thought. "It's just not like them to suddenly want to read a book. Not without a battle at least." Mark walked quietly up the stairs and gently pushed open the boys' bedroom door. Keith and Matt were sitting on the floor with the books, but they weren't reading. They had used them to build bridges for their trains!

"Switch on!" yelled Keith, and Matt pressed the button. The trains screeched around the tracks and over and under the book bridges.

"Oh no!" groaned Mark, shutting the door quickly. "You can't win with these two guys!" With that thought in mind, Mark went to look for his old railroad engineer hat and gloves.

Writing a Realistic Story

PREWRITING *Planning Your Story*

Before you can write your story, you must identify two important elements: (1) a realistic main character and (2) a believable problem for this character to solve.

Create a Character ● Think of friends and other people you know or have read about to get ideas for your main character. You may know someone who loves animals, or someone who loves playing an instrument, or someone who is very short—like Amanda.

THINK IT OVER

Let some of these ideas play around in your brain: Could you write a story about an animal lover? What would this character be like? What might happen to this person in your story? (Don't embarrass anyone by making your character too much like a real person.)

Find a Real Problem ● Suppose your main character (we'll call her Josie) *is* nuts about animals. Here's the situation: Josie wants to keep a stray dog, but she knows her landlord does not allow pets. What will she do? That's her problem. Now think of a *believable* problem for your own character.

LOOKING FOR TROUBLE

This activity will help you brainstorm for problems.

STEP 1: List one or two possible problems next to the categories *school, friends, neighborhood,* and *family.* (Here's a definite friend problem: Your "best bud" may have to quit soccer because of her asthma.)

STEP 2: Decide if your main character could deal with one of these problems. Or think of other problems that might be more closely related to this person. (If you have to, you can always change your character.)

Planning Guide

To help you keep track of all of your planning ideas, you may want to use a "Collection Sheet" like the one below. You don't have to fill in all of the information before you write, and you should feel free to make changes at any time. (Sometimes a sheet like this is very helpful *after* you write your first draft. It helps you see if you have covered all of the basics in your story.)

Collection Sheet

Characters:

(List the main character first. How old are your characters and what will their names be? Think how each of your characters might look, speak, and act.)

Setting:

(Describe where and when the story will take place.)

Problem:

(What problem does the main character need to solve?)

Story Scenes:

(What are some of the things your main character may try in order to solve her or his problem?)

Purpose:

(Will your story be serious, surprising, scary, funny, or sad? One of these feelings can be a guide for your writing.)

TALK About It

Talk about your story ideas with your classmates before (and after) you write your first draft. As you discuss your story, at least one or two more ideas will pop into your mind.

WRITING THE FIRST DRAFT

Most writers would tell you to begin your story right in the middle of the action, but you may start your story any way you want to. Start with "One day last summer . . ." if that feels right to you. (You can always change it later on.)

Start Your Story ● Here are five ways to begin a story.

■ Begin with dialogue:
> *"Put me down!" Amanda shouted.*

■ Begin with a question:
> *How did this super athlete get stuck in such a small body?*

■ Begin with description:
> *The gym smelled like sweat and stale popcorn.*

■ Begin with background information:
> *All through elementary school, Amanda*
> *had been treated like a kid sister.*

■ Begin with the main character introducing herself:
> *I might as well tell you now and get it over with.*
> *I am the shortest person in sixth grade.*

Keep Your Story Going ● Try not to make things too easy for your character. You may have her involved in two or three important actions because of her problem. She may do some talking, thinking, running, fighting, and so on.

End Your Story ● Your story does not have to end on a happy note. Some problems just can't be solved or completely overcome. For example, Amanda Lowe can't make herself grow taller, no matter how many bowls of Wheaties she eats. But she may be able to get her classmates to treat her with more respect.

TAKE NOTE

Most characters change in some way because of their problems. That's something to keep in mind as you write your story.

REVISING *Improving Your Story*

As you review your first draft, make sure that all of the characters' words and actions make sense. Also make sure that your story does not move along too quickly or too slowly. The key is to keep your readers interested.

Add Life to Your Story ● If your story needs to be pumped up, try adding more details, dialogue, and action.

■ Use specific details:

Are there any sights, sounds, smells, and feelings that you could add? Have you described the characters and the setting in your story?

■ Use dialogue and action:

Would you like your story to be more active? Then include more dialogue and action scenes. Notice how the special combination of the two can build excitement:

"Put me down!" Amanda shouted.
"Make me!" Eric dared.
"Okay, you asked for it!"
Amanda twisted and kicked until Eric lost his grip. As she fell, she grabbed hold of his hair . . . .

EDITING & PROOFREADING

Once you have made all of the major changes in your story, read it again to make sure that it reads smoothly and clearly from start to finish. Also check your work for punctuation, spelling, and grammar errors. (Ask a trusted friend or classmate to help you.) Then complete a neat final draft of your story. Proofread this copy before you share it.

Writing Stories from History

Long Ago and Far Away . . .

- *Would you like to go back in time?*
- *Would you like to meet someone from the past?*
- *Would you like to relive a great event?*

You can do all of these things by writing historical stories, stories based on what *could* have happened or what *did* happen at a certain time or place. What's so exciting about this type of writing is that there is so much history to choose from.

A historical story should be part fact and part fiction and believable all the way through.

Writing a Historical Story

PREWRITING   *Planning Your Story*

Think Historically ● When you plan and write a historical story, you may choose a historical period or event and make up characters that could have lived during that time. Or you may choose someone real, making this person your main character.

List Ideas ● The first thing you should do is make a list of different *times, events,* or *people* from history that you might like to write about. For ideas, think of history units you have studied in class and different times and people that you have always been interested in. The sample ideas that follow will help you get started. (Try to list at least five ideas of your own.)

- **Massasoit and the first Thanksgiving** (*an event*)
- **Middle Ages in Europe** (*a historical time*)
- **The Oregon Trail** (*a historical place*)
- **Ferdinand Magellan** (*a famous explorer*)
- **Harriet Tubman** (*a famous freedom fighter*)

Select a Subject ● Once you complete your list, put a check next to the idea that interests you the most. Use this idea as the starting point for your story research. (If you find that one idea doesn't work out so well, you can always try another from your list.)

WRITE
About It
Write freely for 3 to 5 minutes about your subject to help you see what you already know, and what you may need to find out.

Collect Facts ● To collect new information about your subject, start by reading about it in an encyclopedia article, in another basic reference book, or in your history text. Ask your teacher or librarian about other sources of information, too. Take careful notes as you read. (See the sample notes below.)

Sample Note-Taking Page

Listed here are facts that could have been collected for a historical story on the voyage of Ferdinand Magellan.

Facts About Ferdinand Magellan

- a Portuguese sailor who planned to sail around the world
- began his voyage on Sept. 20, 1519
- hardships began immediately (several mutinies)
- ran out of food; crew ate rats and ox hides
- stopped at the Philippines for food
- April 27, 1521, Magellan killed during a battle on the island of Mactan
- of the original 241 sailors only 110 remained
- <u>Trinidad</u> didn't make it back, sailors imprisoned
- <u>Victoria</u> under command of Juan Sebastian del Cano returned to Spain on Sept. 6, 1522
- only Juan Sebastian del Cano and 17 others survived
- Italian crew member Antonio Pigafetta kept a journal

You might find it easier to collect information by starting with a series of basic questions: *Where did Magellan's men sail? Why were they sailing? What happened to them?*

Identify Your Story Elements ● Continue your planning by identifying the basic elements for your story. You may want to use a "Collection Sheet" to help you keep track of your ideas. Use your collection sheet as you write, but feel free to make changes at any time as you go along.

Collection Sheet

Characters:

(Decide how each of your characters might look, speak, and act. Remember to keep the time period of your story in mind.)

Setting:

(Describe the historical time and place of your story.)

Main Action:

(What action will your character be involved in? This action may or may not be true. But it must be believable. Within this main action, there may be some type of problem that needs to be solved.)

Story Scenes:

(What are some of the things your character might do— fighting, planning, eating, etc.—during the main action?)

Form:

(Decide what form your story will take. You may write a basic story, or you may choose another form—a diary or a series of letters. The model on page 175 is told in diary form.)

WRITING THE FIRST DRAFT

Begin Your Story ● Start your story with some dialogue, an action scene, or a brief description. Work in background facts and introduce the main characters as soon as possible.

"Get down, Antonio. They will see you. Get down."

Everything was happening so fast. Captain Magellan was dead, the crew had scattered into the woods, and now we were under attack.

"Juan," whispered Antonio. "Since the captain is dead, you are now in charge. You must get us out of here. You must."

Yes, Antonio was right. I, Juan Sebastian del Cano, was in charge. But get us out of here? How?

Keep Your Story Going ● Remember that your story should be based on historical fact, and it should seem realistic. Keep these points in mind as your main character gets more involved in the story.

End Your Story ● Don't drag your story out. It should end when the main action is completed. Remember, too, that your story does not have to end on a happy note.

REVISING & EDITING   *A Final Checklist*

✔ Do all of the characters' words and actions make sense, considering the historical time? (George Washington wouldn't say something like, "Don't get hyper!")

✔ Does the story build in interest? (Does the main character complete the action or solve the problem in the story?)

✔ Do your sentences read smoothly? (Let a friend read it to you.)

✔ Is your final draft neat and easy to read?

Student Model

Heather Stoll's story is about a baker who lived during the Middle Ages. The story is told in the form of a diary. The introduction and two entries from the diary are shown below:

Here, you will see Genoa, Italy, through the eyes of Piero Baker, a well-to-do baker and pastry maker. Piero's shop is on Mill Road. He is a member of the guild of pastry makers. In his diary, you will find information about different shops, clothes, and products related to the Middle Ages.

Genoa, Italy, in the Middle Ages

September 3, 1348

Today I acquired four bags of flour in return for baking two loaves of bread for Widow Napoli.

Dominic and I finished Lady Sophia's order of trenchers today. She paid me well: ten bags of flour, fourteen gold coins, one yard of silk.

My wife will be pleased to see the latter. She has been awanting for a new dress.

Today I must go to the woods and cut myself a new oven spatula. Mine is sorely burnt and in need of repairs.

September 17, 1348

That clumsy excuse for a helper, Fos, spilled flour all over the floor! Now precious time must be wasted cleaning up.

The order is now more than half done. Lady Sophia is relieved. Already she is hiring minstrels and dancers, and the hall bustles with activity.

Everyone is excited! The fleet must be almost ready to go. They leave tomorrow. It is five days' voyage from the boot of my dear country to Genoa.

Writing Poems, Plays, and Songs

Writing Poems

Writing Songs

Writing Plays

Writing Riddles

Writing for Fun

Writing Poems

Words on High Wind

I write poems when I feel what I have to say needs a special shape and sound. I learned how to write my own poems by first making friends with many of the poems I found in books. Here's how you can do the same.

Ways to Make Friends with a Poem

➤ **Read the poem to yourself several times.**
➤ **Read the poem aloud; listen to what it says.**
➤ **Read it with feeling to friends or classmates.**
➤ **Talk or write about the poem.**
➤ **Copy it in a special notebook.**

Now make friends with one of my poems, following these steps.

EARTH-CLOUD-HILLTOP

WORDS
Words! said the earth.
And the cloud
bumping into the hilltop
said back, Words!
And the words
were born
on a high wind
at the tail end of June,
when the sun brights
the sky so hard
no one can stop laughing.
—Anne-Marie Oomen

What Is Poetry?

Why is poetry such a special form of writing? Let's count the ways.

1 **Poetry looks different.** It's easy to recognize poems. They are written in lines and stanzas (groups of lines), and they usually don't take up much space on a page. Some poems are short enough to fit on the inside of greeting cards. Here is a poem called "Ancestors of the Past." Notice that it is a one-stanza poem containing eight lines.

> I look in the mirror
> And what do I see?
> I see an image of someone
> That looks a little like me.
> Could it be the face
> Or maybe the hair?
> I know who it is now:
> It's my great-great-grandma Claire.
>
> — Phil Ryan

2 **Poetry speaks to the heart as well as to the mind.** You can like a poem for what it says (that's the mind part), and you can like it for how it makes you feel (that's the heart part). It's the "heart part" that really separates poetry from other forms of writing. (**SEE** the lyric model on page 185 for a poem that expresses deep feelings.)

3 **Poetry says a lot in a few words.** Poets create word pictures using "sensory" details that describe sights, sounds, smells, tastes, and other physical feelings.

> I was standing on the street when . . .
> The rusty old black Cadillac **(sight)**
> grunted rack-a-bump-she-bang, **(sound)**
> and heated up my cool spot of air, **(physical feeling)**
> and spewed oily smoke **(smell)**
> all over my mustard-covered foot-long hot dog. **(sight)**
>
> — Anne-Marie Oomen

4 **Poetry says things in special ways.** Poets also create special word pictures by comparing different things. If you've ever written a *simile* ("I climbed slow as an old fly"), then you know what I'm talking about. Another special type of comparison is called a *metaphor*. Can you see what two things are being compared in the following examples?

> Rain
> Rain Rain
> Wet Little Chicken Pox
> On the Window . . .
> 　　　　— Cassie Hoek

> *A gentle wind at night is*
> *my wispy grandmother.*
> 　　　　— Tim Capewell

Helpful Hint　For more about similes, metaphors, and other special comparisons, turn to page 182.

5 **Poetry pleases the ear.** Poets carefully arrange words so that certain sounds stand out. You already know that words sometimes rhyme in poems. But there are a lot of other ways to make poems sound pleasing.

Poets may repeat certain consonant and vowel sounds to help make their poems pleasing to the ear. You can see how this works by reading "Purple Poems." Certain consonant and vowel sounds are underlined. (**SEE** page 183 for more examples.)

> *Purple Poems*
> *Quiet purple clouds rolled in.*
> *Purple rain <u>d</u>rops <u>d</u>rip from*
> *the clouds.*
> *Smooth purple shells <u>w</u>ash*
> *in <u>w</u>ith the <u>w</u>aves.*
> *Purple <u>l</u>ightning st<u>r</u>i<u>k</u>es a tree.*
> *<u>P</u>urple <u>p</u>oems litter the field.*
> 　　　　— Katlyn McKalson

YOU DON'T SSSSSAY

You will also find many of these same elements (like sensory details and similes) in regular writing. They just stand out more in poetry.

Writing a Free Verse Poem

The following guidelines will help you write a free verse poem. Free verse poetry does not follow a specific form, and it does not have to rhyme.

PREWRITING *Planning Your Poem*

Select a Subject ● Write your poem about a person, place, event, object, or idea that you find interesting. You might write about a special room, a friend, a favorite animal, music, and so on.

Collect Your Thoughts ● I decided to write a poem about my favorite animal, dogs. To get started, I wrote freely for a few minutes about one certain dog.

> I knew an alley dog. My stepmom said I was not to touch him ever, but sometimes I crawled down the fire escape and he would sit near me, but we would not touch each other. Once I took him an old sandwich and he was happy. We would watch the sun on the buildings.

WRITING A FIRST DRAFT

Create a Poem ● Here's how a free writing (like the one above) can be the start of a poem. Begin by making line breaks. At first, make these breaks where you naturally hear pauses in the sentences. Then you may try moving words (or parts) around. You may also try adding or changing words. (See how I turned my free writing into a basic poem.)

> The Alley Dog
> Never touch him! my stepmom said,
> but once I fed him an old sandwich,
> and he was happy,
> and sometimes I would
> crawl down the fire escape,
> and he would creep up near me
> and we would watch
> the sun on the buildings.

REVISING *Improving Your Writing*

Add Word Pictures ● Does this first draft contain any specific word pictures or pleasing sounds? Yes, "crawl" and "creep" sound good and are specific. But I wanted to add more word pictures and pleasing sounds, so I thought some more and wrote this new draft.

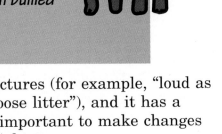

The Alley Dog

Never touch him! my stepmom
shouted loud as a train. But once
I tossed him half my butter sandwich
and he danced like loose litter in wind.
And once I climbed
    slow as an
        old fly
down our fire escape,
and he crept up,
    stop
        and go,
like a car in bad traffic,
and we sat near each other,
and watched how the sun bullied
the cracked brick wall
into the dark.

Now the poem has more word pictures (for example, "loud as a train") and pleasing sounds ("like loose litter"), and it has a shape that is more interesting. It is important to make changes in a poem until it looks and sounds right to you.

Bright IDEA

Try using your poem's subject for a title, as I did in "The Alley Dog." Or use part of your first line (Never Touch Him!) or a word that summarizes your poem (Friendship).

EDITING & PROOFREADING

The following checklist will help you edit your poem.

- ✔ **Make sure that your poem is complete.** Have you left anything out?
- ✔ **Check the line breaks.** Do they add special meaning to your poem? Are they interesting or fun?
- ✔ **Make sure your poem has plenty of specific details.** Do the details paint interesting word pictures? Do they "sound" good? Have you used fresh, new comparisons?
- ✔ **Make sure your poem reads well.** Do you stumble over any words or lines when you read your poem? If so, change them.
- ✔ **Write a final copy of your poem, making all of the corrections.** Proofread this copy before sharing it.

FIGURES OF SPEECH

To create effective word pictures, poets often make special comparisons. These special comparisons are often called **figures of speech**.

- A **SIMILE** compares one thing to something unlike it using *like* or *as*. *Coat hooks hold winter hats like bare branches hold old nests.*

- A **METAPHOR** makes a comparison without using *like* or *as*. *The street is my heart.*

- **PERSONIFICATION** makes a comparison in which something that is not human is described with human qualities. *My eggs stared back like sick eyes.*

- **HYPERBOLE** makes exaggerated comparisons for effect. Sometimes these are funny. *It was so hot we fried.*

The Sounds of Poetry

Listed below are some of the devices poets use to make their poems sound pleasing to the ear. (Use some in your poems.)

Alliteration ● The repeating of the beginning consonant sounds in words like *dance, dare,* and *drop*.

Assonance ● The repetition of vowel sounds in words like *rain, makes, pavement,* and *wavy*.

Consonance ● The repetition of consonant sounds anywhere in the words: *The catcher wore a black jacket.*

End Rhyme ● The rhyming of words at the ends of two or more lines of poetry, as in the first two lines in Robert Frost's famous poem called "Stopping by Woods on a Snowy Evening":

> *Whose woods these are I think I know.*
> *His house is in the village though;*

Helpful Hint Many traditional forms of poetry follow specific rhyme patterns. (**SEE** pages 184-185 for examples.)

Internal Rhyme ● The rhyming of words in the middle of lines:

> *After he had made an out,*
> *a pout rattled around his mouth.*

Onomatopoeia ● The use of words whose sounds make you think of their meanings, as in *buzz, thump,* and *snap*.

Repetition ● The repeating of a word or phrase to add rhythm, or to emphasize a certain idea: *The wind hissed, hissed down the alley.*

Rhythm ● The way the poem flows from one idea to the next. In free verse poetry (the type of poem used as a model on page 177), the rhythm is usually like the natural flow of spoken language. In traditional forms of poetry, words are often arranged into a definite pattern of accented and unaccented syllables. Notice in the following lines how an unaccented syllable is followed by an accented one. This is an example of patterned rhythm:

> *Becáuse I sáw no cáke,*
> *I áte a páper pláte.*

TRADITIONAL POETRY

The forms of poetry that follow have been around for a long time.

Ballad poems tell a story. The ballad is written in four-line stanzas. Often the second and fourth lines rhyme. (Here is the first stanza of my ballad called "Ballad of Skull Rock.")

> *We miners long ago did find*
> *the skull rock on the <u>lake</u>.*
> *The silver lay in open veins,*
> *all shining for the <u>take</u>.*

Cinquain poems are five lines long with a certain number of syllables or words in each.

Syllable Cinquain

Line 1:	Title	2 syllables
Line 2:	Description of title	4 syllables
Line 3:	Action about the title	6 syllables
Line 4:	Feeling about the title	8 syllables
Line 5:	Synonym for title	2 syllables

Word Cinquain

Line 1:	Title	1 word
Line 2:	Description of title	2 words
Line 3:	Action about the title	3 words
Line 4:	Feeling about the title	4 words
Line 5:	Synonym for title	1 word

A **Couplet** is a two-line verse form that usually rhymes and expresses one thought.

> *Back and forth the dancer <u>whirled</u>,*
> *A butterfly with wings <u>unfurled</u>.*

YOU DON'T SSSSS SAY

Some traditional poems are written totally in couplets. Other poems may use only one couplet for special effect.

Free Verse is poetry which does not include patterned rhyme or rhythm. (**SEE** the model on page 181 for an example.)

Haiku is a type of Japanese poetry about nature. It is three lines long. The first line is five syllables; the second, seven; the third, five.

> **Sun moves on rubble,**
> **weeds grow sideways in small cracks,**
> **small vines cling to walls.**

A **Limerick** is a funny verse in five lines. Lines one, two, and five rhyme, as do lines three and four. Lines one, two, and five have three stressed syllables; lines three and four have two.

> There once was a chef named Maurice
> Who always used way too much grease.
>   His chicken was fine;
>   His fries were divine,
> But his dinners just made me obese.

A **Lyric** is a song-like poem which uses sensory details to express personal feelings.

> Up! Up! Bright kites fly, oooh,
>   maroon, and yellow, and easy blue
>   over the evening park.
> I like to think they pull me too,
>   up into that blue, that easy blue,
>   far away from the dark.

A **Quatrain** is a four-line stanza. Notice in this example that the first two lines rhyme, and the second set of lines rhyme. In some quatrains the first and third lines rhyme, and the second and fourth lines rhyme.

> *Not far west of Wyoming there lies*
> *A little town that men despise.*
> *The streets that once glittered with gold*
> *Now are barren, dusty, and cold.*

INVENTED POETRY

Poets have fun inventing new forms of poetry. Here are some invented forms to try.

Alphabet Poetry ● An alphabet poem uses a part of the alphabet to create a funny list poem.

Cats
Don't
Ever
Fly (willingly)

Concrete Poetry ● This is poetry in which the shape or design helps express the meaning or feeling of the poem.

The way to school is d
                      o
                       w
                        n

W I D E streets

FULLOF**BIG**PEOPLE!!!!!

Definition Poetry ● This is poetry that defines a word or an idea creatively.

FRIENDSHIP
Friendship is like stars in the
sky. Like going
to fly with Peace,
and the moon shines
on us while we fly. We walk
through the sky and clouds. And we
share the future in a treasure
chest, topped with diamonds.   —Jessamyn Ansary

Five W's Poetry ● Each line in this type of poem answers one of the 5 W's (who? what? where? when? and why?).

I
Love to 'blade
Along Venice Beach
In the middle of the day
Because people are friendly and get out of your way.

List Poetry ● This is poetry made from a list. Often the title says what the list is.

WHAT'S IN THE BOX UNDER MY BED
eight marbles and a shoestring
a cracker jack ring (I think it's magic)
my two most valuable baseball cards
the mitten that boy dropped
the letter my friend wrote

Name Poetry ● A name poem, or acrostic poem, is formed using the letters of a name or a word to begin each line in the poem.

Fierce   Calm eyes
Righteous   Oozing
Energetic   Over
Dude   Lake water

Phrase Poetry ● This form of poetry states an idea with a list of phrases.

EATING SPAGHETTI
with a twirl of a fork
and the help of a spoon
quickly up to the mouth
before it all falls off

Sensory Poetry ● Each line in this type of poem describes a subject using one of the senses. (**SEE** the bottom of page 178.)

Terse Verse ● This is humorous verse made up of two words that rhyme and have the same number of syllables. The title is the subject.

Joke Books   Kool-Aid   Candy
Smile   Pink   Sweet
File   Drink   Treat

You can try other invented forms of poetry by turning to pages 204-205.

Writing Songs

Goin' Down, Down, Ever Downstream

Have you ever wanted to write a song? Well I have, and I did! I just wrote a song called "Shanty Boat." I'll show you how I wrote it, just in case you want to follow the same steps and write a song of your own.

1 Find a First Line

One day I was thinking about *Huckleberry Finn*, a book about two friends who travel down a river on a shanty boat. I doodled this line in my notebook:

Uncle Sheb lived on a shanty boat.

Hmm. Those words had rhythm. (Say them aloud, loudest on the words in all caps.)

UNCLE Sheb LIVED on a SHANty BOAT.

Those words felt like a song. I tapped my foot to them: and ONE and TWO and THREE and FOUR. I was on my way to becoming a songwriter!

66 Good luck with your songwriting. I'll be listening for you on the radio! By the way, a version of the song "Shanty Boat" has been published as a picture book. 99 I hope you like it.
—Charles Temple

2 Find a "Frame"

As I repeated the first line of my song out loud, a song I already knew came to mind.

FROG WENT A COURTIN'

FROG went a COURTIN' and HE did RIDE,
>   *Uh-huh.*
FROG went a COURTIN' and HE did RIDE,
>   *Uh-huh.*
FROG went a COURTIN', and HE did RIDE,
SWORD and BUCKLER BY his SIDE,
>   *Uh-huh, uh-huh, uh-huh.*

The pattern of rhythm and rhyme from "Frog Went a Courtin' " gave me a **frame** for writing a song about the shanty boat. It also showed me how many beats to put into each line (four beats per line, in this case). The verse from "Frog Went a Courtin' " showed me which words in my song should rhyme.

Important Note: Later, once I'd written the verses of my song, I would make up a new tune of my own.

3 Write the Verses

The words I had written—

>   *Uncle Sheb lived on a shanty boat—*

became the first line of a verse. Now I wanted a line of words to follow each new line in my song, the way "uh-huh" does in the frog song. Lines like these are called **refrains**. Here's the refrain I thought up for the shanty boat song:

>   *Goin' down, down, ever downstream.*

The frog song repeats the words "Frog went a courtin' and he did ride," so I repeated the words "Uncle Sheb lived on a shanty boat." Next I wrote a line to rhyme with "boat," the way "side" rhymes with "ride" in the frog song:

>   *Uncle Sheb lived on a shanty boat,*
>   *Goin' down, down, ever downstream.*
>   *Uncle Sheb lived on a shanty boat,*
>   *That sure was the shabbiest thing afloat,*
>   *Goin' down, down, ever downstream.*

4 Organize Your Verses

I wrote four or five verses before I realized that the song needed an overall **shape**. One way to shape a song is to make it like a story. You can give it a *beginning* (a couple of verses that introduce your characters and their problem), a *middle* (verses that say more about your characters), and an *end* (verses that end the story and tell how the problem was solved).

Find the Beginning

The first verse I wrote really didn't belong at the beginning; it was better for the middle. For a beginning, I wanted to introduce a man who lived on a shanty boat, in a way that would make listeners curious about him. Here's my new first verse:

> My Uncle Sheb never milked him a cow,
> *Goin' down, down, ever downstream.*
> My Uncle Sheb never milked him a cow,
> Nor plucked him a chicken, nor slopped him a sow,
> *Goin' down, down, ever downstream.*

Write the Middle

After a couple of verses that named all the things Uncle Sheb never did, I put in that verse about Uncle Sheb living on the shanty boat, the verse we started with. I added other verses in the middle about what the boat was like and how Uncle Sheb lived on it.

Figure Out the End

Finally, the song needed an ending. I decided to say that Uncle Sheb had died, and I wrote this line:

> They sank that shanty boat, Uncle and all . . .

But I wasn't willing to get rid of him entirely. I turned the shanty into a ghost boat, with someone on deck:

> And an old man stands by the steering oar,
> *Goin' down, down, ever downstream.*
> And an old man stands by the steering oar,
> Guess it could be Sheb, but you can't be sure,
> *Goin' down, down, ever downstream.*

Songwriting Steps

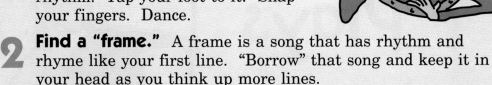

1 Find a first line. Maybe it's a saying, or even something you just heard in the hallway. Say it over and over in different ways until it has rhythm. Tap your foot to it. Snap your fingers. Dance.

2 Find a "frame." A frame is a song that has rhythm and rhyme like your first line. "Borrow" that song and keep it in your head as you think up more lines.

3 Write the verses. Make sure that your lines or verses rhyme in the same places as the lines in your borrowed song. Be sure to consider adding a *refrain* or chorus.

4 Organize your verses. After you've written several verses, it's time to think of a way to organize your song. Will you have a beginning, a middle, and an end?

5 Revise your song.

■ Consider the sound. Do the words work together to make a pleasing sound?

■ Be sure you haven't put too many beats in any line— the test is to tap your foot while you say the line slowly. See if you've put the important words where they'll get the stressed beats.

■ Choose the most vivid words you can—the test here is to ask others if your words make pictures in their minds.

SONGWRITER'S TOOLBOX

Rhyming Dictionary ● Many songwriters use rhyming dictionaries. These books give you gobs of words that rhyme.

Standard Dictionary ● I keep a standard dictionary handy, too, to make sure that a good rhyming word means what I think it does. Don't write something stupid just because it rhymes!

Thesaurus ● I also use a thesaurus. For instance, I couldn't find a rhyme I wanted for "pig," but the thesaurus told me that I could use "sow" instead, and that rhymed with "plow."

Writing Plays

Bringing Ideas to Life

Raise your hand if you like to do things with your friends. (Okay, good.) Next, rub your fingers together if there is something you would like to get, or some problem you would like to solve. (That's right.) And lastly, tap the side of your head if you think you like to daydream or pretend. (Hey, not bad.)

Silly Questions

Why did I ask you to do these silly things? To get you thinking like a playwright. Ideas for plays come from real-life experiences as well as from a writer's lively imagination.

The models and guidelines on the following pages will help you get your fingers and mind working on your first, or next, play.

> A play is really a story in dialogue form. As the characters talk, the story moves on. When you write a play, you bring your personal interests, experiences, and imagination to life.

A Model Beginning

In this model beginning, you will see that Dave and Jessica are in trouble, and they need a way out. That's how plays begin. One or more characters need to solve a problem or figure out how to get something. In between, there's *action*. How will Dave and Jessica keep their dad's mind off fishing? Will their crime be noticed? Those questions will be answered in the rest of the play.

What Will We Tell Mom and Dad?

Characters: DAVE, 12 years old
JESSICA, 11 years old
DAD, their father
MOM, their mother

Place: The living room of a cabin near a river

SCENE 1
(The room is empty. Suddenly, JESSICA
bursts through the door closely followed by DAVE.)

DAVE: (pushing her) It's all your fault!

JESSICA: (pushing him back) It's not! You're the one who couldn't wait till Mom and Dad got home from the store. You just had to go fishing the minute we got to this cabin. I should have never let you talk me into it.

DAVE: I just wanted to surprise them with a fish for dinner. And anyway, you're the one who borrowed Dad's new fishing rod, not me.

JESSICA: But I didn't drop it into the river, did I?

MOM: (calling from offstage) Jessica? Dave? Come help with these groceries.

DAVE: Oh, no! They're home! What are we going to do?

JESSICA: We'll just have to tell them we broke . . .

DAVE: (interrupting her) Tell them? Are you kidding? This vacation will be over before it's even begun. All we have to do is keep Dad's mind off fishing.

JESSICA: But how?

Writing a Play

PREWRITING *Planning Your Play*

Select the Main Parts ● All you really need to get started is at least two characters, a problem, and a place or a setting for the action. People you know may give you ideas for characters. Events that have made you laugh or cry may give you ideas for the problem and action in your play. Places you know may give you ideas for settings. And your dreams and imagination may give you ideas for all three parts.

Collect Details ● Use some form of a "collection sheet" or checklist to help you plan your play. (Ideas to include are listed below.) But remember that part of the fun of writing a play is seeing where your characters will take you. So don't try to plan too many details about your play before you start writing.

Collection Sheet

Main Characters #1 and #2:
(Give each character a name and an age. Describe something about each person's appearance and personality. Decide what role he or she will "play.")

Other Characters:
(Identify any other characters who will be part of your play. You might not know all of these until you actually start writing.)

Setting:
(Describe where and when your play will take place.)

Main Problem:
(What is the main problem faced by the characters?)

Action:
(What things might they do to solve this problem?)

WRITING THE FIRST DRAFT

Before you start writing, review the model on page 193 to see how your play should be set up. Then get to work on your first draft using the suggestions below as your guide.

Start the Play ● The opening part of a play should set the scene for the main action to follow. (Remember that the characters' words and actions are the driving force in a play.)

The main characters should be introduced, the setting should be described, and the main problem should be noted. (The beginning may also describe important events that happened before the start of the play.)

Solve a Problem ● The middle of a play shows the main characters trying to solve their problem or get what they want. (This is the longest part of the play. Each new activity or event could be a different scene.)

In the model, Dave and Jessica could plan all sorts of fun activities to keep their dad from fishing.

Bright IDEA

To create excitement and maybe a little fun in your play, have your main characters get in each other's way.

End the Play ● The ending of a play shows how things finally work out. (Basically, the main characters do or don't get what they want, or they do or don't solve their problem.)

In the model, the dad may finally discover his broken fishing rod. But the kids have been so good that he probably doesn't get too mad at them. Maybe he reminds them of what they should have done instead of what they did.

REVISING *Improving Your Writing*

Read your first draft to yourself. Ask yourself if your play moves along smoothly and clearly from beginning to end. Also decide if there are parts that need to be added or cut. Then read your work out loud, paying special attention to each line. Put a check next to any lines that you want to rewrite.

Write Dialogue ● Writing dialogue is creating talk on paper. Keep this point in mind when you review and revise the first draft of your play. You want your characters to sound like they are really talking. Which of these two sounds more like a real person?

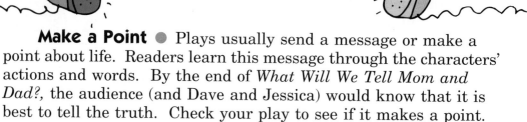

> LEE: *Shar, please call me after you get home from school today.*
>
> *OR*
>
> LEE: *Shar, call me after school, okay?*

Make a Point ● Plays usually send a message or make a point about life. Readers learn this message through the characters' actions and words. By the end of *What Will We Tell Mom and Dad?,* the audience (and Dave and Jessica) would know that it is best to tell the truth. Check your play to see if it makes a point.

Ask a small group of classmates to read the different parts in your play. Listening to your play will help you find the parts that need to be changed.

EDITING & PROOFREADING

Check Your Writing ● Check the revised version of your writing for spelling, mechanics, and grammar errors. Then write a final draft of your play, following the form used for the model beginning on page 193. Proofread this draft before sharing it.

What Will We . . .

As you remember in the model beginning on page 193, Dave and Jessica have a problem. They've broken their dad's new fishing rod, and they don't want him to find out. How might that play continue? Student writer Faith Brawley continued the play with this scene, which adds a little more suspense to the plot.

SCENE II

(The family has just finished dinner and is chatting in the living room.)

MOM: *(So, what did you guys do while we went grocery shopping?)*

JESSICA: *(in a shaky voice)* Well, we um . . .

DAVE: *(interrupting JESSICA)* We played a game of cards.

JESSICA: *(glaring at DAVE)* We also went for a swim. I pushed Dave in the water. I thought he could use a cooling off.

DAD: Oh, that reminds me. Do you guys want to go fishing tomorrow or would you rather go on a nature walk?

DAVE & JESSICA: *(at the same time)* NATURE WALK!

DAD: Okay, that settles that. We'll go on a nature walk.

MOM: *(yawning)* It's getting kind of late.

JESSICA & DAVE: *(exiting the living room)* Okay, Mom, we'll see you tomorrow.

JESSICA: That was a close one!

DAVE: *(his heart skipping a beat)* You're telling me!

JESSICA: *(feeling horrible)* I don't want to keep lying about this! I'm going to tell Dad!

DAVE: *(in a panic)* You can't tell him. We're already too deep in this to try and get out.

JESSICA: I suppose so . . .

To become a good playwright, you should read a lot of plays. A good place to start is the magazine called *Plays: The Drama Magazine for Young People*, published by Plays, Inc. Most libraries have it.

Writing Riddles

Exercising Your Mind

Question: *Why is the letter e like a question mark?*

Answer: *It's found at the end of every riddle.* (Get it?)

Why do so many people enjoy asking and hearing riddles? Maybe it's because there's a laugh at the end of most riddles—and because there's a surprise there, too. Can you "crack" the following riddle?

*Inside an ivory box is
a crystal sphere.
Inside the crystal is
a heart of gold.
What is it?*

(An egg)

Are you ready to write a riddle or two of your own? You can start with the "Crack Up" and "What Am I" riddles.

> 66 *Telling riddles is a form of mental exercise. Since so many riddles depend on puns (little jokes) and wordplay, they develop your language skills. And because many of them are crazy, they encourage your imagination to grow.* 99
> — Lorraine Sintetos

"CRACK UP" RIDDLES

Riddle #1 *Why is it hard to find a home for a gloomy whale?*
No one wants a pet that size (sighs).

Riddle #2 *Where's the best place to buy a part for a clock?*
A secondhand shop (second hand).

In each of the "crack up" riddles above, the answer contains a *pun* (a word that sounds like a word with another meaning). In the first riddle, "size" and "sighs" are pronounced the same, but have different meanings and spellings. Both, however, make sense in the answer. In the second riddle, *secondhand* has two meanings: a "secondhand" shop is a place to buy things; a "second hand" is a clock part.

Writing a "Crack Up" Riddle

1 ▶ **Brainstorm for words that sound alike.**

> *Example:* peace (noun) piece (noun)
> *(Your words should be the same part of speech.)*

2 ▶ **Pick a pair of words and think of a sentence (or a phrase) in which either word makes sense.**

> He just wants a little peace (a little piece).

3 ▶ **Ask yourself questions.**

> Who might want a little peace?
> *(someone around a lot of noise)*

> Who might want just a little piece?
> *(a kid being served something yucky)*

4 ▶ **Create a riddle question with this pattern:**
Why is a _____ like a _____ ?

> **Why is a teacher with noisy students like a boy being served spinach pie?**
> Both just want a little peace (piece).

"WHAT AM I" RIDDLES

"What Am I" riddles have been around for a long time. In this type of riddle, you try to guess what object or idea is being described. Here are two different ways to write them:

Use Metaphors

You can describe the appearance of an object as if it were something else. (By doing this, you are creating a comparison called a *metaphor*.) In the riddle on the first page in this chapter, the shell of an egg is compared to an ivory box, the white of the egg is a crystal sphere, and the yolk is compared to a heart of gold.

> *Inside an ivory box is*
> *a crystal sphere.*
> *Inside the crystal is*
> *a heart of gold.*

Use Personification

Or you can describe an object as if it were a living thing. (This is called *personification*.) In the riddle below, a shout is described as if it could fly, and we normally think of wings as belonging to living things.

> *I have no wings, but I can cross the widest*
> *street without touching the ground.*
> *What am I?*

(A shout.)

Use Surprise Endings

You can use your imagination to combine details that sound ordinary, but then take an unexpected funny twist.

> *What is gray, has big ears, and squeaks?*
> *(It sounds like a mouse. But it could be*
> *an elephant wearing new shoes!)*

Writing a "What Am I" Riddle

1 ▶ **Start by making a list of everyday objects and ideas.**

LIST: flower, night, bookshelf, scissors, football, skateboard, radio

2 ▶ **Choose one noun (to be the answer to your riddle) and describe it.**

CHOOSE: *night*
DESCRIBE: *dark, quiet, soft, comes slowly every day, can be scary, not human*

3 ▶ **Ask yourself, "What different thing can I compare it to?" (metaphor) or "Can I describe my noun as a living thing?" (personification)**

COMPARE: Study your list of descriptive words for ideas. Suppose you decide to describe the night as if it were a black cat. Both are dark and quiet.

4 ▶ **Write your riddle.**

WRITE: *I'm dark and have no legs, though I sneak into your house slowly and quietly every day. What am I?*

(Night)

THINK IT OVER

Try exercising your mind by creating a "What Am I" rhyming riddle. Here's an example:

*The more times you use me,
the shorter I'll grow.
The more I do of my work,
the less of yours will show.
What am I?*

(An eraser.)

Writing for Fun

Ideas for Friends and Family

Writing is the least expensive hobby I know. It has other advantages, too: you can write all your life, whether it's rainy or sunny, summer or winter. You can do it lying down, sitting, or standing on your head, and you can do it every day, on your own, outside of school. There are at least 700 kinds of writing besides homework. None of them are fattening, and most are very enjoyable.

Starting with Stories

Even though we listen to stories and tell stories, one thing we don't do very often is write stories down. I don't mean the kind we imagine or make up. Nearly everyone has written made-up stories from the time they were able to put words on paper. I mean the kind of stories that really happened.

> 66 Stories make it wonderful to be human. You won't find a horse telling a tale to another horse, or a bullfrog chuckling over a favorite joke. People do these things all the time, however. 99
> — Peter Stillman

Writing Family Stories

Every family needs someone to save, or preserve, stories about important people, places, and events. You are the perfect person for this job. Here are a few ideas to get you started.

Name Stories . . . your name first ● Write about how your first and middle names were chosen. If you don't know, go to the source. Ask a parent or guardian. There is a story behind every name. This one, the story of your name, will be the first in a collection of stories about the _____ family.

. . . other family names ● Now check into other family names that interest you. Are there favorite first names or middle names in your family? How about nicknames? Last names? Tell their stories.

Birth Stories ● Find out about the day you were born. Ask your parents. What was the weather like? What time of day did you arrive? What important events were going on in the world that day?

Holiday Stories ● Write about the way your family celebrates holidays—Thanksgiving, Christmas, Hanukkah, New Year's Day, Easter, birthdays. Are there any special holidays that only your family celebrates?

Recipe Stories ● Your family has favorite recipes. Write up three or four. This way, they will always be available. (You may even want to put together a family recipe book.)

Heirloom Stories ● Many families have special pieces of furniture, jewelry, or paintings that have been handed down from generation to generation. These objects are called *heirlooms*. What are the stories behind your heirlooms? Where did they come from? Why are they valuable to your family?

Bright IDEA

Here are some topics to get you thinking about more family stories:

superstitions, spooky events, disasters, oddball relatives, rascals, pranks, and special sayings

Storyboards

The very first stories were recorded in picture form. We still create stories with pictures, but now we usually add a few words. Stories written in this way can be presented on a **storyboard** like the following example.

It's easy to make storyboard blanks, and it's fun to fill them in. Storyboard stories can be about your family, and they can also be goofy, like the one about Spot. Make enough blanks. Not all stories will fit in six frames.

Four Kinds of Playful Poems

Found Poems ● Visit a local store that features many different products. With pencil and notepad in hand, list as many items as you care to. Later, create a poem by combining some or all of the items you have listed. Here is the start of such a poem:

> *On the shelves*
> *of our general store*
> *you can find*
> *eyebolts, stovebolts, U-bolts, and carriage bolts;*
> *birdfood, catfood, dogfood, and fishfood; . . .*

Dictionary Poems ● Flip to any page of a dictionary and jot down phrases that appeal to you from the definitions of at least three words. Then arrange and rearrange the phrases until they make sense. Be sure to title your work. (Can you think of a title for this one?)

A trick of magic
kept in motion,
of quick movement,
of great joy:
writing in a journal.

Telephone Number Poems ● Telephone numbers aren't poems, but your phone number has a poem hidden inside it. You can find it by letting each number represent either syllables or whole words. Let's say your phone number is 362-4814. The first line of your poem will have three syllables (or words), the second will have six, the third will have two, and so on. Here's an example:

Our cat starts (3 syllables)
most mornings on my lap (6 syllables)
before
stalking stuffed mice
or dashing downstairs to explore.
He
likes things the same.

Lifelong Poems ● Many poems are really lists. A long time ago, I began one with the title "Things I Love." Here are the first two lines:

Horse tracks in the snow
Rain on my cabin roof

It's a very long poem now, because I add to it often, sometimes just one line, sometimes more. Start your own "Things I Love" list today. Promise yourself that you will keep at it for a month, at least one line a day. You're in for some surprises.

Another good title for a lifelong poem is simply "I Am . . . ." See where it takes you, one "I am" at a time.

I am . . . the rainbow on a soap bubble.

Research Writing

Using the Library

Writing a Summary

Writing a Classroom Report

Using the Library

Ask the Experts!

Suppose you are asked to write a report about whales. You can use your own experience. You can talk to other people. However, if you get seasick just thinking about boats, or if the people you know don't have a whale of a tale, there are other people who can help! And, there's a place you can "meet" them and "hear" their stories and ideas—

THE LIBRARY.

Where You'll Find It

Card Catalog—books, recordings, videos, etc.

Encyclopedias—general information about a topic

Magazine Guide—magazine articles

Special Reference Books—special information on everything from *aardvarks* to *zyzzyvas*

Using the Card Catalog

In the ocean, you need sonar and trained people to find whales. In the library, whether you're looking for giant whales or invisible atoms, you'll need the **card catalog**. Cards in the card catalog are placed alphabetically in drawers (or on computers). Here are some guidelines:

■ **Title Cards:** There is a **title card** for every book in the library. If a title begins with *A, An,* or *The,* skip to the next word.

Example: The title card for *The Pig-Out Blues* is in the P drawer under *Pig-Out.*

■ **Author Cards:** Every book has an author(s) or an editor. The name on the **author card** is listed last name first.

Example: Elsholz, Carol.

■ **Subject Cards:** Many books are also listed on **subject cards.** They are filed alphabetically and come before title cards beginning with the same word.

Example: The subject card DINOSAUR—HISTORY comes before the title card *Dinosaur Fossils.*

Inside the Card Catalog

To find out if your library has a certain book, look in the card catalog (or computer) for the *title* of the book. If you don't know the title, look up the *author*. Finally, if you don't know the title or the author, look under the general *subject* of the book.

Sample Catalog Cards

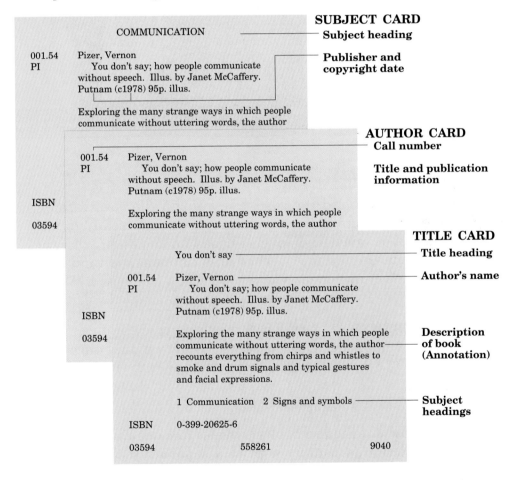

SUBJECT CARD

COMMUNICATION — Subject heading

001.54 | Pizer, Vernon — Publisher and
PI | You don't say; how people communicate | copyright date
without speech. Illus. by Janet McCaffery.
Putnam (c1978) 95p. illus.

Exploring the many strange ways in which people
communicate without uttering words, the author

AUTHOR CARD — Call number

001.54 | Pizer, Vernon
PI | You don't say; how people communicate | Title and publication
without speech. Illus. by Janet McCaffery. | information
Putnam (c1978) 95p. illus.

ISBN

03594 | Exploring the many strange ways in which people
communicate without uttering words, the author

TITLE CARD

You don't say — Title heading

001.54 | Pizer, Vernon — Author's name
PI | You don't say; how people communicate
without speech. Illus. by Janet McCaffery.
ISBN | Putnam (c1978) 95p. illus.

03594 | Exploring the many strange ways in which people | Description
communicate without uttering words, the author— | of book
recounts everything from chirps and whistles to | (Annotation)
smoke and drum signals and typical gestures
and facial expressions.

1 Communication   2 Signs and symbols — Subject
headings

ISBN | 0-399-20625-6

03594 | 558261 | 9040

 Once you have found the card in the card catalog, copy down the call number (and the title and author) of the book. This will save you the trouble of looking it up again later if you don't find the book right away.

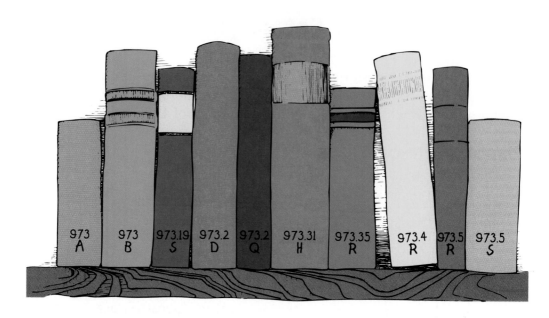

Finding a Book

Once you have found the card you want in the card catalog, and carefully copied down the call number, you are ready to look for your book. You may find several books on the shelf with the same numbers *on the top line*. When this happens, you must look at the letters and numbers *on the second line*. See how 973 / A comes before 973 / B in the illustration above.

Using Call Numbers ➤ Some call numbers contain decimals and are longer than other call numbers. Don't let that throw you. For example, **973.19** might seem *larger* than 973.2. In fact, it is only *longer*, not larger, because 973.2 is really **973.20**. Keep this in mind as you search for your book.

Finding Novels ➤ Fiction books (novels) are not numbered like other books. Fiction is usually kept in a separate section of the library where the books are arranged on the shelf by the author's last name.

Finding Biographies ➤ Biographies and autobiographies are also arranged on a separate shelf by the last name of the person written about. (Ask your librarian for help locating these special shelves.)

Using a Computer Catalog

There are different ways to tell a computer what you want. The simplest way is to use *keywords* and *logical operators*.

Using Keywords ➤ A keyword is a word related to your research topic. When you enter a keyword, the computer will look for it and list any records containing the word.

***Sample Keyword:* dinosaurs**

Using Logical Operators ➤ You can combine keywords to narrow or enlarge your search. Logical operators are the words you use between your keywords. The three logical operators—*and*, *or*, and *not*—tell the computer what to do.

---

and Use **and** to narrow your search. *And* tells the computer that *both* terms must be together before it selects them.

> ***Sample Search:* dinosaurs *and* Jurassic**

or Use **or** to enlarge your search. *Or* tells the computer to list either *one* or *both* terms if it finds them.

> ***Sample Search:* Tyrannosaurus rex *or* dinosaurs**

not Use **not** to narrow your search. *Not* tells the computer that the first keyword must be in the record and the second term must not be in the record. (*Not* is sometimes typed as *and not*.)

> ***Sample Search:* dinosaurs *not* carnivores**

Using the On-line Catalog ➤ After you've entered your keywords, a list of results (called **hits**) will appear on the screen. If you're using an on-line catalog, you will get a list of book titles. When you select a title, the screen will show you the record for that title. You will see the same information you would find on a card-catalog card: *title, author, copyright date,* and *call number*.

Using the Encyclopedia

An **encyclopedia** is a set of books (or a CD) with articles on every topic imaginable. The topics (or articles) are arranged alphabetically, just like a dictionary. Most encyclopedia articles begin with the basic facts. The further you read, the more details you will find. You will also find a list of related topics at the end of each article.

Using the Index

To help you find specific information about your topic, use the *Index* volume. (You will find it after the *WXYZ* volume.) The index tells you all the other places in the encyclopedia where you will find information, pictures, or other topics related to your subject. For example, here are some index entries for *Whale* from the *World Book Encyclopedia Index:*

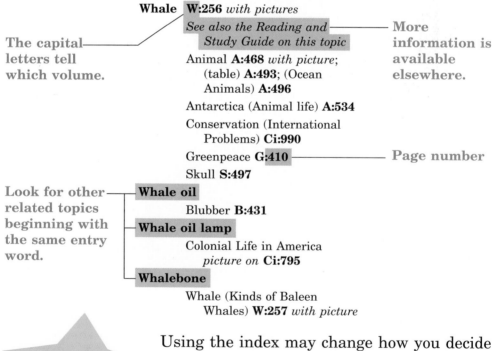

The capital letters tell which volume.

Whale W:256 *with pictures*
  See also the Reading and Study Guide on this topic —— More information is available elsewhere.
  Animal **A:468** *with picture*; (table) **A:493**; (Ocean Animals) **A:496**
  Antarctica (Animal life) **A:534**
  Conservation (International Problems) **Ci:990**
  Greenpeace **G:410** —— Page number
  Skull **S:497**

Look for other related topics beginning with the same entry word.

Whale oil
  Blubber **B:431**
Whale oil lamp
  Colonial Life in America *picture on* **Ci:795**
Whalebone
  Whale (Kinds of Baleen Whales) **W:257** *with picture*

Bright IDEA

Using the index may change how you decide to write about your subject. You might, for example, get a new idea from a story about whales in the American colonies, or about Greenpeace's fight to save whales today.

Using Other Reference Books

Reference books contain useful facts and information. You probably are most familiar with encyclopedias, dictionaries, and atlases. Other reference books can be just as helpful and are sometimes more up-to-date. Some popular titles are listed below:

- **The World Almanac and Book of Facts** contains facts and statistics about entertainment, sports, business, politics, history, religion, education, and social programs.

- **Great Lives** gives biographical information about well-known people in science, medicine, world government, sports, and the environment.

- **Encyclopedia of Presidents** contains one volume on each United States president.

- **Asimov's Chronology of Science & Discovery** discusses developments in science from 4,000,000 B.C. to the present.

THINK IT OVER

Many realistic fiction books contain information you might find helpful in a report. *Julie of the Wolves*, for example, contains a great deal of factual information about wolves.

- **Eyewitness Books** cover many science topics and have excellent color photographs.

- **Enchantment of the World** covers population, government, geography, and history.

- **Index to National Geographic** lists all the articles published in *National Geographic Magazine*.

- **Guinness Book of Records** lists records of all kinds, from science and medicine to sports and space.

Understanding the Parts of Reference Books

When you use a nonfiction book to find information for school writing, you should know the *parts* of the book and how they can help you use that book more efficiently. Below, you will find a short description of each part of a book.

➤ The **title page** (usually the first printed page in a book) lists (1) the complete title of the book, (2) the author's name, (3) the publisher's name, and (4) the place of publication.

➤ The **copyright page** is next and gives you the year the book was published. (Remember, if the book is too old, it may no longer be a good source of information.)

➤ The **preface, foreword, introduction,** or **acknowledgment** comes before the table of contents and tells what the book is about. It may also explain why the book was written.

➤ The **table of contents** shows you the divisions of the book (units, chapters, and topics). You can use it to find major topics covered in the book.

➤ The **body** is the main section of the book.

➤ The **appendix** follows the body. Here you will find extra information such as maps, charts, tables, diagrams, letters, or copies of official documents.

➤ The **glossary** is the dictionary part of the book. It lists terms or special words used in the book and explains each of them.

➤ The **bibliography** lists books or articles used by the author to help write the book. (You can use this list to find other books on the same topic.)

➤ The **index** lists all the topics in the book alphabetically. It will tell you whether the book contains the information you need and on which page you will find it.

Using the *Children's Magazine Guide*

The *Children's Magazine Guide* is another useful guide for finding information in the library. This guide is an organized list of all the latest magazine articles, articles you may find useful for a number of classroom reports or writing assignments.

To use the *Magazine Guide*, simply select the issue that covers the time period you are interested in. Once you have found the right issue, look for your subject. (The subjects are all listed in alphabetical order.)

If you can't find your subject, think of related topics. For example, if you are writing a report about *fossils*, you might look under *dinosaurs* or *prehistoric animals*.

Reading the Guide

When you find a magazine article you would like to read, copy down the title and date of the magazine and give it to the librarian. The librarian will get the magazine for you or show you where you can look for the article yourself. Here's a sample magazine entry from the *Children's Magazine Guide*:

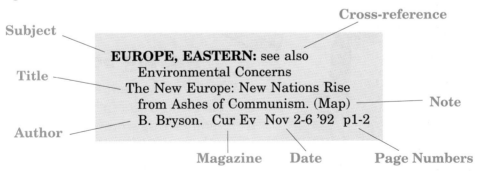

- **Subject** of the magazine article. Subjects are listed alphabetically.
- **Title** and **Author** of the magazine article.
- **Magazine** in which the article appears. A key to the abbreviations of magazine names is located on the inside front cover of the guide.
- **Date** (month, week, and year) the magazine was published.
- **Page Numbers** where the article can be found in the magazine.
- **Notes** give you more information about what's included in the article.
- **Cross-references** tell where more information can be found.

Writing a Summary

Learning and Remembering

Think of all the reading you do in school. For daily assignments, you are asked to read handouts, chapters, and stories. Then on your own, you are expected to do additional reading for special reports and projects. That's a lot of reading. You need a strategy or method to help you understand and remember the important ideas in these assignments. One such strategy is **summary writing**.

The Big Squeeze

When you write a summary, you select only the most important ideas from something you have read. You then combine these ideas into a clear and simple mini-report. Writing a summary tests how well you understand something you have read. It is a very effective learning tool, one that you will use again and again as a student. To see how a summary is written, refer to the model and guidelines that follow.

The process of writing a summary is a little like squeezing out toothpaste. You squeeze out just what you need and leave the rest in the tube.

Original

This article from a reference book describes the changes leaves undergo in the fall. (From *The Green Kingdom,* Volume 6 of *Childcraft—The How and Why Library.* © 1993 World Book, Inc.)

Why Leaves Change Color in Autumn

Inside a leaf there are millions of tiny packages of color—yellow, orange, and green. The yellow is called xanthophyll, the orange is carotene, or carotin, and the green is chlorophyll. The green color covers up the others, and that's why leaves are green all summer.

Near the end of summer, the green chlorophyll fades and disappears. Then the yellow xanthophyll and orange carotene can be seen. That's why many leaves turn yellow and orange in autumn.

All summer, water goes into each leaf through tiny tubes in the leaf's stem. Leaves make sugar, which is a plant's food. Sap carries the sugar out of the leaf to other parts of the plant. Near summer's end, a thin layer of cork grows over the tubes and seals them up. No more water can get into the leaf. Sugar often gets trapped inside leaves when the tubes are sealed up. This sugar may cause the sap to turn red or purple and make the leaves look red or purple.

When leaves are dry and dead, they turn brown.

Model Summary

In autumn, changes take place inside a leaf causing it to change colors. The green chlorophyll that covers a leaf begins to fade away. This allows the other colors (yellow and orange) to be seen. Also, the tiny tubes inside a leaf close up at the stem and hold in sugar and sap. The sugar may turn the sap red or purple which shows through the leaf. Then, once the leaf dries up, it turns brown.

Writing a Summary

Planning Your Summary

Skim and List ● Learn as much as you can about a reading selection before you try to summarize it.

➤ Skim it once to get the general meaning. Then read the selection carefully, paying special attention to key words that are **boldfaced** and *italicized*.

➤ Next, list the main points on your paper.

➤ Check your list against the reading selection to make sure you haven't missed anything.

WRITING THE FIRST DRAFT

Use Your Own Words ● Write your summary in clear and complete sentences. Use your own words, except for key words.

➤ The first sentence should state the main idea of the selection. (**SEE** the next page for help.)

➤ Include only the most important information in the rest of your summary. Do not get too detailed.

➤ Arrange your ideas in the most logical order.

➤ Add a concluding sentence, if one seems to be needed.

 **TAKE NOTE** Writing a summary is really a lot like writing a paragraph. The first sentence in a summary is the topic sentence. The sentences that follow must support the topic sentence.

Improving Your Work

Review It Carefully ● Ask yourself the following questions:

➤ Have I included all of the important ideas?

➤ Have I stated these ideas clearly and in my own words?

➤ Could another person get the main idea of the selection by reading my summary?

Finding the Main Idea

A Closer Look at Summarizing

The main idea in the model reading selection is stated right in the title: "Why Leaves Change Color in Autumn." That's easy. But what happens when you can't figure out or find the main idea? Try one or more of the following activities.

Self Check ● Make sure you have followed all of the steps listed under "Planning Your Summary" on page 218.

Big Questions ● Ask yourself some important questions. What is the biggest, largest, or most important idea in this reading material? What do I want to remember about this material a month from now? (How much do I have to squeeze out?)

Sharing Session ● Talk about the selection with a classmate. What do each of you think the reading is about? Work out any differences in your thinking until both of you agree on the main idea.

Reading Strategies ● Use a reading strategy like KWL (**K**now, **W**ant, **L**earn) to help you focus your attention on the important points in the reading material. (**SEE** pages 237-243 for more on these strategies.) Once you discover the main idea of a reading selection, all of the other parts of your summary should naturally fall into place.

Summarizing is an important part of other longer forms of writing, especially book reviews, classroom reports, and news stories. Look at the guidelines for writing a summary when using these other forms of writing.

Writing a Classroom Report

Flying Fish, Ocean Acrobats

Your teacher says, "Today, students, we're going to begin our reports on fish."

"Oh, no! Not another report," you think. "Sometimes they can be so *boring*." But wait a second. Your teacher is now saying this report should be on something different about fish, not the same old stuff. Maybe you've seen a "fish story" on television, in a magazine, or as part of a movie. Or maybe you have a personal story to tell.

No *Fishy* Topics!

When you write a report, you should find a topic that you would like to know more about, a topic that is truly interesting—one that you would enjoy reading about, writing about, and sharing with others.

> **Just as we've helped many of our students write reports, we'll show you how the whole process of researching, organizing, and writing your report might go. You can begin by turning to the next page and reading the report we wrote. Then, on the pages which follow, we will show you the process we used to write it. We hope it helps.**
> —*Peter & Connie Roop*

FLYING FISH, OCEAN ACROBATS

BEGINNING
The report begins with an action-packed story.

In the ocean, two hungry dolphins pick up speed. They see a school of flying fish. Sensing danger, the flying fish swim faster. Soon they are going 20 miles an hour. The dolphins are closer. Suddenly the flying fish break the surface, spread their side fins, and take off.

They soar over the waves at 40 miles an hour. The dolphins swim beneath them, gobbling any that drop down too soon. The rest of the flying fish skim the surface, beat their tails, and take off again.

MIDDLE
A number of fascinating facts are included in the body.

Flying fish, the dragonflies of the deep, use two sets of fins as wings to fly. Their front fins lift them out of the water while their back fins help them soar over the surface. Their flights are actually glides, some of them as long as three football fields. Because they are only gliding, the fish can't fly long distances like birds. The record for the longest flight is 1,214 yards on a flight that lasted 90 seconds.

Most flying fish glide 4 feet above the water. But some have been known to soar as high as 45 feet, high enough to sail over a house.

Quotes are also added from an interview.

Flying fish often land in fishing boats. One fisherman recalled meeting a flying houndfish, a cousin of the flying fish. "It came sailing through the air and before I could move, it struck me like a spear. Its snout went through my calf and stuck itself in the boat's side. I was pinned there in such agony I was hardly conscious, but then the fish tore itself loose and was off again."

END
A final thought is added to keep the readers thinking.

Their ability to escape enemies by taking to the air makes flying fish very successful sea creatures. They have been gliding since the days of the dinosaurs. Their special skill will probably keep them soaring for ages to come.

As Simple As A B C

There are three major steps to follow when you write a classroom report. This chapter will help you understand and follow this three-step plan:

    A. Select a good topic.
    B. Collect information about that topic.
    C. Connect that information into a well-written report.

A   SELECT A GOOD TOPIC

The first thing you have to do when you write a report is to find a good topic. A good topic is one that is interesting and *specific*. (*Fish* is a general topic; *goldfish* is specific. More about that later.) You also have to find a topic that works well for your assignment. To do that, you need to explore all the possibilities.

1 **Create a web, list, or cluster.** Start with the general topic assigned by your teacher, or one you've chosen, and jot down as many ideas about that topic as you can. We needed to write a report on fish for a local magazine, but the specific topic was up to us. Below is the web we created to help us find a specific topic.

General Topic Web

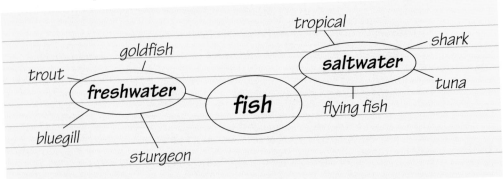

 Notice that we began our web by dividing it into the two biggest fish topics or categories we could think of: **freshwater** and **saltwater fish**.

2 **Let your web (list, cluster) sit.** After a couple of hours (even a full day), go back to your web and find an item or two that interests you the most.

After looking closely at our web, we sensed we wanted to write about saltwater fish. This became our chosen subtopic. We were now one step closer to our specific topic.

3 **Ask general questions.** Once you've decided upon your subtopic, begin another web. This web will hold all the questions you'd like answered about your topic. Knowing we were headed for the ocean depths, we drew the one below.

Subtopic Web

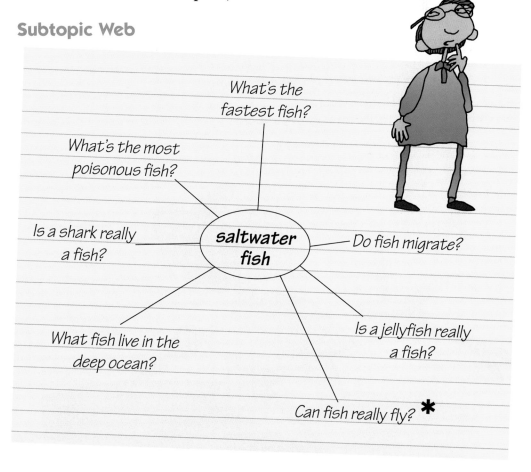

* As we worked on our second web, we began to think about doing our report on flying fish. So we starred this question. We were beginning to find out what really interested us.

4 **Ask specific questions.** By the time we finished our second web, we knew that we wanted to do our report on flying fish. To help us decide what we would include in our report, we made a list of questions that we wondered about. We figured our readers would wonder about the same things.

Specific Topic List

> ### flying fish
> Can we interview someone who's seen one?
> Who eats them?
> How high do they fly?
> Are they called by other names?
> How long have they been around?
> What do they eat?
> Are there any good stories about them?
> How fast do they go?

B   COLLECT INFORMATION

Once you've decided on your specific topic and collected your questions, it's time to start doing your research. Here are some suggestions for helping you gather information.

1 **Use a gathering grid.** This activity will help you to organize your information. Because you'll need to make a huge grid, it's best to use a big piece of paper (one 11- x 17-inch or two 8 1/2- x 11-inch pieces taped together). Then draw lines like the ones shown on our sample grid on the next page, and do the following:

➤ Write your topic in the upper left-hand corner.

➤ List your questions down the left side of your grid.

➤ List all the sources of information across the top. (See number 3 below for more on *sources*.)

2 **Ask open-ended questions.** As you list your questions on your grid, try to make them open-ended. An open-ended question is one that requires more than a "yes" or "no" answer. For example, the question "Do flying fish fly?" will not give you as much information as "How do flying fish fly?"

3 **Find good sources of information.** As you know, it's impossible to write a *good* report without a *good* topic and *good* information. Here are some sources you can use.

● **Use your school and public libraries.** (***SEE*** the chapter in this handbook about using libraries, pages 207-215.)

● **Find experts on your topic to write or talk to.** (***SEE*** page 125 for interview techniques and pages 142-147 for writing business letters.)

● **Ask your teacher, a parent, or your friends what they know.** (You might be surprised! Take your notebook and ask away.)

YOU DON'T SSSSAY

Some schools have a computer information service which you can use to find all kinds of material. Ask your teacher if your school has this service.

Gathering Grid

Sources of Information

Flying Fish	Books	Encyclopedias	Interviews	Magazine Articles
What eats flying fish?				
What do they eat?				
How fast do they go?	fly at 40 mph <u>How Fish Fly</u>, p. 2			
How & why do they fly?	tails flap 50 beats/sec. <u>How Fish Fly</u>, p. 2			
How far can they fly?	some glide as far as 3 football fields <u>Flying Fish</u>, p. 42			
Any good stories?			fisherman-Abe Short interview in writer's notebook	
Has anyone seen one fly?				Yes! See index card. "Has anyone seen one?"
Other names?		"dragon flies of the deep" <u>World Book</u>		
How long have they been around?	since dinosaur days, <u>Yesterday, Today & Tomorrow</u>, p. 92			
What do they look like?		5"-18" long <u>World Book</u>		

Your Questions

4 **Answer your questions.** Fill in the answers to your questions, as we have, right on your grid. At times you'll have more information than the grid will hold. Note cards can then prove very helpful.

5 **Use note cards, if needed.** Books, encyclopedias, interviews, magazines! There can be a lot of information to write down for a report. Your grid will help you keep track of all your facts, but you may find that some of the facts just won't fit. That's when you may need to use note cards. Simply write the question across the top of a 4- x 6-inch note card and list all your answers on the card.

Quotes: When you read something in a book or magazine that you want to use word for word, copy down the quote just as it was written. Do the same for what is said in interviews. (Remember to use quotation marks before and after a quote.)

Sample Note Cards

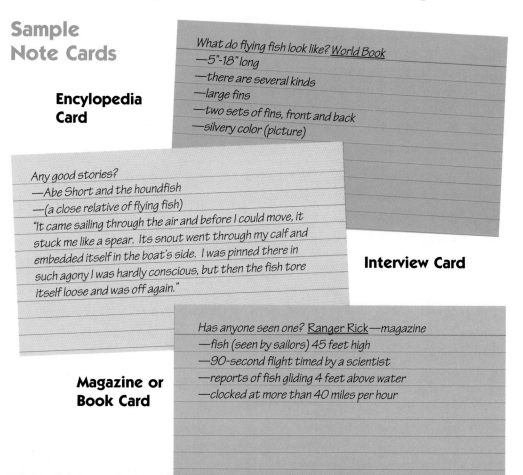

Encylopedia Card

What do flying fish look like? *World Book*
—5"-18" long
—there are several kinds
—large fins
—two sets of fins, front and back
—silvery color (picture)

Any good stories?
—Abe Short and the houndfish
—(a close relative of flying fish)
"It came sailing through the air and before I could move, it stuck me like a spear. Its snout went through my calf and embedded itself in the boat's side. I was pinned there in such agony I was hardly conscious, but then the fish tore itself loose and was off again."

Interview Card

Has anyone seen one? *Ranger Rick*—magazine
—fish (seen by sailors) 45 feet high
—90-second flight timed by a scientist
—reports of fish gliding 4 feet above water
—clocked at more than 40 miles per hour

Magazine or Book Card

6 **Check your information.** It is important that you take time to look over all your information before you start writing your report. By using different kinds of information, you will keep your readers interested. Try to include some of the following:

- quotes from experts or people with experience
- stories that sound as if you were an eyewitness
- colorful or powerful words that fit your topic
- interesting diagrams and drawings
- humorous or surprising information about the topic

CONNECT YOUR IDEAS

Once you have answered all your questions and organized all your information, it's time to begin writing your report. Here are some tips to help you make your report clear and interesting.

1 **Begin your report with a hook.** Most writing needs a good **hook**, something that will start it off with a bang. Starting with a *short story* is one way to begin. The two-paragraph story at the beginning of our report is our *hook*.

FLYING FISH, OCEAN ACROBATS

In the ocean, two hungry dolphins pick up speed. They see a school of flying fish. Sensing danger, the flying fish swim faster. Soon they are going 20 miles an hour. The dolphins are closer. Suddenly the flying fish break the surface, spread their side fins, and take off.

They soar over the waves at 40 miles an hour. The dolphins swim beneath them, gobbling any that drop down too soon. The rest of the flying fish skim the surface, beat their tails, and take off again.

Other Ways to Begin . . .

- ■ with a quote from an interview (*"It came sailing through the air and before I could move, it struck me like a spear."*)

- ■ with a dramatic statement (*Flying fish soar as high as 45 feet, high enough to sail over a house!*)

- ■ with a character or subject introduction (*You're about to meet a strange creature, one that you'll not soon forget.*)

- ■ with description (*In the ocean, two hungry dolphins pick up speed. They see a school of flying fish. Sensing danger, . . .*)

2 **Tie your facts together.** Now it's time to tie your facts together in an interesting way. Simply listing the facts you've gathered would turn out like a shopping list: useful, but boring! But linking your facts together from beginning to end can change a list into an interesting report.

THINK IT OVER

Our third and fourth paragraphs report fascinating facts about flying fish. By linking them to the hook (the first story in our report) and to what comes next (the quote from our interview), we have created an interesting "body" for our report.

Flying fish, the dragonflies of the deep, use two sets of fins as wings to fly. Their front fins lift them out of the water while their back fins help them soar over the surface. Their flights are actually glides, some of them as long as three football fields. Because they are only gliding, the fish can't fly long distances like birds. The record for the longest flight is 1,214 yards on a flight that lasted 90 seconds.

Most flying fish glide 4 feet above the water. But some have been known to soar as high as 45 feet, high enough to sail over a house.

3 **Use quotes and charts.** In your report, include someone's actual words. That's a **quote.** A person's real words are almost always interesting. A strong quote from a real person brings your report to life. Our quote was one of many we could have picked from, but it said so much and was so exciting, we chose it over all the others.

Helpful Hint — Use charts or diagrams if you think they would make your report more interesting or easier to understand.

Flying fish often land in fishing boats. One fisherman recalled meeting a flying houndfish, a cousin of the flying fish. "It came sailing through the air and before I could move, it struck me like a spear. Its snout went through my calf and stuck itself in the boat's side. I was pinned there in such agony I was hardly conscious, but then the fish tore itself loose and was off again."

4 **End with a strong point.** End your report with another story (a short one) or a strong point. Because flying fish have been around since the days of the dinosaurs, we ended our report by suggesting that the flying fish's unique ability has helped it survive in the past, and will help it survive in the future.

Their ability to escape enemies by taking to the air makes flying fish very successful sea creatures. They have been gliding since the days of the dinosaurs. Their special skill will probably keep them soaring for ages to come.

5 **List your sources.** Your teacher may ask you to make a list of the materials (sources) you used to write your report. In that case, you will need to include a **bibliography** page at the end of your report. To make a bibliography page, simply list your sources alphabetically by the author's last name, or by the title if there is no author given. Follow the examples listed below.

BOOKS Author (last name first). Title. City where the book is published: Publisher, copyright date.

> Athenton, Pike. *Fish with Wings*. Miami: Marine Press, 1990.

MAGAZINES Author (last name first). "Title of the article." Title of the magazine date (day month year): page numbers of the article.

> Bay, Marianne. *"Something Fishy Going Up."* At Sea 7 June 1992: 34-35.

Note: Indent the second and third lines 5 spaces.

ENCYCLOPEDIAS "Article title." Title of the reference book. Edition (if stated). Year published.

> *"Flying Fish." The World Book Encyclopedia. 1993 ed.*

FILMS, SLIDES, VIDEOTAPES Title. Medium (film, videocassette, etc.). Production company, date. Time length.

> *Flying Fish and Flightless Birds—Nature's Mistakes? Videocassette. Classroom Science Productions, 1993. 30 min.*

INTERVIEWS Person you interviewed (last name first). Type of interview. Date.

> *Short, Abe. Personal interview. 15 Aug. 1993.*

ON-LINE SOURCES (Simplified Entry) Author (last name first). "Title of article." Title of file year or date of publication. On-line. Name of computer network. Date of access. Available: electronic address

> *Abrams, Marietta S. "Fascinating Fish." Aquatic World Quarterly Apr.-June 1995. On-line. Internet. 10 Dec. 1995. Available HTTP://www.ppc.new.edu*

Writing a Report: A Summary Checklist

SELECT A GOOD TOPIC

1. Create a web (list, cluster).
2. Let your web sit.
3. Ask general questions.
4. Ask specific questions.

COLLECT INFORMATION

1. Use a gathering grid.
2. Ask open-ended questions.
3. Find good sources of information.
4. Answer your questions.
5. Use note cards, if needed.
6. Check your information.

CONNECT YOUR IDEAS

1. Begin with a hook.
2. Tie your facts together.
3. Use quotes and charts.
4. End with a strong point.
5. List your sources.

CHECK YOUR REPORT

1. Have you used clear, complete sentences?
2. Are your paragraphs well organized?
3. Have you covered the topic completely?
4. Have you used quotation marks correctly?
5. Have you checked your spelling, usage, and punctuation?
6. Is your report written (or typed) neatly?

Other Ways to Present a Report

Ask your teacher if you can try a different format for sharing what you've learned about your topic. Here are some other ways to do a report:

➤ **Write a poem.** (*SEE* the "Writing Poems" chapter.)

➤ **Perform a play.** (*SEE* the "Writing Plays" chapter.)

➤ **Write a song.** (*SEE* the "Writing Songs" chapter.)

➤ **Do and describe an experiment.** (*SEE* the "Writing Explanations" section.)

➤ **Draw a cartoon or series of cartoons.** (Include information in bubbles or as captions.)

➤ **Give a speech.** (*SEE* the "Giving Speeches" chapter.)

➤ **Write a historical story.** (*SEE* the "Writing Stories from History" chapter.)

➤ **Take pictures and make a photo essay.**

MINI LESSON   To give you an idea of how different forms of writing can work for a report, practice converting our report, "Flying Fish, Ocean Acrobats," into one of the forms listed above.

The Tools of Learning

Improving Your Reading

Using Reading Strategies

Reading Pictures

Using Reading Strategies

A Plan of Action

When you read, you want the ideas on the page to make sense. You want to enjoy what you read. You also want to be able to remember and use the information. So how can you become a better reader? One way is to follow the simple plan we've suggested below:

- **Read often.**
- **Read everything.** (stories, books, newspapers, magazines, even computer screens)
- **Change your speed as you read.**
- **Use reading strategies.**

When you re-read something or take notes, or talk about what you have read, you are using reading strategies. That's what we are going to talk more about in this chapter: how to use reading strategies to make you a better student. We hope you find it helpful.

What Are Reading Strategies?

A **strategy** is a plan or way of doing something. There are many strategies readers can use, and good readers use them often. They use them *before, during,* and *after* reading. Here are some strategies to help you read your textbook materials.

➤ Before Reading

Before you begin reading, try to get "the big picture," or overall point, of the material. Here are some strategies to help you preview what you are about to read:

■ Think about the title and then ask yourself some questions:

1. *What do I know about this topic?*

2. *What would I like to know?*

3. *What is this chapter or article probably going to be about?*

■ Next, preview the pages by looking at the major headings, **boldfaced words**, *italicized words*, and picture captions.

■ Look for a summary at the end of the chapter and read it carefully.

■ Also look for charts, graphs, pictures, and diagrams, and think about what each is "saying" about the topic.

➤ During Reading

As you read, try to be an alert, active thinker!

■ Look for the answers to any questions you may have.

■ Stop every so often and ask yourself, "What did I just read?" Then answer your own question.

■ Make a list of key words, phrases, or summary sentences.

 Try to figure out the author's purpose or pattern of organization. (Read "Purpose Patterns" on the next page.)

PURPOSE PATTERNS

Picking out the author's purpose as you read is another helpful reading strategy. Here are four common "purpose patterns" you can look for when you read:

The Sharing-Experience Pattern ● Writers often share their personal experiences with their readers. Watch for words like "I" or "us." You can usually read this material quickly. As you are reading, ask yourself, "Why is the writer telling this story?"

The Question/Answer Pattern ● Look for questions as you read, especially at the beginning of chapters or paragraphs. Remember, the author's purpose is to give you the answer to each question. Don't stop until you find it.

The Opinion/Reason Pattern ● Watch for "I believe . . ." or "In my opinion . . . ." A reason should follow the opinion. Find it.

The Fact/Proof Pattern ● Watch for a factual statement followed by evidence or "proof." The proof might be a list of facts, a series of examples, or a chart. Read slowly. (If you don't understand the factual statement, look up individual words you don't know or ask someone for help.)

➤ *After Reading*

After you have finished reading—but before you close the book or put the materials away—look over the pages again. Here are some reviewing tips:

■ Ask yourself some questions:
1. *What do I know now that I didn't know before I read this?*
2. *If I had to tell someone what I just read, what would I say?*

■ Talk about what you have just read with anyone who will listen.

■ Write a summary of what you've read. (**SEE** pages 216-219.)

Reading Strategies You Can Use

SRN (Survey, Read, Note)

SRN is an easy reading strategy to use when you read non-fiction. Simply divide your notebook paper into two columns and *survey*, *read*, and *take notes*.

1 **Survey.** Read the title, major headings, subheadings, **boldfaced** and *italicized* words, picture captions, and the summary.

2 **Read.** Before you read each section, write the heading or subheading in the left-hand column of your paper.

3 **Note.** When you finish reading a section, write the key words, phrases, or ideas in the right-hand column next to each heading.

Geography

A Land of Many Climates—pages 46-47

Introduction	Climate has two main parts: temperature and precipitation
Temperature	= how cold or warm a place is In the U.S., northern Alaska is one of the coldest places because it is near the North Pole. Hawaii is one of the warmest places because it's near the equator. High places, like the mountains, are cooler than the land level with the ocean.
Precipitation	= rain and snow Plants need precipitation and warm weather to grow. When a place has cold winters and warm summers, plants will grow during the summer, known as the growing season.

MAPPING

Mapping is another good reading strategy, especially when you read textbooks. All you have to do is write the subject in the center of the page and draw a map of what you're reading. Mapping helps you do several important things:

- pick out the main topic *before* you begin reading
- focus on the subject and remain alert *during* reading
- review, summarize, and use the information *after* reading

Sample Reading Map

Below is a sample reading map drawn during a reading assignment in math. Notice how easy it is to understand this information about triangles when you are able to "see" it.

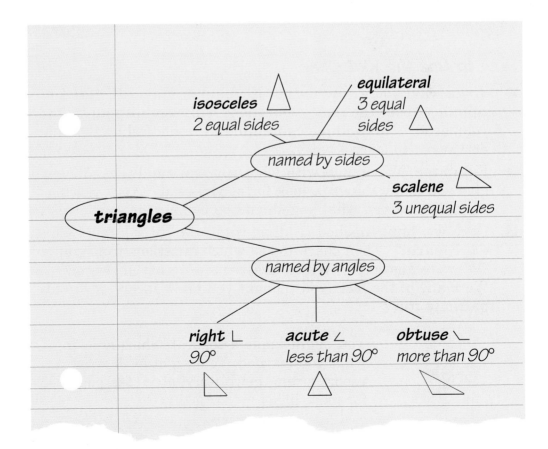

KWL *(Know, Want, Learn)*

KWL is a good strategy to use by yourself or with a partner. Simply divide your page into three columns and put a **K,** a **W,** and an **L** above each.

Famous Walls Around the World		
(K) What do I **know?**	**(W)** What do I want to **learn?**	**(L)** What did I **learn?**
1. There are lots of them: Great Wall of China, the Vietnam Memorial, etc. 2. Each was built for a different reason.	1. How long is the Great Wall of China? 2. When was it built? 3. Who built it? Why? 4. How many walls are there?	1. The Great Wall was built more than 2,000 years ago. 2. East and west sections were made of different materials. 3. There are lots of walls! The Wailing Wall, the Berlin Wall . . .

How to Use the KWL Chart

■ Write what you **know** in the "K" column. This will start you thinking about the topic. Questions will begin popping into your head. This will lead you into the second column, "What do I **want** to learn?"

■ Fill in the "W" column with what you **want** to learn. This will give you many things to look for as you read. (Your teacher may also tell you what you should be looking for as you read.)

■ Once you have finished reading, fill in the "L" column: "What did I **learn?**" Then check to see which questions from column "W" were answered. Which questions were not answered? Were any of the facts you thought you knew incorrect or only partially true?

Bright IDEA

You might make a separate chart showing what you learned. You might even write a report, poem, news story, etc. (**SEE** page 233 for more ideas.)

WRITING TO LEARN

Listed here are many of the common writing-to-learn strategies you can use before, during, and after you read. Experiment with a number of them until you find the ones that work best for you.

First Thoughts ● Write down your first impressions of the reading material—either before you read or soon after you start reading. This will help you focus your thoughts.

Stop 'n' Write ● Whenever you feel the need, stop and write down your thoughts and feelings about interesting (or confusing) ideas in your reading. Write freely in brief bursts of 2-3 minutes.

Clustering ● In the center of a page, write a word that relates to an important idea in the reading. Circle that word. Then think of other related words or ideas and write them around your key word. (**SEE** page 26 for a sample.)

Dialogues ● Have two people discuss an idea from your reading. (You can be one of the speakers.) Then write a short summary of this discussion. This will bring your reading to life.

Pointed Questions ● Keep asking yourself why . . . why . . . why in your writing. Keep asking until you reach a dead end or a natural stopping point.

Retelling ● Pretend your friends did not read what you did, but they need to know the information. Think about what you would tell them and write it down. Then practice retelling it out loud.

Many teachers will tell you that writing is the best strategy you can use to understand and remember what you've read. Try it and see for yourself.

Elements of Literature

Like most people, you know a good story or book when you read one. But can you put into words why you liked it? The following glossary of what "goes into" a story (the elements) will help you understand and write about what you've read.

Action is everything that happens in a story.

The **antagonist**, or villain, is the person or thing fighting against the hero of a story. *Example:* The Joker is Batman's antagonist.

An **autobiography** is a story the writer tells about her or his own life.

A **biography** is a story the writer tells about another person's life.

A **character** is a person in a story.

A **comedy** is a story that makes you smile, or even laugh.

Conflict is the "problem" in a story. There are five basic types of conflict.

➤ *Man vs. Man:* A character has a problem with one or more of the other characters.

➤ *Man vs. Society:* A character has a problem with society—the school, the law, tradition.

➤ *Man vs. Himself:* A character struggles with himself, trying to decide what to do about some problem.

➤ *Man vs. Nature:* A character is in conflict with some element of nature—bitter cold, extreme heat, a tornado.

➤ *Man vs. Fate (Destiny):* A character fights against a problem that seems too big to control.

Dialogue is the talking between characters in a story.

Drama is the form of literature commonly known as plays.

Mood is the feeling a reader gets from a story: happy, sad, peaceful.

The **moral** is the lesson a writer is trying to teach in his or her story. A children's story might have a moral such as "Treat others as you would like to be treated."

A **myth** is a story created to explain a mystery of nature.

The **narrator** is the person or character who is telling the story. For example, Harold the dog tells the story of the family he lives with in the book *Bunnicula*; so the narrator is actually a dog.

A **novel** is a book-length story created from the author's imagination.

The **plot** is the action of the story. The plot is usually a series of incidents which build on one another from the beginning to the end of the story.

The **plot line** shows the action in a story. It has five parts: *exposition, rising action, climax, falling action,* and *resolution*:

PLOT LINE

➤ The **exposition** (usually at the beginning of the story) explains what happened before the story starts, the setting of the story, and often introduces the characters.

➤ The **rising action** is the central part of a story during which various problems arise, and it leads up to the climax.

➤ The **climax** is the turning point in the action of a story.

➤ **Falling action** is the part of a story which follows the climax, or turning point; it has the action or dialogue needed to bring the story to an end.

➤ The **resolution** is the end of a play or story when the problems are solved.

The **point of view** is the angle from which a story is told. This depends upon who is telling the story.

➤ A **first-person** point of view means that one of the characters is telling the story:

> Yes, **I'd** been told that dragon-flies could not sew **my** mouth shut, but Mom didn't know everything.

➤ A **third-person** point of view means that someone outside of the story is telling it:

> Yes, **she'd** been told that dragonflies could not sew **her** mouth shut, but her mom didn't know everything.

The **protagonist** is the hero of the story.

Romance is writing that shows life as the author or reader might like it to be rather than as it really is. Often, a romance is full of evil spies, adventure, and superheroes.

The **setting** is the time and place of a story.

The **theme** is the *subject or message* being written about.

The **tone** is the author's feeling about a piece of writing. The author's tone may be *serious, funny, angry, sad,* and so on.

The **total effect** of a piece of writing is the overall influence it has on you, the reader—the way it makes you feel and the ideas it gives you.

A **tragedy** is a story about a hero or heroine who is destroyed by a personal weakness, or flaw: envy, jealousy, greed, etc.

Turn to *Writing Poems* on pages 182-187 for additional information on the "elements" of poetry.

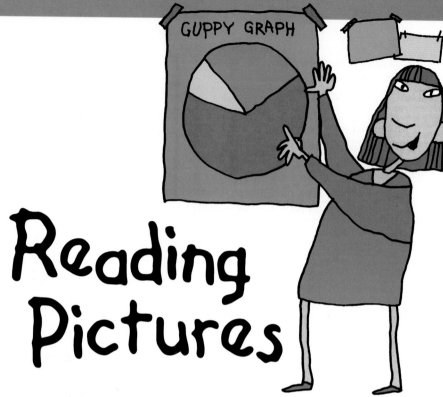

Reading Pictures

A Picture Is Worth . . .

Did you know that the first writing ever invented didn't have any words? It used pictures instead. Egyptian kids who lived about 5,000 years ago learned by "reading" a kind of picture writing called *hieroglyphics:*

KLEOPATRA

Native American tribes also used picture writing to "talk" to other tribes that didn't speak their language. That's one useful thing about pictures—they mean the same thing to everybody. "Bear" is **oso** in Spanish, **ours** in French, and **honaw** in Hopi, but everybody understands ➤

➤ Symbols

The pictures used in picture writing are called "symbols." A **symbol** is just a simple picture or drawing that stands for something. Sometimes it's easy to tell what a symbol means, because it looks just like the thing it stands for.

Signs and Symbols ● But sometimes symbols stand for things that you can't really draw a picture of—like the equal sign. Nobody knows what "equals" looks like, but everybody who knows basic math knows that = means "equals."

There are lots of different symbols. Some are used by just about everybody. Some are used only in certain subjects. When you study a new subject, you have to learn the symbols used in that subject.

Here are a few examples of signs and symbols used in different subjects. How many do you know?

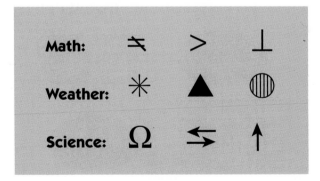

If you see a symbol, and you don't know what it means, look in the appendix or glossary of the book. You may also look under "Signs and Symbols" in the table of contents of your dictionary.

➤ Diagrams

A **diagram** is like a map, but instead of a place, it shows . . . almost anything! You could draw a diagram of a bicycle, a computer, or the bones in the human hand.

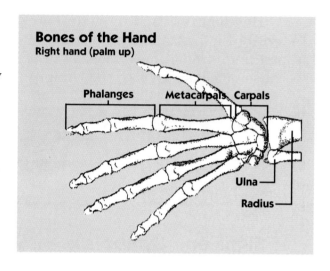

Bones of the Hand
Right hand (palm up)

Phalanges   Metacarpals Carpals

Ulna

Radius

Picture Diagram ●

A picture diagram is a drawing that shows how something is put together, how the parts relate to one another, or how the thing works. Diagrams may leave out some parts, showing only what you need to learn. This diagram of a hand leaves out the skin and muscles so that you can see the bones.

Line Diagram ● In a way, line diagrams are like symbols:
They can show something that you can't really see. For example, a family tree is a diagram of how your relatives are related. It helps you get a picture of where everybody fits, but your parents aren't really hanging over your head! (Are they?)

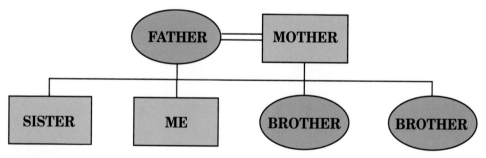

FATHER   MOTHER

SISTER   ME   BROTHER   BROTHER

THINK IT OVER

If a diagram is picturing motion, it usually shows things moving from left to right. A diagram that pictures time usually shows it moving from top to bottom (like in the family tree). Look for clues like this to help you "read" diagrams.

➤ Graphs

Graphs are pictures which help us see how two things are related. They are pictures of information—information about how things changed over time, or information about how things compare to one another.

There are different kinds of graphs for different kinds of information. The most common kinds of graphs are **bar graphs, line graphs,** and **pie graphs.**

Bar Graph ● A bar graph shows how two or more things compare to one another at the same time. When you read a bar graph, it's important to remember that it's like a snapshot taken at one point in time.

The bars of a bar graph can go up and down or sideways. Either way, the graph pictures exactly the same information.

Both bar graphs below show the number of guppies in the 4th-grade aquarium compared to the number in the 5th-grade aquarium at the end of the school year.

Model Bar Graph

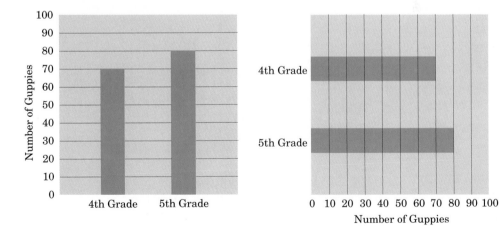

**Number of Guppies
in 4th and 5th Grade
Aquariums at End
of School Year**

**Number of Guppies
in 4th and 5th Grade
Aquariums at End
of School Year**

Line Graph ● A line graph always begins with a "grid." The horizontal (left-to-right) side of the grid stands for **passing time**. The vertical (top-to-bottom) side stands for the **subject** of the graph (whatever is passing through time). The line which passes through the grid allows you to study the subject as it passes through time.

The line graph below shows how many guppies were in the 5th-grade aquarium in each month of the school year so far. Guppies are the *subject* of this graph, and *time* is measured in months (September through June).

Model Line Graph

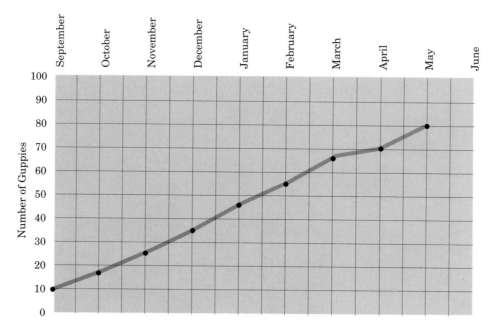

**Number of Guppies
in the 5th Grade Aquarium Each Month**

Sometimes a line graph will contain dots or points on the line to help make it easier to read. (See the dots in the graph above.) Other times, the line will have no markings on it. You have to picture the points in your mind's eye.

Pie Graph ● A pie graph shows how each part of something compares to the other parts and to the whole "pie." This pie graph shows what part (or percentage) of the total number of guppies is contained in each grade or classroom aquarium. You can see at a glance which classrooms have lots of guppies, and which have few. (If there are 100 guppies in the whole school, the 5th-grade class would have 62 guppies, because 62% of 100 is 62.)

Model Pie Graph

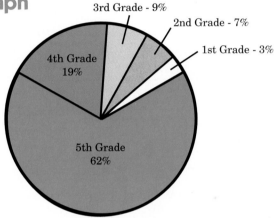

3rd Grade - 9%

2nd Grade - 7%

1st Grade - 3%

4th Grade
19%

5th Grade
62%

**Part (or Percentage)
of the Total Number
of Guppies in Each Grade**

YOU DON'T SSSSS SAY

If you have trouble understanding a graph, remember the following hints. They should help you see things more clearly:

■ A **line graph** tells you how things changed over time.

■ A **bar graph** compares things at the same time.

■ A **pie graph** shows how things compare to one another; it also shows what percentage of the whole thing each part takes up.

■ Every graph has a subject (just like a paragraph): figure out what the subject is.

■ Some graphs simply repeat information that's already spelled out in words; other graphs tell you more about a topic.

➤ **Tables**

Like diagrams and graphs, tables try to "show" how certain things are related. Tables have *rows* (going across) and *columns* (going down). Rows contain one kind of information, while columns contain another kind of information. The table makes it easy to see how the different kinds of information fit together.

Schedule ● The table below is a bus schedule. The rows show days of the week; the columns show times of day. A check mark means a bus leaves on that day, at that time.

	8 a.m.	Noon	6 p.m.
Mon. – Fri.	✓	✓	✓
Saturday	✓	✓	
Sunday		✓	
Holidays	✓	✓	✓

Distance Table ● Another common kind of table is a distance or mileage table. To read a distance table, find the place you're starting from. Then, find the place you're going to in the opposite part of the table. Finally, find the place where the row and the column meet—that's how far it is from one place to the other.

	Los Angeles	Seattle	Baltimore
Los Angeles	0	1,141	2,701
New York	2,787	2,912	197
Tampa	2,591	3,096	997

MINI LESSON Read the two tables above and answer the following questions:

■ If you wanted to take a bus on the Fourth of July to visit your grandmother, what time of day could you leave?

■ If you live in Los Angeles, and your grandmother lives in Seattle, how many miles will you travel on that bus?

Conversion Table ● Another very useful table is a conversion table. This is a table that converts (changes) information from one form to another. Some popular conversion tables show how to change American measurements to metric measurements and dollars to foreign money.

American Measurements		Metric
1 inch		2.54 centimeters
1 foot	12 inches	0.3048 meter
1 yard	3 feet	0.9144 meter
1 pint		0.4732 liter
1 quart	2 pints	0.9463 liter

Custom-Made Tables ● Tables show more than schedules, distances, and conversions. They can show all kinds of information. Imagine that for a science project you needed to guess how much some things weigh, and then weighed them to find out how well you guessed. You could make a table like this:

Things I weighed	estimated weight	actual weight	difference
my hamster	1 pound	7 ounces	9 ounces
my cat	10 pounds	8 pounds	2 pounds
my dog	100 pounds	68 pounds	32 pounds
my friend	100 pounds	75 pounds	25 pounds
my mom	250 pounds	118 pounds	132 pounds
me	90 pounds	75 pounds	15 pounds

Bright IDEA

For more practice reading tables, turn to the "Useful Tables and Lists" section. Make sure you look at the entire table first to get the "big picture." Then look closely at the labels so you understand how each table works.

Improving Your Spelling and Vocabulary

Building Vocabulary Skills

Becoming a Better Speller

Building Vocabulary Skills

Becoming More Wordwise

Think of your vocabulary as all the words you are able to use. These are the words you use when you are reading, writing, and talking. They are the tools in your language tool kit. The more tools you have, the better you will be able to think and communicate.

Smarten Up!

Having more words at your command also helps you become a better listener and reader. Let's say you hear this comment: "Jim *donated* $10 to the group." By knowing what "donated" means, you would know that Jim does not expect to get his money back. Then you hear, "Carlos *lent* $10 to the group." By knowing what "lent" means, you would know Carlos expects to get his money back.

So how can you "smarten up" and become a better listener and reader? Just read (and follow) the suggestions given in this chapter.

Strategies for Building Your Vocabulary

1 **Read, read, read!** Books, magazines, and newspapers contain many more new words than you will ever encounter in conversations or on television. So spend time reading.

2 **Use context clues.** When you are reading and come across a word you don't know, you can use the other words in the sentence (a word's *context*) to figure it out. The tips that follow will help you use context clues.

- Study the sentence containing the word as well as the sentences which come **before and after**.

- Search for clues that tell you what part of speech the word is (*noun, verb, adjective*, etc.).

- See if a **synonym** or an **antonym** is given:

    *Carmen thought the field trip was **tedious—not interesting**, as they said it would be.* (If the trip was "not interesting," what could "tedious" mean? Does this meaning fit the sentence?)

- Search for clues which appear in a **series of words**:

    *Luis loaded the group's equipment into the van. He put the **amplifiers and speakers** in first, and then loaded the **guitars and synthesizers**.* (If you know what speakers and guitars are, can you guess what the other equipment might be?)

3 **Keep a vocabulary notebook.** Keep a special place in your writer's notebook for new words. Divide the page into three columns and label them as shown below:

Vocabulary		
Words	Definitions	Sentence
chuck (verb)	1. To toss or throw 2. To pat or tap	He chucked his old shirt.

4 Turn to a thesaurus.

A thesaurus is a book of words and their synonyms—words which mean pretty much the same thing. It will help you find the best way to say something. Here are just some of the words (synonyms) you'll find listed under *happy* in the thesaurus.

happy: **joyful, elated, glad, cheerful, radiant**

As you can see, a **thesaurus** helps you find just the right word. It is a "backward" dictionary. You go to a dictionary when you know the word but need to find its meaning. You go to a thesaurus when you know the meaning but need a different word.

Look Up the Right Word ● For example, you can use a thesaurus to find just the right word for *scare* in the following sentence:

Jose wanted to _____ his classmate with the rubber spider.

Simply look up the word *scare* as you would in a dictionary. You will find a long list of words that mean something similar to *scare*. (As you can see below, it is located between *scarce* and *scatter*.)

Entry words		Another form of the entry word	
scarce	scanty, sparse, rare *plentiful* SCARCITY		
scare	frighten, alarm, startle, unnerve, terrify, horrify, appall		*Synonyms*
scatter	disperse, distribute, spread, separate, part, split up, squander, strew *gather, collect*		*Antonyms*

Choose the Right Word ● Look over the list of synonyms and choose the word that works best for your sentence. In the example, the best word is *startle:*

Jose wanted to __startle__ his classmate with the rubber spider.

5 **Use a dictionary.** Use your dictionary to look up each new word you discover. (The guide words at the top of each page will help you find it.) In addition to helping you understand the meanings of words, here are some other things a dictionary can help you with.

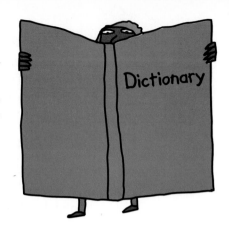

Spelling ● If you don't know how to spell a word, try looking it up by how it sounds.

Capital Letters ● A dictionary shows if a word needs to be capitalized.

Syllable Division ● A dictionary shows where you can divide a word. Heavy black dots divide a word into syllables. A (-) shows where hyphens are needed.

Accent Marks ● An accent mark (´) shows which syllable should be stressed when you say a word.

Pronunciation ● To remember a word and its meaning, you must know how to say it. A dictionary will spell each word phonetically (as it sounds).

Parts of Speech ● A word can be used in different ways. The dictionary will tell you the part of speech of each word you look up.

Word History ● Some words have stories about where they came from or how their meanings have changed through the years. This information appears inside brackets [ ].

Synonyms and Antonyms ● Synonyms (words with similar meanings) are sometimes listed with sample sentences. Antonyms (words with opposite meanings) may be listed last.

Meaning ● Some words have only one meaning. Some words have several meanings, and you will have to choose the best one.

Bright IDEA

A dictionary can also help you use *old* familiar words in *new* ways. If you read all of the different meanings for a word, you may discover another way to use it. (For example, the word *set* has over 100 different meanings!)

Sample Dictionary Page

Guide word —— **crawdad**

craw·dad \'krȯ-ˌdad\ *n, dialect* : CRAYFISH 1 —— Usage label
craw·fish \'krȯ-ˌfish\ *n* 1 : CRAYFISH 1 2 : SPINY LOBSTER
¹**crawl** \'krȯl\ *vb* 1 : to move slowly with the body close to —— Different
the ground : move on hands and knees 2 : to move along meanings
slowly (the bus *crawled* along) 3 : to be covered with or
have the feeling of being covered with creeping things (the
floor was *crawling* with ants) — **crawl·er** *n*
²**crawl** *n* 1 : the act or motion of crawling 2 : a swimming
method in which the swimmer lies facing down in the water
and moves with overarm strokes and a thrashing kick
crawl·way \'krȯl-ˌwā\ *n* : a low passage (as in a cave) that
one must crawl through
cray·fish \'krā-ˌfish\ *n*
1 : any of numerous
freshwater inverte-
brates that are crus-
taceans and are usu-
ally much smaller —— Art
than the related lob-
sters 2 : SPINY LOB-
STER

crayfish 1

Accent marks —— **dash·board** \'dash-ˌbō(ə)rd, —— Pronunciation
-ˌbȯ(ə)rd\ *n* 1 : a screen on the
front of a usually horse-
pulled vehicle to keep out
water, mud, or snow 2 : a
panel across an automobile or
airplane below the windshield
usually containing dials and
controls
Parts of —— **dashed** \'dasht\ *adj* : made up of
speech a series of dashes
da·shi·ki \də-'shē-kē\ *n* : a usually brightly colored one-piece
Word history —— pullover garment [derived from
danshiki, a native word for this
garment in a language of eastern Africa]

dashiki —— Caption

¹**same** \'sām\ *adj* 1 : resembling in every respect (the
same answer as before) 2 : not another (we went to the —— Examples of
same school) 3 : very much alike : COMPARABLE (on the common uses
same day last year)
Synonyms —— **syn** SAME, IDENTICAL, EQUAL mean not different or not
differing from one another. SAME suggests that the things
being compared are really one thing and not two or more
(we both saw the *same* truck but at different times) IDEN-
TICAL usually suggests that two or more things are just
like each other in every way (these plates are *identical*)
EQUAL suggests that the things being compared are like
each other in some specific way (two singers of *equal*
talent)
²**same** *pron* : the same one or ones
Spelling and —— **Sam·o·yed** \'sam-ə-ˌyed, 'sam-ˌȯi-ˌed\ *n* : any of a breed
capital letters of medium-sized white or cream-colored dogs developed
in Siberia

Pronunciation —— \ə\ abut   \aù\ out   \i\ tip   \ȯ\ saw   \ù\ foot
key \ər\ further   \ch\ chin   \ī\ life   \ȯi\ coin   \y\ yet
\a\ mat   \e\ pet   \j\ job   \th\ thin   \yü\ few
\ā\ take   \ē\ easy   \ŋ\ sing   \th\ this   \yu̇\ cure
\ä\ cot, cart   \g\ go   \ō\ bone   \ü\ food   \zh\ vision

Syllable
division

6 Study word parts and forms.

You can figure out the meanings of new words by learning about the three word parts:

- **prefixes** (common word beginnings)
- **suffixes** (common word endings)
- **roots** (common word bases)

For example, knowing that the prefix "non" means "not" helps you figure out the meaning of the word "nonsense": something that does *not* make sense. Knowing that the suffix "less" means "without" helps you figure out the meaning of "senseless": without sense.

Use Word Parts ● Before you can use word parts well, however, you must learn the meanings of some of the most widely used prefixes, suffixes, and roots in our language. For instance, the prefix *astro* is found in the word *astronomy* where it means *star*; it is also found in the words *astrodome* and *astronaut,* where it also means *star*.

Use Word Forms ● Look for other forms of words you already know. Suppose you know that the word "judge" means "to decide or settle something." When you see or hear the words *judgment, judgmental,* and *judicial,* you'll already have some idea of what they mean.

On the next nine pages, you will find a list of the most common prefixes, suffixes, and roots in the English language. Look them over and see if you recognize any. Then learn as many as you can—a few at a time.

PREFIXES

Prefixes are those word parts which come *before* the root word (pre=before). Prefixes often change the meaning of a word.

ambi, amphi *[both]*

ambidextrous *(skilled with both hands)*
amphibious *(living on both land and water)*

anti *[against]*

antifreeze *(a liquid that works against freezing)*
antipollutant *(designed to work against pollution)*

astro *[star]*

astronomy *(study of the stars)*
astronaut *(star traveler, space traveler)*

auto *[self]*

autobiography *(writing about yourself)*
autonomy *(self-government)*

bi, bin *[two]*

binocular *(having to do with both eyes)*
biweekly *(every two weeks)*

cent *[hundred]*

centimeter *(1 / 100 of a meter)*
century *(a period of 100 years)*

circum *[around]*

circumference *(the line that goes around a circle)*
circumnavigate *(to travel completely around)*

co *[together, with]*

coauthor *(one who writes with at least one other person)*
copilot *(one who flies with and assists the main pilot)*

ex *[out]*

exit *(the act of going out)*
expel *(drive out)*

fore *[before, earlier]*

forecast *(predicting something before it happens)*
forefather *(a related person who lived at an earlier time)*

hemi, semi *[half]*

hemisphere *(half of a sphere)*
semicircle *(half of a circle)*

hyper *[over]*

hyperactive *(overly active)*
hypersensitive *(overly sensitive)*

inter *[among, between]*

intermission *(a pause between the acts of a play)*
international *(of or between two or more nations)*

macro *[large]*

macrocosm *(the world as a whole)*
macrodent *(having large teeth)*

mal *[badly, poorly]*

maladjusted *(poorly adjusted)*
malnutrition *(poor nutrition due to improper diet)*

micro *[small]*

microfilm *(a very small film)*
microscopic *(so small it can be seen only under a microscope)*

mono *[one]*

monochrome *(one color)*
monorail *(a vehicle which runs on one track)*

non [absence of, not]

nonfat (absence of fat)
nonfiction (not fiction)

oct [eight]

octagon (a shape with eight sides)
octopus (a sea animal having
eight armlike tentacles)

penta [five]

pentagon (a figure or building
having five angles or sides)
pentameter (a line of verse com-
posed of five metrical lines)

poly [many]

polychrome (many colors)
polygon (a figure having many
angles or sides)

post [after]

postscript (a note added after the
end of a letter)
postwar (after a war)

pre [before]

predict (to tell about something
before it takes place)
preview (showing something
before the regular showing)

pseudo [false]

pseudonym (false or assumed
name)
pseudopod (false foot)

quad [four]

quadrant (one quarter of a circle)
quadruple (four times as much)

quint [five]

quintet (a group of five musicians)
quintuplet (one of five children
born in a single birth)

re [again, back]

return (to come back)
rewrite (to write over again)

sub [under]

submerge (put under)
subsoil (layer of weathered material under the surface soil)

trans [across, beyond]

transoceanic (crossing the ocean)
transplant (to move something
from one place to another)

tri [three]

triangle (a figure that has three
sides and three angles)
tricycle (a three-wheeled vehicle)

un [not]

uncomfortable (not comfortable)
unhappy (not happy)

uni [one]

unicycle (a one-wheeled vehicle)
unique (one of a kind)

NUMERICAL PREFIXES

Prefix	Symbol	Equivalent	Prefix	Symbol	Equivalent
tera	*T*	trillionfold	**deci**	d	tenth part
giga	*G*	billionfold	**centi**	c	hundredth part
mega	*M*	millionfold	**milli**	m	thousandth part
kilo	*k*	thousandfold	**micro**	u	millionth part
hecto	*h*	hundredfold	**nano**	n	billionth part
deca	*da*	tenfold	**pico**	p	trillionth part

SUFFIXES

Suffixes come at the end of a word. Sometimes a suffix will tell you what part of speech a word is. For example, many adverbs end in the suffix *ly*.

able *[able, can do]*

agreeable *(able or willing to agree)*
capable *(able to do something)*

al *[relating to]*

gradual *(relating to "grades" or degrees)*
manual *(relating to the hands)*

ed *[past tense]*

called *(past tense of call)*
learned *(past tense of learn)*

er *[one who]*

baker *(one who bakes)*
teacher *(one who teaches)*

er *[used to compare things]*

neater *(more likely to be neat than another)*
tougher *(more likely to be tough)*

ess *[female]*

actress *(a female actor)*
lioness *(a female lion)*

est *[used to show superiority]*

fastest *(most able to move rapidly)*
hottest *(highest of all temperatures)*

ful *[full of]*

careful *(full of care)*
helpful *(full of help)*

ic *[like]*

metallic *(like metal)*
poetic *(like poetry)*

ily *[in some manner]*

happily *(in a happy manner)*
steadily *(in a steady manner)*

ing *[an action or process]*

talking *(to talk)*
writing *(to write)*

ist *[one who]*

artist *(one who does art)*
chemist *(one who specializes in chemistry)*

less *[without]*

careless *(without care)*
hopeless *(without hope)*

ly *[in some manner]*

bashfully *(in a bashful manner)*
quickly *(in a quick manner)*

ment *[act of, result]*

achievement *(result of achieving)*
movement *(act of moving)*

ness *[state of]*

carelessness *(state of being careless)*
restlessness *(state of being restless)*

ology *[study, science]*

biology *(study of living things)*
geology *(study of the earth, rocks)*

s *[plural, more than one]*

books *(more than one book)*
trees *(more than one tree)*

sion, tion *[state of]*

action *(state of doing something)*
infection *(state of being infected)*

y *[inclined to]*

cheery *(inclined to be cheerful)*
itchy *(inclined to itch)*

ROOTS

Knowing the **root** of a word—especially a difficult word—can help you understand and remember it much better. This can be very useful when learning new words in all your classes.

acid, acri [*bitter, sour*]

acrid (*bitter or sour taste or odor*)
antacid (*works against stomach acid*)

ag, act [*do, move*]

agent (*someone who acts for another*)
agitate (*to cause to do something*)

ali, alter [*other*]

alias (*a person's other name*)
alternative (*another choice*)

am, amor [*love, liking*]

amiable (*friendly*)
amorous (*loving*)

anni, annu, enni [*year*]

anniversary (*happening at the same time every year*)
annually (*yearly*)
centennial (*once every 100 years*)

anthrop [*man*]

anthropoid (*manlike*)
anthropology (*study of mankind*)

aster [*star*]

aster (*star flower*)
asterisk (*starlike symbol*)

aud [*hear, listen*]

audible (*can be heard*)
auditorium (*a place to listen*)

bibl [*book*]

Bible (*sacred book of Christianity*)
bibliography (*list of books*)
bibliophile (*a book lover*)

bio [*life*]

biography (*writing about a person's life*)
biology (*study of life*)

centri [*center*]

centrifugal (*moving away from the center*)
concentric (*having a common center*)

chrom [*color*]

chromosome (*color body in genetics*)
monochrome (*one color*)

chron [*time*]

chronological (*in order of time*)
synchronize (*together in time*)

cide [*kill*]

genocide (*race killer*)
homicide (*human killer*)

cise [cut]

incision (a thin, clean cut)
precise (cut exactly right)
incisors (the teeth that cut or tear your food)

cord, cor [heart]

cordial (heartfelt)
coronary (relating to the heart)

corp [body]

corporation (a legal body)
corpulent (having a large body)

cosm [universe, world]

cosmos (the universe)
microcosm (a small world)

cred [believe]

credit (belief, trust)
incredible (unbelievable)

cycl, cyclo [wheel, circular]

bicycle (a cycle with two wheels)
cyclone (a circular wind)

dem [people]

democracy (people rule)
epidemic (on or among the people)

dent, dont [tooth]

denture (false teeth)
orthodontist (someone who straightens teeth)

derm [skin]

dermatology (the study of skin)
epidermis (outer layer of skin)

dic, dict [say, speak]

dictionary (a book of words people use or say)
predict (to tell about something in advance)

dynam [power]

dynamite (powerful explosive)
dynamo (power producer)

equi [equal]

equilibrium (a state of balance; equally divided)
equinox (day and night of equal length)

fac, fact [do, make]

factory (a place where people make things)
manufacture (to make by hand)

fer [bear, carry]

conifer (a cone-bearing tree)
ferry (carry from place to place)

fide [faith, trust]

confident (trusting oneself)
fidelity (faithfulness to a person or cause)

fin [end]

final (the last or end of something)
infinite (having no end)

flex [bend]

flexible (able to bend)
reflex (bending or springing back)

flu [flowing]

fluid (waterlike, flowing substance)
influence (to flow in)

forc, fort [strong]

force (strength or power)
fortify (to make strong)

fract, frag [break]

fracture (break)
fragment (a piece broken from the whole)

gastr [stomach]

gastric (relating to the stomach)
gastritis (inflammation of the stomach)

gen [birth, produce]

congenital (existing at birth)
genetics (study of inborn traits)

geo [earth]

geometry (measuring the earth)
geography (study of the earth)

grad [step, go]

gradual (step-by-step)
graduation (taking the next step)

graph [write]

autograph (self-writing)
photograph (light-writing)

greg [herd, group]

congregation (a group functioning together)
segregate (tending to group apart)

hab, habit [live]

habitat (the place in which one lives)
inhabit (to live in)

hetero [different]

heterogeneous (different in birth or kind)
heterosexual (with interest in opposite sex)

homo [same]

homogeneous (of same birth or kind)
homogenize (to blend into a uniform mixture)

hum [earth]

exhume (to take out of the earth)
humus (earth; dirt)

hydr [water]

dehydrate (take water out of)
hydrophobia (fear of water)

ject [throw]

eject (to throw out)
project (throw forward)

leg [law]

legal (related to the law)
legislature (persons who make laws)

log, ology [word, study]

psychology (mind study)
zoology (animal study)

luc, lum [light]

lumen (a unit of light)
translucent (letting light come through)

magn [great]

magnificent (great)
magnify (increase to a greater size)

man [hand]

manicure (to fix the hands)
manufacture (to make by hand)

mania [madness]

kleptomania (abnormal tendency to steal)
maniac (a mad person)

mar [sea, pool]

marine (related to the sea)
marsh (a wet, grassy area)

medi *[middle, between]*

  mediterranean *(lying between lands)*
  medium *(in the middle)*

mega *[great]*

  megalopolis *(great city or an urban region)*
  megaphone *(great sound)*

mem *[remember]*

  memo *(a note; a reminder)*
  memorial *(a remembrance of someone)*

meter *[measure]*

  meter *(a unit of measure)*
  voltameter *(instrument to measure volts)*

migra *[wander]*

  emigrant *(one who leaves a country)*
  migrant *(someone who wanders from place to place)*

mit, miss *[send]*

  emit *(send out; give off)*
  missile *(an object sent flying)*

mob, mot *[move]*

  mobile *(capable of moving)*
  promotion *(to move forward)*

mon *[warn, remind]*

  admonish *(warn)*
  monument *(a reminder of a person or an event)*

morph *[form]*

  amorphous *(with no form or shape)*
  metamorphosis *(change of form)*

mort *[death]*

  immortal *(something that never dies)*
  mortuary *(a place for the dead)*

multi *[many, much]*

  multicultural *(including many cultures)*
  multiped *(an organism with many feet)*

nat *[to be born]*

  innate *(inborn)*
  nativity *(birth)*

neur *[nerve]*

  neuritis *(inflammation of a nerve)*
  neurologist *(a physician who treats the nervous system)*

nov *[new]*

  innovation *(something newly introduced)*
  renovate *(to make like new again)*

numer *[number]*

  enumerate *(to find out the number)*
  innumerable *(too many to count)*

omni *[all, every]*

  omnipresent *(present everywhere)*
  omnivorous *(all-eating)*

onym *[name]*

  anonymous *(without a name)*
  pseudonym *(false name)*

ortho *[straight]*

  orthodontist *(someone who straightens teeth)*
  orthodox *(straight or usual belief)*

pac *[peace]*

  Pacific Ocean *(peaceful ocean)*
  pacify *(make peace)*

patr *[father]*

  patriarch *(the father of the family)*
  patron *(special guardian or father figure)*

path, pathy *[feeling, suffering]*

  empathy *(feeling with another)*
  telepathy *(feeling from a distance)*

ped *[foot]*

pedal (lever for a foot)
pedestrian (one who travels by foot)

pend *[hang, weigh]*

pendant (a hanging object)
pendulum (a weight hung by a cord)

phil *[love]*

Philadelphia (city of brotherly love)
philosophy (love or study of wisdom)

phobia *[fear]*

acrophobia (fear of high places)
agoraphobia (fear of public, open places)

phon *[sound]*

phonics (related to sounds)
symphony (sounds made together)

photo *[light]*

photograph (light-writing)
photosynthesis (action of light on chlorophyll)

pop *[people]*

population (the number of people in an area)
populous (full of people)

port *[carry]*

export (carry out)
portable (able to be carried)

proto *[first]*

protagonist (the first or leading character)
prototype (the first model made)

psych *[mind, soul]*

psychiatry (hearing of the mind)
psychology (study of the mind)

rupt *[break]*

interrupt (break into)
rupture (break)

sci *[know]*

conscious (knowing or being aware of things)
omniscient (knowing everything)

scope *[see, watch]*

kaleidoscope (instrument for viewing beautiful forms)
stethoscope (instrument for listening to sounds in the body)

scrib, script *[write]*

manuscript (written by hand)
scribble (write quickly)

sen *[old]*

senile (showing the weakness of old age)
senior (an older person)

sequ, secu *[follow]*

consecutive (following in order, one after another)
sequence (one thing following another)

spec *[look]*

inspect (look at carefully)
specimen (an example to look at)

sphere *[ball, sphere]*

hemisphere (half of a sphere)
stratosphere (the upper portion of a sphere)

spir *[breath]*

expire (breathe out; die)
inspire (breathe into; give life to)

strict *[draw tight]*

boa constrictor (snake that constricts its prey)
constrict (draw tightly together)

tact, tag *[touch]*

contact (touch)
contagious (transmission of disease by touching)

tele [far]

telephone (far sound)
telescope (far look)

tempo [time]

contemporary (those who live at the same time)
tempo (rate of speed)

tend, tens [stretch, strain]

extend (to make longer)
tension (tightness caused by stretching)

terra [earth]

terrain (the surrounding earth or ground)
terrestrial (relating to the earth)

therm [heat]

thermal (related to heat)
thermostat (a device for controlling heat)

tom [cut]

anatomy (cutting apart a plant or animal to study it)
atom (cannot be cut or divided)

tox [poison]

intoxicated (poisoned inside)
toxic (poisonous)

tract [draw, pull]

traction (the act of pulling or gripping)
tractor (a machine for pulling)

typ [print]

prototype (first print)
typo (a printing error)

vac [empty]

vacant (empty)
vacuum (a space empty or devoid of matter)

val [strength, worth]

equivalent (of equal worth)
evaluate (find out the worth)

vert, vers [turn]

divert (turn aside)
reverse (turn back)

vid, vis [see]

supervise (oversee or watch over)
video (what we see)

viv [alive, life]

revive (bring back to life)
vivacious (full of life)

voc [call]

vocal (calling with your voice)
vocation (a calling)

vor [eat greedily]

carnivorous (flesh-eating)
herbivorous (plant-eating)

zo [animal]

zodiac (circle of animals; the constellations)
zoology (study of animal life)

Becoming a Better S-p-e-l-l-e-r

A Self-Help Guide

You write about good ideas. You use vivid words. You make **sure** the words in your final drafts are spelled correctly.

Why? *Beecus speling erers ar harrd tu rede. And besides, people won't know how smart you really are ef yew spel lack thes.*

So you want to spell correctly. But how do you do that? Here are four things you can do:

1 Make a spelling dictionary.

2 Use strategies for remembering spellings.

3 Learn to proofread for spelling.

4 Learn some basic spelling rules.

1 Make a spelling dictionary.

Use a Notebook ● To make a spelling dictionary, take a small notebook and label the pages with the letters of the alphabet. (Put one letter on the top of each page.) Then, each time you have to look up a spelling word in the regular dictionary, write that word in your spelling dictionary. Next time you can look it up in your spelling dictionary.

 Study the words in your spelling dictionary whenever you can. Before long you will be able to spell these words without looking them up.

2 Use strategies for remembering spellings.

Use Your Senses ● Experts say one of the best ways to remember spellings is to use your senses: seeing, hearing, and feeling. Here's a *sensory system* you can use to study for spelling tests:

➤ **Look at the word as you say it aloud.**

➤ **Write the word. Name each letter as you write it.**

➤ **Read the word aloud again.**

➤ **Check to make sure you spelled the word correctly.**

➤ **Cover the word and write it again. Name each letter as you write it. Check your spelling.**

Use Sayings ● By remembering (and making up!) a few sayings, you can avoid some very common spelling errors.

You have a PAL in your princiPAL.   *People say BRrrr in FeBRuary.*

I always want SecondS of deSSert.   *Writing papER is stationERy.*

Use Acrostics ● You can also use *acrostics* to help you spell better by making up sentences for difficult words.

GEOGRAPHY – Giraffes eat old, greasy rugs and paint houses yellow.

ARITHMETIC – A rat in the house might eat the ice cream.

3 Learn to proofread for spelling.

After you have revised your writing assignments so that they make sense, you must edit them for punctuation, grammar, and spelling errors. We suggest that you check spelling last. Here are some suggestions for you to use.

Read from Bottom to Top ● Start with the last line of your draft and read from bottom to top. This will force you to concentrate on each individual word.

Use an index card or a half sheet of paper right beneath the line you are studying. Once you finish checking one line, move the index card up to the next one.

Correct the Misspellings ● Put a line through any misspelled word and make the correction right above it. (*Remember:* If you skip every other line when you write your draft, it is much easier to make corrections.)

Circle the Puzzlers ● If you are not sure about a spelling, circle it. Go back to the circled words when you have finished checking your entire paper. (For help, use your own spelling dictionary, the spelling list in this handbook, or a regular classroom dictionary.)

Ask for Help ● Finally, have a friend or classmate check your corrections and look for other spelling errors in your writing.

Special Note: If you used a computer, make sure to run your work through the spell checker. Also check it yourself for names, homonyms (*inn* instead of *in*), wrong words, and so on. Your spell checker will not find these kinds of errors for you.

Turn to the following pages for help:
- ✔ **Commonly misspelled words** (pages 358-361)
- ✔ **Possessives and Plurals** (pages 349, 355)
- ✔ **Using the right word** (pages 362-369)

4 Learn some basic spelling rules.

You can avoid some spelling errors by learning a few basic spelling rules. As you will see, most of these rules deal with adding endings to words.

➤ **Words Ending in Y** ● When you write the plurals of words that end in *y*, change the *y* to *i* and add *es*. If the word ends in *ey,* just add *s*.

bully, bullies   monkey, monkeys

➤ **Consonant Ending** ● When a one-syllable word with a short vowel needs an ending like *-ed* or *-ing*, the final consonant is usually doubled.

bat, batted   get, getting

➤ **I Before E** ● For words spelled with *i* and *e*, remember this: "*i* before *e,* except after *c*, or when rhyming with *say*, as in *neighbor* and *weigh*."

believe, receive, sleigh

> **EXCEPT**   Here are some exceptions: ***either, neither, their, height, weird,*** and ***seize***.

➤ **Silent E** ● If a word ends with a silent *e*, drop the *e* before adding an ending (suffix) which begins with a vowel.

use, using, useful
believe, believing, believable
nine, ninety, nineteen

> **EXCEPT**   Notice that you do ***not*** drop the *e* when the suffix begins with a consonant *(-ful, -ty, -teen)*.

Improving Your Speaking and Listening

Giving Speeches

Performing Poems

Improving Viewing Skills

Improving Listening Skills

Giving Speeches

Speak to the Clouds

When I was about your age, I loved to swing. But we didn't have a swing, so I went to Angie's place. Not only could I swing at Angie's, I could also sing at her house because no one could hear me. I sang songs that seem corny now, and even though I was alone, I pretended I was a star on a TV show! I still love to swing and sing. What has changed is that I now love to have an audience, not just when I sing, but also when I talk.

❝ Like you, I talk to express my ideas and opinions. I also speak to groups as part of my job, and every time I give a speech, I feel like the young girl I used to be. I get excited. My heart pounds. It's as if I were swinging up into the clouds. ❞
— Gloria Nixon-John

Writing a Speech

How do you feel when you are asked to speak in front of others? Do you get a little nervous or excited? Do you enjoy sharing your feelings and ideas with others, especially your classmates?

If you're like most people, you enjoy talking about things you're interested in or know a lot about. (You probably don't enjoy talking about topics that don't interest you or topics you don't know much about.) That's why it's so important to select the right topic whenever you are asked to give a report or speech in class.

Types of Speeches

The first question you have to ask yourself when you begin searching for a good topic is "Why am I giving this speech?" Is it to share information, to demonstrate something, or to change people's minds?

➤ **Speech to Inform:** Give information (facts, figures, history, etc.).

➤ **Speech to Demonstrate:** Show others how to do something.

➤ **Speech to Persuade:** Present facts to change people's minds.

The Steps in the Process

No matter what type of speech you choose to write, you should follow these eight steps from start to finish. That's why I wrote this chapter—to help you through each step in the process.

1 PICK THE TOPIC CAREFULLY.

2 NARROW YOUR TOPIC.

3 GATHER ENOUGH INFORMATION.

4 PREPARE AN EXCITING INTRODUCTION.

5 WRITE AN OUTLINE.

6 WRITE YOUR SPEECH. *(OPTIONAL)*

7 PRACTICE YOUR DELIVERY.

8 PRESENT YOUR SPEECH.

1 PICK THE TOPIC CAREFULLY.

When you are asked to write and give a speech, you should begin by picking a good topic. Here are some questions you can ask:

- **What do I know a lot about?**
- **What would I like to know more about?**
- **What do I do for fun?**
- **What do I read about?**
- **What do I talk about with my friends?**

(***SEE*** "Selecting a Subject" on pages 26-27 for more help.)

2 NARROW YOUR TOPIC.

Let's suppose that my teacher asked me to give a **demonstration speech** for my class. I own and love horses, so "horses" is a natural choice. Horses . . . now that's a big topic. Too big for one speech. So I decide, since I can bring props with me, I'll bring in my saddle and demonstrate how to put a saddle on a horse.

If my teacher had asked me to give an **information speech**, I could have informed my audience about the care and costs of keeping a horse. Or, if my teacher had asked me to give a **persuasive speech**, I could have tried to convince my audience that anyone can enjoy riding horses.

Pick your topic the way you would pick the food and music for a party. Who will be present? If you were inviting grandparents, would you play rap music? If all of the guests were 10 or 11, would you serve lima beans and brussels sprouts? Of course not!

3   GATHER INFORMATION.

Remember, books and magazines are not the only sources of information!

- **Talk or write to experts in your school, family, or neighborhood.**
- **Observe and take notes on people, places, and events.**
- **Watch videos, movies, and TV programs.**
- **Scan the newspaper.**
- **Remember things from your own experience.**

To make your ideas clearer, you might look for drawings, photos, videotapes, or props you can use during your speech.

4   PREPARE AN EXCITING INTRODUCTION.

Now that you have chosen and narrowed your topic and gathered information, it's time to prepare an introduction. Writing an introduction will help you think about *what* you want to say and *how* you're going to say it. Here are some tips:

➤ *Use a famous quote.*
  ". . . forbid that I should go to a heaven in which there are no horses."   —Theodore Roosevelt

➤ *Ask an interesting question.*
  Did you know that horses have a language of their own?

➤ *Tell a story.*
  One day two summers ago, I was riding my horse in the field down the road from our house when suddenly . . .

➤ *Make a striking statement.*
  Horses understand body language better than people do. The slightest twitch of your body can tell a horse to move.

➤ *Refer to a recent incident.*
  At the last Olympics, the U.S. basketball team won a Gold Medal. So did the U.S. horse-jumping team.

5 | WRITE AN OUTLINE.

After you've written an introduction, you should write an outline of what you plan to say in your speech. You can do this on note cards or on a sheet of paper. As you'll see, I used only short phrases to remind me of what I wanted to say.

I wrote out my introduction and conclusion word for word so that I could learn them so well I wouldn't stumble.

Introduction: #1

    The average horse weighs between 1,000 and 1,600 lbs. When you consider I weigh just a small fraction of that, it seems amazing that I can get on the back of such a large animal and convince him to take me where I want to go. The things I know about the personality of each horse help, but I also depend on other things, including the equipment: the bridle, bit, reins, and saddle. And since the saddle goes on first, let's start there.

Sample Outline

#2

Equipment Needed:

Saddle, saddle pad, girth, bench or "wooden horse."
Drawing of horse.
Show and Tell the Following:
  I. Prepare the horse
     mentally and physically.
    Talk to horse.
    Rub under his mane.
    Stroke his neck.

  II. Stand left of horse.
                                    #3
     Place the saddle pad below his withers.
     (Use diagram on the board to show where the
      withers are.)
 III. Place saddle on top of pad.
     Watch toes!
 IV. Fasten girth first on left, then right.
     Tighten from right.
     Tighten a second time.

Conclusion: #6

    Putting a saddle on a well-groomed, happy, and healthy horse is a cinch! I really could go on and talk about my horses all day. I could talk about bridles and bits. I could talk about breeds of horses, even how to braid a tail or mane, but then I wouldn't have time for a trail ride today, and that just won't do!

6   WRITE YOUR SPEECH.

You may decide to give your speech using only your outline. However, if you decide to write out your speech, follow your outline and write it the same way you would any other piece of writing. Keep your purpose (to inform, demonstrate, or persuade) and your audience in mind. Also remember to use words and sentences that will sound good to your audience. (**SEE** "All About Writing" on pages 3-7 for additional help.)

7   PRACTICE YOUR DELIVERY.

You've heard that practice makes perfect, but how can you practice a speech? Simple. First look at the reminders in step 8 below; then do one or more of the following:

- **Practice in a quiet place where you can listen to yourself.**
- **Practice in front of friends or parents and ask for their suggestions.**
- **Practice with an audio or video tape recorder and pick out the spots you need to practice more.**

8   PRESENT YOUR SPEECH.

When you are ready to give your speech, remember these points:

- **Look at the audience.**
- **Speak loudly and clearly.**
- **Speak in a slow, natural tone. Look at your notes only when you need a reminder.**
- **Use clear, correct language. Do *not* use slang, or such sounds as *ah, dah,* or *um.***
- **Stand up tall. Don't slump, sway, or lean.**

The Final Speech: A Student Model

If you follow all eight steps in the process, you should end up with a speech that is interesting to both you and your audience—just like the model below written by Angela Zischke of Lansing, Michigan.

Lansing, My Hometown

Hello. My name is Angela Zischke. I have lived in Lansing, Michigan, my whole life (10 years), and all of it has been great. There are a lot of places to visit that are fun, but my personal favorite is the capitol.

The capitol is educational and fun at the same time. It has just been restored and was rededicated on November 19, 1992. There now is a lot of history in the building, which makes it a lot more interesting. For instance, they have Civil War flags on the bottom floor where you look up at the dome. In the dome there are beautiful paintings of goddesses and the past governors of our state. There are also beautiful chandeliers. The stairs are lined with many wonderful wood carvings. I think the best views are looking up at the dome and looking down from the fourth floor.

Another good thing is that the capitol has tour guides and pamphlets to help you. If you ask, the tour guides will take you into the Senate and House of Representatives rooms. On the ceiling in the House of Representatives room are all of the 50 state seals in the order they were brought into the country.

On the first floor of this beautiful limestone building (below the dome) is a glass floor. Don't worry about walking on it, though, because the floor is very well supported.

I hope you can come and visit the capitol someday. If you can, make sure to make your reservation for a tour guide. Then you can see everything I did.

Performing Poems

Perform It!

You're Melinda Castillo and you've written this wonderful poem about spring. If you could just *do* something with this, you think, something more than putting it into your portfolio. You talk with your friends. You read them your poem. Several of them agree; your poem IS terrific! Now you need to figure out what to do!

Flamingo of Spring

the Flamingo of Spring
walks through winter.
the Flamingo of Spring
brightens everyone's daisies.
the Flamingo of Spring
welcomes the baby animals
to the world.
the Flamingo of Spring
stands on one leg
in a shimmering lake.
the flowers open to
a beautiful song made
by the Flamingo of
Spring.

Moving Poetry from Page to Stage

So what do you do if you have a wonderful poem to share? You perform it! Perform it right there in your classroom, at parents' night, for a community group. You can form your own theater company and perform wherever you like. Here's what you need to do: *form a team, find a poem, script the poem, score the poem,* and *perform the poem.*

1 Form a Team. You can always perform alone, but it is more fun performing as a team. Your team can be made up of two, three, or four performers, but avoid teams of five members or more. You may start out working with one partner. Later, you may find that some poems really need one or two more partners.

2 Find a Poem to Perform. Look through your portfolio, your classroom anthologies of student work, books of poems you've published.

Collect Several Poems ● Read each poem carefully to yourself and then out loud to your partners. Collect a variety of poems, maybe several that are funny, and one or two that are serious. Don't worry too much about a poem's length. If you find a short poem you really like, try to find another poem to go with it.

Choose the Right Poem ● Poems that contain a lot of action are easiest to perform. Poems that tell about ideas and feelings are sometimes harder to perform. However, such poems can really get your imagination going. Here are some questions you can ask about each poem to help you decide:

1. **Who is the main speaker in the poem?**
2. **What other characters (people, animals, things) appear?**
3. **Where and when does the poem take place?**
4. **What actions (physical or mental) are in your poem?**

If you have more characters in your poem than you have team members, ask the players to take two or more parts, using a different voice for each character.

3 **Script the Poem.** After you have selected the poem you want to perform, make a copy for each person in your group. This will make it much easier to "script" the poem. (Scripting a poem means dividing it into speaking parts.) Let's imagine that your team has chosen to perform "I'm Glad," a short poem by an unknown author:

> I'm Glad
>
> I'm glad the sky is painted blue,
> And the earth is painted green,
> With such a lot of nice fresh air
> All sandwiched in between.

You might think, "Four lines divided by four performers equals one line per performer. Simple!" But poetry is *not* simple mathematics!

A "Scripted" Poem ● Instead of dividing the lines by the number of actors, divide them according to the characters in the poem. Remember, characters can be people, places, things, or animals. In "I'm Glad," we find four *characters:* the sky, the air, the earth, and I (the narrator who tells the story).

Cast: 1 = Narrator
2 = The sky
3 = The earth
4 = The air

Two Scripting Possibilities:

All: "I'm Glad," author unknown
1: I'm glad the sky is painted
2: blue
1: And the earth is painted
3: green
1: With such a lot of
4: nice fresh air
2 & 3: All sandwiched in between

All: "I'm Glad," author unknown
1: I'm glad
2: the sky is painted blue
1: And
3: the earth is painted green
1: With such a lot of
4: nice fresh air
2 & 3: All sandwiched in between

4 **Score the Poem.** Next, your team must "score" its poem. (Scoring a poem simply means to name emotions [feelings] and motions [movements] for each line of poetry.) Scoring your poem will help you to understand and perform it better. Consider this familiar poem called "The 5:15" by an unknown author:

> The 5:15
> The peanut sat on the railroad track.
> Its heart was all aflutter.
> The 5:15 came rushing by—
> Toot! Toot!
> Peanut Butter!

A "Scored" Poem ● Here is one way to score this poem, which has been scripted for three characters:

Cast: 1 = Peanut, 2 = Engineer, 3 = Bystander

	Line	Emotion	Motion
1:	The peanut sat on the railroad track.	*(excited)*	sit on chair
1:	Its heart was all aflutter.	*(frightened)*	pat heart or bite nails
1:	The 5:15 came rushing by—	*(surprised)*	jump back as if to dodge passing train
2:	Toot! Toot!	*(threatening)*	raise and lower hand as if pulling chain of whistle
3:	Peanut Butter!	*(happy)*	pretend mouth is full of peanut butter

YOU DON'T SSSSSAY

You don't need emotions and motions for every word or line. Sometimes you can simply tell the poem, letting the words stand on their own. Try to find a balance between *telling* and *performing*.

5 **Perform Your Poem.** After you have scripted and scored your poem, practice reading it out loud. You don't need a stage or special lights for your final performance. The front of the classroom will do just fine. (You can use simple costumes and props, if you want.)

Five Performance Tips

- **Stand and move with confidence.** Always stand up (or sit up) straight. Do not fidget. Standing (or sitting) tall will help you talk to your audience with confidence.

- **Face your audience.** As a rule, do not turn your back to the audience, even a little. It helps to think of your audience as one person (who happens to be very wide and hard of hearing).

- **Introduce the poem and the poet.** Before your performance, stand shoulder to shoulder facing the audience. As a team, using your clear, confident, outside voices, announce the title of the poem and then the poet's name. Then move quickly into your starting positions for the performance.

- **Use your "outside" voice.** Always speak clearly and loudly enough to be heard by *everyone*. Try to find a voice somewhere between soft-spoken and yelling. This clear, loud voice is your outside voice, the one you use while playing outside.

- **Exit quietly.** When your performance is over, pause for a moment, take a bow if you wish, then leave your performance space.

Now You Try It!

The following poem was written by a group of students at Beverly Elementary School, Edmonds, Washington. It is scripted for four people. Experiment with different ways of scripting and scoring this poem. (**SEE** pages 284-285.)

The Salmon People
by students from Beverly Elementary School

1 2 3 4: I am salmon,

1: I am fast;

2: A fish that likes to swim in the past.

1 2 3 4: I am going somewhere!

3: To Seattle,

4: To the Kingdome.

1 2 3 4: To the Salmon People who live in the ocean.

1: I have magic wings that help me fly.

2: I can swim through a river of stars.

3: My skin is slippery like a wet bar of soap.

4: My scales shine like fluorescent fingernails;

1 2 3 4: Pink, orange, yellow, green, blue, and purple

1 2: Salmon People have long gold and silver hair.

3 4: Their skin is different colors;

1 2 3 4: Mixed together like the rainbow.

1: I need food.

2: I'm going on a mission

2: To survive.

3: To talk to the people;

3: To help the people.

4: Can the people help me?

1 2 3 4: Be kind to the salmon.

Improving Viewing Skills

Becoming a Smart Viewer

According to a recent survey, Americans watch an average of 26 hours of television a week. And that's the *average*. Some of us watch as much as 40 hours of TV a week! Most of that time is spent watching entertainment (and commercials). The rest of it is spent getting information, either from the news or from educational specials.

Even if you spend very little time watching television, it's important for you to be a smart viewer. And that's just what this chapter can help you become!

As you watch television, it is shaping what you *know*, what you *believe*, and what you *buy*. You need to become an intelligent viewer—you need to know what to look for and what questions to ask.

Watching the News

Let's start with a sample news story. WGIP sends a camera person and a news reporter to Brown Elementary School to document your trip to a local pond. You've been studying pond life for weeks, and you can hardly wait to get out there to see and feel a *real* one. By 9:00 a.m. you're off. The day goes well, you *think*, and you're all excited because you know you'll see yourself on TV tonight.

Six o'clock comes, and you're sitting in front of the TV, hot dog and juice in hand—rah, rah—and before you know it . . .

THERE YOU ARE!

But guess what? The good TV folks didn't show you gently pulling your crayfish out of the pond and carefully drawing it; they showed you fooling around with Cary during one of those "off" moments. Instead, the news showed Devon doing what *he* was supposed to be doing! You're mad because you know very well they filmed *you* with the crayfish, too!

THINK About It

The story you've just read teaches a simple lesson: All of us, from kids to camera people, report what *we* see and hear, and what *we* feel is most important. Sometimes we don't see the whole story. As long as we remember this, we can watch the news, or any TV program, intelligently.

Questioning the News

➤ *Is it complete?*

A news story must answer all the basic questions (**5W's and H**) about the event. It must tell . . .

Who was involved: *Tom and Jerry, the 5th-grade gerbils,*

What happened: *escaped*

When it happened: *last night.*

Where it happened: *The cage is kept on the windowsill.*

Why it happened: *When the janitor opened the window,*

How it happened: *the cage fell out the window, and its door came open. Tom and Jerry scrammed.*

➤ *Is it fair?*

It can be hard to decide when a news story is fair. The story about the class studying pond life certainly didn't seem fair, at least not to all the students. Here are some things to look for:

Sound Bites ● A sound bite is a short film clip of someone speaking. Sometimes a sound bite is too short and doesn't tell the whole story, or it makes the person look bad. Let's say you are listening to a report on the two candidates for mayor of your town. Are you seeing all of what each candidate said, or just a short part of it? Do you think each candidate was treated fairly?

Equal Time ● Even though there is an *equal-time* law for elections, this law doesn't have to be followed for news stories. Let's say the story is about a tough new law against handguns. The story does not have to give equal time to people who are for it *and* to people who are against it. But to be fair, it should.

Choice of Sources ● A fair story will include *reliable* sources (people) who have different views on an issue. If a news story uses the governor as a source in favor of a tough new gun law, and a convicted robber as a source against it, is the story fair? Probably not.

TALK
About It

What are a news reporter's responsibilities?
Is all the news you watch really news?
Which local TV station has the best newscast?

Watching Television Specials

Has your teacher ever asked you to watch a certain TV show? Maybe it was a special on beavers in Alaska or the Berlin Wall in Germany. Television can "put you there" in ways that no other medium (books, magazines, etc.) can. However, even educational programs need to be viewed correctly. Here are some helpful hints:

Viewing Guidelines

✔ Before viewing, consider what you already know about the subject, and think of questions you would like answered.

✔ If your teacher gives you questions to answer during the show, make sure you understand them before you leave school.

✔ While watching the special, take a few notes—not only on the facts, but on how you feel about what you see.

✔ After the special, talk with somebody about it, or write about it in your journal.

Sample Journal Entry

Saturday, January 7, 1993
Lake Baykal   The Deepest Lake in Russia

It's so deep and so cold, it's got life in it that's found nowhere else in the universe! That's because it was formed 25 million years ago. Here are some animals you can only find in Lake Baykal.
            golomyanka and other kinds of fish
            Baykal seal
It's beautiful and wild—336 rivers flow into it, but only one flows out. It's frozen from January to May—that's a long time!

Improving Listening Skills

"Now Listen Carefully!"

Since this page and the next are about listening, maybe you could find a partner to read them out loud while you listen. But if that isn't possible, do the next best thing: continue reading.

Do you know that we spend more time listening than we do speaking, reading, and writing combined? Our ears make it possible for us to *hear* what is being said around us. But it is our minds that make it possible for us to *listen*. You see, listening is more than just hearing—it is thinking about what we hear. It is making sense of all the "noise" that comes at us 14-16 hours a day, seven days a week, week after week.

Good Listener Checklist

Because we are human, we don't always listen (are you listening?). We are easily distracted. We sometimes daydream. We sometimes *hear* people when we should be *listening* to them. So how can you become a better listener, both in and out of school? Here's a whole page of suggestions. I hope they help!

✔ **Listen with a good attitude;** you'll learn more.

✔ **Listen with your ears *and* your eyes;** you'll hear more.

✔ **Listen for specific directions;** you'll know what you're supposed to do.

✔ **Listen for the main ideas;** you'll stay on track.

✔ **Listen for key words (first, second/before, after);** you'll keep things in the right order.

✔ **Listen for the speaker's tone of voice;** you'll get the true meaning.

> A good listener is not only popular everywhere, but after a while he gets to know something.

✔ **Take notes or make drawings;** you'll remember things longer.

✔ **Think about what you hear;** you'll understand better if you relate ideas to different things you already know.

✔ **Picture what you hear;** you'll see things more clearly.

WRITE About It

Write down questions about the things that aren't clear. Also, sum up everything in writing as a test of how well you listened.

Improving Your Thinking

Getting Organized

Thinking and Writing

Thinking Clearly

Getting Organized

Becoming a Better Thinker

All of us are thinkers. We think all the time (except maybe when we're sleeping). Because you are a student, you have to learn to think well. To think well, you have to be able to gather many different kinds of thoughts, or details, and organize them in the right way.

Then you have to use these organized thoughts to help you understand things better, solve problems, make decisions, and support your opinions.

That's what this section of your handbook is about: helping you become a better, more organized thinker.

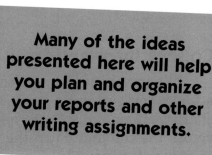

Many of the ideas presented here will help you plan and organize your reports and other writing assignments.

Using Graphic Organizers

One very effective way to organize your thoughts is to use *graphic organizers*. (Graphic organizers are shapes created from lines, circles, and boxes.) When you are gathering ideas, you can use these shapes to help you collect and organize your details. Because you can *see* where each detail should go, it is much easier to keep your thoughts organized.

Collect Details ▶

If you are trying to collect details to describe something, you can draw a circle with lines or spokes around it. Write the name of the person or thing you want to describe in the circle (the key word). List the important details on the spokes around the circle.

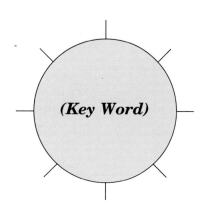

(Key Word)

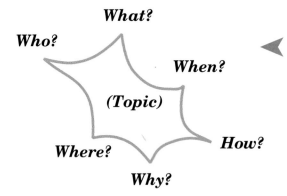

Who? **What?** **When?** **(Topic)** **Where?** **How?** **Why?**

◀ Ask Questions

Another good way to organize your thoughts and details is to ask the 5 W's & H questions. You can use a web like the one shown here to help you see your answers.

Collect Information

When you need to collect and organize lots of information on a topic, you can use a "gathering grid." Simply draw a grid or chart with as many boxes as you need. Then label each box across the top and down the side to fit your topic. Fill in the grid as you collect your information. (**SEE** page 226 for a sample grid.)

Compare and Contrast

The design shown here (called a Venn diagram) can be used to organize your thoughts when you need to compare or contrast two subjects.

Put the important details for one of these subjects in the area marked with a *1*. Put the details for the second subject in area *2*. In area *3*, list the details the two things have in common. Now you can clearly see the similarities and differences.

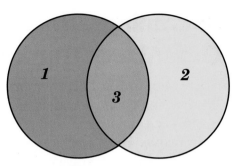

Venn Diagram

TAKE NOTE   When you want to compare, talk about the details in area *3*. When you want to contrast, talk about how the details in area *1* are different from the details in area *2*.

Outline

Sometimes you will need to make an organized list of the details (facts, examples, reasons) you collect. One kind of list is the outline. Use it when you have lots of different ideas or topics that need organizing.

An outline also works well when you have a lot of notes or ideas that you need to organize for a report or speech. Simply put the topic at the top and organize your details underneath it.

(Topic)

I. _____

   A. _____

   B. _____

   C. _____

II. _____

   A. _____

   B. _____

   C. _____

Bright IDEA   Try to come up with graphic organizers of your own. Compare them with the ones your classmates have invented.

Becoming an Organized Thinker

Becoming a better, more organized thinker isn't easy—but it can be done. It simply takes time and a desire to improve. Here are some helpful guidelines to get you going.

1 **Be patient . . .** Don't expect quick, easy answers to every problem or challenge you face. Good thinking often takes time— time to plan, read, and listen.

2 **Set goals . . .** Think about what you can do now (*short-term goals*) and what you will have to do later (*long-term goals*). (**SEE** page 319.)

3 **Think logically . . .** Don't settle for the first answer that pops into your head. Look at all sides of a question; then support your thoughts with good reasons, examples, and facts. (**SEE** "Thinking Clearly" on pages 308-313.)

4 **Ask questions . . .** Ask questions about what you read, what you hear—even what you see! If you think you know *what* something is, then ask *why, who, when, where, how, how much, why not.*

5 **Think about your thinking . . .** Try to "watch" yourself as you think and work; then change the way you think if necessary (slow down, speed up, zoom in, back up).

6 **Write things down . . .** Writing can help you think more clearly. It can also help you discover things you didn't know you knew. It can even help you sort through your thoughts and do more with them than you ever imagined.

7 **Use graphic organizers . . .** Keep your thoughts organized by using lists, outlines, or graphic organizers. (**SEE** pages 296-297.)

Your Basic Writing and Thinking Moves

The following chart shows you the kinds of "thinking moves" you can use to help you gather and organize your thoughts.

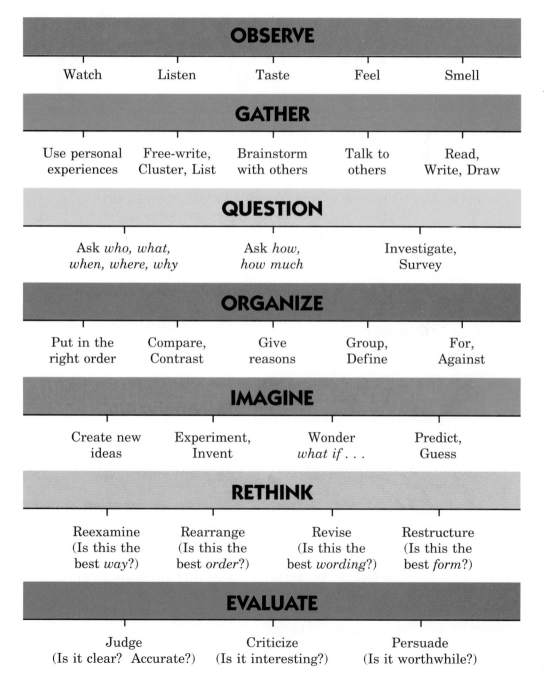

OBSERVE

| Watch | Listen | Taste | Feel | Smell |

GATHER

| Use personal experiences | Free-write, Cluster, List | Brainstorm with others | Talk to others | Read, Write, Draw |

QUESTION

| Ask *who, what, when, where, why* | Ask *how, how much* | Investigate, Survey |

ORGANIZE

| Put in the right order | Compare, Contrast | Give reasons | Group, Define | For, Against |

IMAGINE

| Create new ideas | Experiment, Invent | Wonder *what if . . .* | Predict, Guess |

RETHINK

| Reexamine (Is this the best *way*?) | Rearrange (Is this the best *order*?) | Revise (Is this the best *wording*?) | Restructure (Is this the best *form*?) |

EVALUATE

| Judge (Is it clear? Accurate?) | Criticize (Is it interesting?) | Persuade (Is it worthwhile?) |

Thinking and Writing

Learning to Think

We go to school to learn how to read, how to write, how to speak. But before we can do any of these things—or at least do them well—we have to "learn" how to think. You will use many different kinds of thinking in school. Thinking is often divided into six general categories:

- ■ **Recalling**
- ■ **Understanding**
- ■ **Applying**
- ■ **Analyzing**
- ■ **Synthesizing**
- ■ **Evaluating**

An explanation of each of the six kinds of thinking follows. These explanations will help you understand the different kinds of thinking and how you can use them in your writing.

■ Recalling

The most basic type of thinking you do in school is **recalling** information. This is the type of thinking you do when you are asked to remember something you talked about in class or read about in a textbook. Because your teacher will expect you to recall the most important information, make sure that you listen and read carefully.

➤ Use Recall on Tests

When you answer test questions, you are *recalling* information. Let's say you are studying pollution in your science class. As one part of this unit, you read about acid rain, a serious pollution problem that is killing lakes around the world.

As a basic test question, your teacher might ask you to list five important facts that you have learned about this kind of pollution. The sample answer below shows the kind of information you might list (recall) to answer this test question.

Test Question: *List in complete sentences five important facts you have learned about acid rain.*

Answer

1. Acid rain is caused by pollution from cars and some electric-power plants.
2. When acid rain is still in clouds, it can blow far away from where the pollution started.
3. Acid rain kills plants and trees.
4. When acid rain falls on lakes and rivers, it kills fish.
5. The worst acid rain contains as much acid as lemon juice.

■ Understanding

Your teachers will often ask you to do more than just recall or make a list of what you remember about a topic. They will ask you to show that you **understand** the information well enough to talk or write about it.

➤ Read, Study, and Understand

To really *understand* information from a textbook, you must be a careful reader and take notes. Then, to test whether you understand the material you've read, do one of three things— summarize it in writing, review the main points out loud, or teach it to someone else. If you *can't* do at least one of these three, read it again.

➤ Write to Show Understanding

Understanding is also important when you work on paragraphs and essay test questions. Let's say your science teacher asks you to explain acid rain. Your teacher is really asking you to recall the important facts and details about this kind of pollution *and* show that you understand it by writing clearly about it. The paragraph below is a sample of what you might write. (Also **SEE** pages 330-331.)

Assignment: *In a paragraph, explain acid rain.*

Model Understanding Paragraph

Acid rain is a kind of pollution. It starts when chemicals from cars and power plants go into the air. In the atmosphere, the chemicals mix with the tiny drops of water that make up clouds. When rain falls from the clouds, the acid chemicals are in the rain. The acid kills plants, trees, and fish.

■ Applying

When you are asked to **apply** information, you are being asked to *use* what you've learned. If, for example, you have been learning to play an instrument, you may be asked to apply what you have learned by playing a scale or a short solo.

➤ Use What You've Learned

You will often be asked to *apply* what you have learned in school. Let's say that as part of a pollution unit, your science teacher hands you the following assignment:

Assignment: *Write a letter to a company in your area that might be causing pollution. Explain what you've learned about acid rain. Ask the company to explain to you what they are doing to prevent pollution at their plant.*

Model Letter

Dear Mr. Gray:

In school, I learned that power plants that make electric power by burning coal are a big cause of acid rain. Power plants release the chemicals that cause acid rain. The chemicals mix with clouds and can be blown far away, even to other countries, before the acid rain falls. When it falls, it can kill plants and animals.

I am worried that your power plant could be causing acid rain. Please write to me and tell me if your plant pollutes the air with the chemicals that cause acid rain. If so, please tell me what you are doing to stop polluting the air.

Sincerely,

■ Analyzing

As you get older, you will be asked to study information very carefully and in many different ways. This is called **analyzing**. When you analyze, ask yourself these three questions:

➤ Decide the Purpose

First: "What is the purpose of this assignment?" Is it to show how things are alike (comparing) or different (contrasting)? Is it to put similar ideas into groups (grouping)? Is it to give reasons (cause and effect)? Or is there another purpose?

➤ Select Facts and Details

Second: "Which facts and details are the right ones to use for this assignment?" Let's say the purpose of the assignment is to compare two planets you've been studying. You will want to select the *same kind* of information (facts and details) for both planets. Then you can make a comparison. (**SEE** page 297.)

➤ Organize the Facts and Details

Third: "How should the facts and details for this writing assignment be organized?" In order of importance? In time order (the order in which they happened)? In order of location (the order in which they are located)?

Assignment: *In a paragraph, discuss the causes of acid rain.*

Model Cause and Effect Paragraph

Acid rain is caused by air pollution. But not all air pollution causes acid rain. It is only caused by certain chemicals. When coal or gasoline is burned, chemicals called nitrogen oxides and sulfur dioxide are released into the air. They mix with the water droplets in clouds. When the water droplets fall as rain, the acid chemicals are still there. The acid in acid rain kills trees and fish.

■ Synthesizing

If your teacher were to stop in the middle of a story or an experiment and ask you what you think might happen next, you would be **synthesizing**. You would be using what you already know to create new information. You would be thinking like an artist, a songwriter, or an architect.

➤ Think About It

Suppose your teacher asks you to take the information you just learned in your pollution unit and do something unusual with it—something that will force people to think about it or look at it in a new way.

➤ Use a New Form

One thing you could do is use a different or creative kind of writing form. Instead of writing an ordinary paragraph, you could write a title-down paragraph (or a list poem). Or you could use one of the other forms of writing. (***SEE*** pages 34-35.) By putting what you have learned into a new or an unusual form, you are forcing yourself (and your audience) to look at things differently. You are *synthesizing* information.

Title-Down Paragraph: ACID RAIN

Acid rain starts with air pollution.
Cars are one source of air pollution that causes acid rain.
Industry is another source of air pollution that causes acid rain.
Damage from acid rain lasts for years.

Rain that is polluted kills plants and animals.
Acid snow is just as harmful as acid rain.
In Canada, forests and lakes are dying from acid rain caused by
   U.S. pollution.
Nitrogen oxides are one group of chemicals that cause acid rain.

■ Evaluating

Evaluating is one of the most advanced levels of thinking and writing you will be asked to use. When your teachers ask you to evaluate, they are asking you to judge or defend what you have learned. It's the kind of thinking a judge or lawyer has to do.

➤ Study the Subject

When you are asked to evaluate information, you are being asked to think like an expert. To become an expert, you must know all the important facts and details on the topic. You must know its good and bad points, its strengths and weaknesses.

➤ Write an Evaluation

To write an evaluation, start with a sentence which tells the reader how you feel about the subject. Then add facts and details which prove that your ideas are correct.

Let's say that as part of that unit on pollution, you are asked to *evaluate* the latest attempts to stop acid rain. After studying your notes and reading more on the subject, you feel you have enough information. The following paragraph is an example of what you might write for this assignment.

Assignment: *Evaluate the latest attempts to stop acid rain.*

Model Evaluating Paragraph

The latest attempts to stop acid rain are not strong enough. In most places, the main chemical in acid rain is sulfur, which forms a gas (sulfur dioxide) when it is burned at electric-power plants. Most new power plants must have "scrubbers" that keep sulfur from getting into the air, preventing acid rain. But studies show that unless more plants are required to use scrubbers, acid rain will keep getting worse.

Guidelines for Thinking and Writing

If you are asked to . . .		you should be ready to . . .
Recall list *label* *cluster* *name* *identify* *define* *memorize*		**Remember what you've learned** ■ by listing important details ■ by defining terms ■ by clustering information
Understand *review* *show* *summarize* *explain* *describe*		**Show that you understand what you've learned** ■ by giving examples ■ by explaining how something works
Apply *select* *choose* *organize* *illustrate* *demonstrate* *locate*		**Use what you've learned** ■ to select the most important details ■ to organize information ■ to make something work
Analyze *compare* *classify* *contrast* *divide* *tell why* *map* *break down* *examine*		**Examine material closely to understand it better** ■ by making connections between this and other things ■ by studying cause and effect
Synthesize *combine* *develop* *invent* *design* *compose* *create* *predict* *imagine*		**Reshape material into a new form** ■ by inventing a better way of doing something ■ by predicting what will happen next
Evaluate *judge* *rate* *recommend* *measure* *persuade* *argue* *convince*		**Judge the worth of the material** ■ by pointing out its strengths and weaknesses ■ by evaluating its clearness, accuracy, value, etc.

Thinking Clearly

Use Your Brain!

You don't have to *be* a brain to *use* your brain. In fact, as you read this page, you are already using your brain. You are observing, comparing, analyzing, evaluating, and solving problems. Plus, you've been using these skills since you were very young, without even "thinking" about it.

So, even though you've been practicing since you were very young, you will want to know how you can become an even better thinker—a clearer thinker. You can do it by . . .

- using facts and opinions correctly,
- avoiding fuzzy thinking,
- making good decisions,
- and solving problems.

This chapter will help you better understand and practice these four important thinking skills.

Why think? Thinking saves time, prevents accidents, leads to success, and helps you figure things out—that's why.

Using Facts and Opinions Correctly

An **opinion** is what someone *believes* is true. A **fact** is a statement which can be *proven* to be true. Look at the difference between the opinion and the facts below. The opinion states a personal belief about paper recycling. The facts are specific and can be proven. (Facts can be used to support an opinion.)

> *Opinion:* Recycling paper should be required by law.
>
> *Fact:* If paper is not recycled, trees must be cut down to make more paper.
>
> *Fact:* We are running out of places to dump our trash, and much of our trash is paper.

➤ Write an Opinion Statement

Once you've formed an opinion in your mind, you must word it well so that others will understand what you are saying. Follow the simple recipe below to help you write a good opinion statement.

> *Recipe:* A specific subject (*recycling paper*) + your specific opinion or feeling (*should be required by law*) = a good opinion statement.

Opinions which include strong words such as *all, best, every, never,* or *worst* are difficult to support. (Recycling *all* paper should be required by law.)

➤ Support Your Opinion

When you support or back up your opinion, make sure you use clear, provable facts. Otherwise, your reader probably won't believe you. Let's say you are supporting the opinion that paper recycling should be required by law. Look at the difference between the following ideas:

> *Provable Fact:* Recycling paper would save trees.
>
> *Not a Provable Fact:* Recycling paper would help everyone.

Avoiding Fuzzy Thinking

When you're trying to get others to agree with you, it's important to think clearly, write clearly, and stick to the facts! There's really no room for fuzzy thinking. Here are some suggestions to help you keep your thinking clear.

Don't make statements that jump to conclusions.

"Because ozone is a gas found in smog, ozone is bad."

Discussion: This statement jumps to a conclusion. It says that ozone is bad because it is part of smog, which is bad. But ozone can be good. The natural ozone in the atmosphere protects the earth from the sun's rays.

Don't make statements that make things seem worse—or better—than they are.

"Many Americans recycle their newspapers, so we're saving the trees that would have to be cut down to make new paper for newspapers."

Discussion: This statement makes things sound better than they are. It sounds like most newspapers are recycled, so no trees need to be cut down to make newspapers. But only about 27 percent of all newspapers are recycled, and it takes more than 30 million trees to make the newspapers that we still throw away each year.

Don't make statements that are half-truths.

"Acid rain is 2,000 times more acidic than unpolluted rain."

Discussion: This statement makes it sound like *all* acid rain is 2,000 times more acidic than unpolluted rain. Some is, but some is only 10 times more acidic. The statement makes part of the truth sound like the whole truth.

Don't make statements just because most people agree with them.

"Acid rain is not a bad problem, because most people I talked to don't think it is."

Discussion: This statement is based on the idea that if most people believe something, it must be true. But "most people" can be wrong. They may not know how bad acid rain really is.

Don't make statements that compare things that aren't really like each other.

"When acid rain falls, it's like liquid fire falling on the earth."

Discussion: This statement compares acid rain to something that is really much worse. The worst acid rain is about as acidic as lemon juice. That's bad for the earth, but not as bad as liquid fire!

Don't make statements that are based on feelings, not on facts.

"All big factories should be shut down because they cause air pollution."

Discussion: This statement is based on feelings, and there are no facts to back it up. First, not all big factories cause air pollution. Second, there are other ways to stop air pollution besides shutting down factories.

MINI LESSON After you've read each of the six **don't** statements, go back and read them again. Then rewrite each of the six samples so that they are no longer fuzzy. Compare answers with your classmates.

Making Good Decisions

We make decisions every day. We decide what to wear to school, where to sit at lunch, what book to read for our next report. Many of these decisions can be made with very little planning.

Other decisions are much more difficult and take a good deal of time and thought. When you face a tough decision, here are some guidelines you can use:

1. Define your goals.
❑ What are you trying to figure out or accomplish?
❑ What decision do you have to make?

2. Make a list of your options or choices.
❑ What are some of the things you could do?

3. Study your options.
❑ Look carefully at each option.
❑ What are the pluses and minuses of each?

4. Rank the options.
❑ Put your options in order from best to worst, from easiest to most difficult, from quickest to longest, etc.

5. Choose the best option.
❑ Consider all your options; then choose the best one.

The best option for *you* might not be the best option for someone else. Each person and each situation is different.

6. Review all the steps.
❑ Let some time pass. Then go through the process again to see if your thinking has changed.

Solving Problems

Just like doctors, lawyers, and auto mechanics, you have to solve problems every day. Some are big problems; some are small. And, like anyone else, you will need a plan for solving these problems. First, you will need to identify the problem. Next, you will need to collect information about the problem, think of possible solutions, and choose the best one.

Sometimes you do all of this in a split second; other times, it can take you days or even weeks to solve a problem. For these harder problems, here are some guidelines you can follow:

1. Identify or name the problem.
  ❏ What is the problem?

2. Collect information.
  ❏ What exactly is wrong or needs to be done?
  ❏ What caused the problem?

3. Think of possible solutions.
  ❏ What can be done right now?
  ❏ What can be done a little at a time?

4. Try out the solutions.
  ❏ Try to imagine each solution in action.
  ❏ Use trial and error to test your solutions if you can.

5. Choose the best solution.
  ❏ Think of what's best for others as well as for you.
  ❏ Put your plan into action.

6. Evaluate the result.
  ❏ If you had it to do over again, would you choose the same solution?

Improving Your Learning Skills

Writing as a Learning Tool

Completing Assignments

Working in Groups

Taking Tests

Keeping Good Notes

Writing as a Learning Tool

Dear Students,

Before you read the following pages, I would like to share a few thoughts with you about writing . . . and how you can use writing to learn.

When I first learned to write, I understood that it was important for communicating with others—friends, teachers, relatives. But now, after many years of writing and publishing books, I see that my writing helps me figure things out, find and organize my thoughts, and keep in touch with the outside world.

As a teacher and an author, I've learned this for myself, and as a father, I've enjoyed watching my daughters learn the same thing. The following stories may explain what I mean, and also help you use **writing as a learning tool**.

Sincerely,

Toby Fulwiler

Megan's Story . . .

One day, when I was reading the newspaper, my fifth-grade daughter, Megan, asked me, "Dad, how do you make a speech?" She was supposed to give a short speech to her class explaining how to do something, and she wanted to explain how to stencil. (She had been helping her mother stencil heart designs.)

Make a List

I suggested that she first make a list of all the things she wanted to tell about stenciling. "Just list what comes to mind," I said. Here's what she came up with:

> what stenciling is used for
> where you can buy supplies
> the origin of stenciling
> dictionary definition
> show sample
> make one

First Things First

A good list, I thought, and asked her another question. "In what order do you want to say these things?" Here is what she wrote:

> dictionary definition
> what stenciling is used for
> the origin of stenciling
> show sample
> make one
> where you can buy supplies

When Megan wrote her first list, ideas spilled out of her head. As soon as she saw her ideas on paper, she saw how she could rearrange them. The first list made the second list possible!

Because writing, unlike speaking, stays put, it lets you see your thinking *outside* of your head. You can look at your ideas; you can do something with them.

Anna's Story . . .

Megan was the reader and writer in the family, but Anna, my second daughter, thought of herself as a nonwriter. As it turns out, Anna actually was a writer—an *undercover* writer.

One day Anna and I were watching *The Cosby Show*, but she wasn't really paying attention. Instead, she was carefully unfolding small, crumpled sheets of paper and arranging them on her lap.

An "Undercover" Writer

I asked, "What are you doing?"
Without looking up, she replied, "Sorting my notes."
"What notes?"
"The ones from school."
"What do you mean?"
"The notes I get from my friends."
"How many do you have?"
She stopped unfolding and counted each sheet: "One hundred and twelve," she said.
"Wow! That's a lot, and you've only been in school a few weeks. What are they about?"
"Oh, you know, finding out what people are doing or who they're fighting with. I'm organizing them."

Writing for Real Reasons

Of course, Anna *wrote* notes, too, and these undercover notes taught her a lot. Without realizing it, she understood that writing means connecting with real people (her friends) for real reasons. The same was true for Megan. Once she listed ideas about her subject, her speech-making job became easier, and her stencil-making speech took shape.

WRITE About It

Try some "real" writing yourself. Each day for a month, write out your ideas for doing tomorrow's school assignments. See if this doesn't help you do even better assignments the next day.

Completing Assignments

Learning Made Easier

How do you learn? Is learning easy for you? Do you sometimes wish it could be easier? Well, maybe we can help. Understanding *how* you learn can help you become a better learner.

When it comes to learning in school, there are three pieces to the puzzle: you, your teachers, and your texts.

Your teachers start the learning process by introducing a unit of study. Your texts (this includes books, CDs, videos, etc.) give you the information for the unit. Your job is to read and study this material until you become the best student you can be.

Let's Get Started!

We'll help you do your job by showing you how to set goals, manage your time, and complete your assignments. It's as easy as 1, 2, 3!

Setting Goals

Before you started school, you set goals for yourself all the time—like learning to ride a bike or dribble a basketball.

Now, years later, you're still setting goals—learning to play an instrument, earning money to buy something, turning your next assignment in on time. Setting goals for yourself and reaching them is what growing up is all about.

No one plans to fail; they just fail to plan.

Some Helpful Guidelines

1 Be realistic. Learn to set realistic goals for yourself. Becoming the editor of your school newspaper, although a big challenge, is a realistic aim. But can you learn to play the guitar in a day? Probably not. It's better to do some things step-by-step. For example, you might plan to do one part of a science project each day for a week. Or, each time you play in a sport, you might try to improve just one specific skill.

2 Work toward your goal. Continue working toward your goal—no matter what happens! If you choose to keep a journal, set aside a specific time each day to write in it. If you want to improve in a certain sport, set up a time to talk to your coach or an older friend about improving your skills.

Remember, there will be times when you won't be able to write or practice—when you are sick, for instance. Find another time to make it up.

3 Reward yourself. When you reach one of your goals, reward yourself in some small way. Let's say you've decided to keep a daily journal for the whole school year. When you have faithfully written in your journal every day for two weeks, do something special, or tell a parent or teacher. They'll be proud of you!

Managing Your Time

Are you a *procrastinator*? Do you sometimes put off doing things that you should do? Well, the truth is, we all procrastinate at times. But if you put things off all the time, then you need to learn about time management.

Steps in the Process

1 **Make a daily list.** Write down things you *need* to do today, perhaps in a small spiral notebook. Number your "To Do" list from the most important to the least important, and cross each one off as you complete it.

2 **Keep a weekly schedule.** A weekly planner shows you what you have to do during the week. It helps you plan your study time and your fun time. Use the following model or design your own.

WEEKLY PLANNER

Day	Assignment	Due Date	Activities	Study Time	Fun Time
Monday					
Tuesday					

 Figure out what time of the day you think and work best. Use this time for your toughest assignments and most important work.

3 **Turn big jobs into little ones.** When you have a big assignment to do, it can seem really overwhelming. One way to make it seem easier is to turn it into smaller jobs. Figure out how many days you have to complete the assignment, and how much you need to do each day. Working 15 minutes a day for two weeks beats two or three hours of work the night before your project is due.

Doing the Assignments

1 Plan ahead.

- First of all, be sure you know exactly what your assignment is, and when you have to turn it in.
- Decide how much time you'll need to complete your assignment. Then, set aside study time in your daily schedule to get it done.
- Plan when and where you will do your assignment. This should be a quiet place where you can work without interruptions. (Ask your family to "hold your calls.")

2 Get off to a good start.

- Gather all the materials you will need to complete your assignment (paper, pens, folders, journal, notebook, handouts, dictionary, handbook).
- Read over all your teacher's directions so that you know exactly what you have to do for the assignment.
- Set a goal for yourself to get a certain amount of the assignment done before you take a break. Stick to that plan!

3 Get the job done.

- Use a study-reading strategy to help you complete your reading and studying. (**SEE** pages 238-242 in "Using Reading Strategies.")
- Keep an "Ask the Teacher" list for things you don't understand.
- Make sure your work is neat and doesn't contain any careless errors. Turn it in on time.

Working in Groups

Listening, cooperating, and clarifying are often called "people skills" because they help people work and learn better in groups.

Making Your Group Work

What was it like the last time you worked in a group? Did your teacher ask you to work with other students in the class? Did you work with a group of kids in the neighborhood or at a club meeting? Did you have a good time? Did you accomplish something?

Getting Started

Working in a group can be fun if everyone gets along and gets the job done. In this chapter, we'll look at how you can use "people skills" to help make your next group a success. You can begin by *making a plan*.

Making a Plan

Every job you do should begin with a plan. Your group's task is no different. Members should ask themselves these questions:

- What is our task or assignment?
- What do we need to do in order to accomplish this task?
- What job or jobs will each group member do?
- What deadlines must we meet?

Try using an outline like the one below to help your group make its plan. Remember to share ideas and listen carefully to one another. Be sure everyone agrees with the plan and is willing to do the jobs assigned to them.

Group Plan

A. Our task is _____
   (Is it to solve a problem, answer questions, research a topic?)

B. Things we need to do: _____
   1. _____
   2. _____
   3. _____
   (Add more lines if you need them.)

C. Jobs for each group member:
   Name _____ Job _____
   Name _____ Job _____
   Name _____ Job _____
   (Some sample jobs: writer or recorder, researcher, artist, coordinator)

D. This is our schedule:
   By this date _____, we will have this done: _____
   By this date _____, we will have this done: _____

Skills for Listening

Listening is important when you work in groups. People can only work together if they listen to one another. Imagine a group of fire fighters at a huge fire. If they didn't listen to one another, they could never cooperate well enough to put out the fire.

➤ **Just listen.** Remember, listening means *thinking about* what is being said. So, you can't truly listen and do something else at the same time. Don't draw pictures, write notes to your friends, or make animals out of paper clips while you're listening.

➤ **Listen actively.** You'll have to try hard to keep your mind on what's being said. It's natural for your mind to wander. Because you can think faster than people can talk, your mind races ahead and gets off the track. To stay on track, do the following:

M·m·m·m·m·m·

- **Look at the person who is speaking.**
  This works because your mind thinks about what your eyes see.

- **Listen for key words and phrases.**
  For example: "The only solution is . . ." or "Here's what I think we should do."

- **Write down a few notes.**
  It's not the same as writing notes to your friends, because you're writing about what's being said.

➤ **Ask questions.** If you don't understand something, ask about it. But don't interrupt the person who is speaking unless you're really lost. Wait until she or he is finished. Then ask a good, clear question such as, "Karen, you're saying we should do a report instead of making a model, because a report will be easier—right?"

THINK IT OVER

Listening is not as easy as it sounds!
To **hear,** you need only your ears.
To **listen,** you need your ears *and* your mind.

Skills for Cooperating

Cooperating means working with others to reach a shared goal.

➤ **Give your ideas and opinions.** It's important to let other group members know what you think. When you like someone's idea, say so! When you don't, it's okay to say so. But don't say, "That's a stupid idea!" Say, "I don't think that will work *because* . . . ." (When you give your opinion, you should give your reasons, too.)

➤ **Be willing to change your opinions.** Listen to other opinions with an open mind. Remember, when you work with a group, you are trying to reach a decision everyone agrees with.

➤ **Don't get personal.** Try not to criticize or say anything too personal. And if you hear a personal comment, remind the speaker that this is a group project and everyone needs to work together.

Skills for Clarifying

Clarifying means "clearing up." If someone in the group is confused, the group can't work together toward the goal. Here's how you can help clear up confusion:

➤ **Remember your goal.** Remind everybody what the group's goal is. Also, suggest steps that will help you reach the goal. For example: "First, let's decide whether to do a report or make a model. Then let's decide what each person's job will be."

➤ **Re-explain it.** If someone doesn't understand something, ask if anyone else in the group can think of a new way to explain it.

➤ **Stay on track.** Also, if someone gets off track, say something as simple as, "I think we should get back to the main point."

Making a Group Decision

Successful groups make decisions by *consensus*. *Reaching a consensus* means getting everyone in the group to agree with the decision. How do you get everyone to agree? Here are some tips:

Reaching a Consensus

- Ask everyone in the group for ideas about a certain problem, and listen while they explain them.
- Discuss each idea and how it will (or won't) help solve the problem.
- Select the idea everyone agrees will help the most.
- If more than one idea is selected, try to combine these ideas into one plan, a plan everyone can agree on.

Remember, to reach a consensus, you must get everyone to agree with a group decision. That doesn't mean that everyone thinks it's the *best* idea; it means that it is the idea that everyone in the group agrees to accept.

Evaluating Your Work

Well, how did your group do? The proof that your group *succeeded* is a *successful* product. Before you hand in your assignment, judge the work your group accomplished. You can do this by having everyone answer and discuss these questions:

- Does our final product meet all the requirements of the assignment?
- Did group members do their jobs and contribute to the final product?
- Are we proud to say that this is our product?

If you have to answer "no" to any of these questions, you may want to go back and revise your work. Then answer the questions again.

Group Sharing

One kind of group work you'll do in school is "group sharing." One of the most common topics for group sharing is books you have read. Here are some guidelines to help you share with your group.

Before You Begin: Make a list of the things you plan to say about the book. Here are some ideas:

The Plot

What events stand out in your mind? Why?

What parts of the story remind you of your own life? In what way?

What other stories is this one like?

The Characters

Who are your favorite characters?

Do any of the characters remind you of people you know?

Overall Effect

Do you think the title fits the book?

What is the author trying to tell the reader about life?

Who else should read this book?

Helpful Hint After you have told a little about your book, you might actually read your favorite part.

As You Share: Get into small groups (no more than six) and sit facing each other. Decide who's going to start.

- Listen carefully to one another and write down your reactions and questions.

- Add to what the others say about the book. Make sure you share your personal thoughts about the book as well.

Taking Tests

Getting Your Act Together

You're having a test? Well, it had to happen sooner or later! Taking a test is a good way for you—and your teacher—to find out what you have learned. (And what you haven't learned!) But tests don't have to be a big deal. If you follow these two simple rules, you'll do just fine: **be prepared** and **pay attention**.

To do well on tests, you must do well in class. You must organize yourself, your time, and your work—from the very first day.

Test-Taking Strategies

On the following pages, you'll find lots of good strategies and hints for helping you do your best on tests. There are hints for objective tests, hints for essay tests, and hints to help you remember things better. We hope they help!

Preparing for the Test

Ask questions . . .

- What will be on the test? (Ask your teacher for examples.)
- What kind of test will it be? (Multiple choice? Essay?)

Organize your notes . . .

- Reread your class notes carefully. (Get any notes or materials you may have missed.)
- Rewrite your most important notes or put them on note cards.

Review for the test . . .

- Skim the lessons in your textbook. (Also look over old quizzes and worksheets.)
- Recite difficult material out loud as you review.

 Use lists, diagrams, rhymes, or any other special memory aids. (**SEE** pages 334-335.)

Taking the Test

Listen attentively . . .

- Listen carefully to your teacher. How much time will you have? Can you use your notes, a dictionary, or your handbook?

Read carefully . . .

- Skim the whole test quickly, so you know which questions will take the most time.
- Then go back and read the directions carefully. Be on the lookout for words like *always, only, all,* and *never.*
- Don't spend too much time on any one question.

Check closely . . .

- Double-check to be sure you have answered all the questions. (Check each answer if you have time.)
- Ask your teacher about any questions which still confuse you.

The Essay Test

When you answer an essay question, you are doing more than just writing. You are reading, thinking, organizing—*and* writing. Here are some suggestions to help you improve your essay answers.

Understanding the Essay Test Question

Your essay answer will be much better and clearer if you take the time to read before you write. The first step is to read the question carefully, at least twice, to be sure you understand what is being asked.

Pay special attention to the "key words" that are found in every essay question. These key words will tell you what kind of thinking and writing you'll need to do to answer the question correctly.

Key Words

Compare/contrast ● (*Compare and contrast* the water quality before and after the chemical plant moved to our town.) To *compare*, you should use examples to show how two things are alike in several ways. To *contrast*, you show how they are different.

Define ● (*Define* ultraviolet light.) To *define*, you must tell what the word or subject in the question means. You do this by showing just what this thing is, and what it does.

Describe ● (*Describe* the sun's spectrum.) To *describe*, you must tell how something or someone looks, feels, sounds, etc.

Explain ● (*Explain* how the Underground Railroad operated.) To *explain*, you must tell how something happens or show how something works (step-by-step).

List ● (*List* as many reasons as you can for the American Revolution beginning when it did.) To *list*, you must include a number of examples, reasons, or other details, in list form.

Prove ● (*Prove* that Abraham Lincoln worked hard as a boy.) To *prove*, you must present facts and details (proof) which show clearly that something is true.

Planning and Writing the Essay Answer

1 Reword the question. After you've read the question carefully, you can change it into the first sentence of your answer. This is easy . . . all you need to do is drop the key word and rearrange the remaining words into a topic sentence. (Sometimes you may need to add words, too.)

> **Question:** *List* three reasons why Abraham Lincoln is remembered as a great president.

> **Topic Sentence:** *Abraham Lincoln is remembered as a great president for three reasons.*

 The question was changed into a topic sentence by dropping the key word (*list*) and arranging the rest of the words into a sentence.

2 Organize the main points. Put all the details in the best order before you start writing your answer.

> I. *Lincoln was a great president.*
>   A. *He kept our nation together.*
>   B. *He abolished slavery.*
>   C. *He ended the Civil War.*

3 Write your essay answer. Your first sentence will be your topic sentence. The other sentences will add the information you need to make your answer clear and complete. Use connecting words to make sure your answer reads smoothly. Double-check your answer, by rereading the question and your notes or outlines, to be sure you included everything you needed to.

> *Abraham Lincoln is remembered as a great president for three reasons. One reason is that he kept our nation together when slavery was tearing it apart. Because he was able to keep the country together, he was also able to abolish slavery in all the states. Even though it took four years to do, he was able to bring the Civil War to an end. Because Lincoln did all these things, the United States became a strong, slave-free nation.*

The Objective Test

To really shine on an objective test, keep the following hints in mind as you take the test.

TRUE/FALSE TEST

➤ Read the entire question before answering. For an answer to be true, the *entire answer* must be true. If only part of it is true, you must choose false.

➤ Watch for words like *all, every, always, never*. Statements with these words in them are often false.

Questions: Read carefully each sample true/false question below. Then decide how you would answer each.

_____ 1. Plastic can never be recycled.

_____ 2. All plastic can be recycled.

_____ 3. Vinyl is a kind of plastic used to make tires.

Answers: All are false. Some plastic—but not *all*—can be recycled. In number 3, the first half is true (vinyl is a kind of plastic), but vinyl is *not* used to make tires.

MATCHING TEST

➤ Before you make any matches, read both lists quickly.

➤ Check off each answer as you make your match, unless you are told that you might need to use an answer more than once.

Questions: Match the product (on the left) to the recycled material that it is made from (on the right).

_____ Asphalt	a. Motor oil
_____ Mulch for plants	b. Christmas trees
_____ Motor oil	c. Tires

Answers: (c) Asphalt, (b) Mulch, (a) Motor oil

MULTIPLE CHOICE TEST

➤ Read the directions carefully to see if you are looking for the *correct* answer or the *best* answer.

➤ Answer each question in your mind *before* looking at the choices. Then read *all* the choices before answering.

 Look for negative words like *not, never, except, unless.* They can change the entire meaning of the question.

Questions: Read the following questions carefully. How would you answer each?

1. Plastic can never be recycled to make
   (a) packaging   (b) park benches   (c) tires

2. Motor oil can't be recycled except to make
   (a) tires   (b) plastic jars   (c) motor oil

Answers: 1. (c) Plastic is *never* recycled to make tires.
2. (c) Motor oil *can't* be recycled except to make motor oil.

FILL IN THE BLANKS

➤ Count the number of blanks in each question. It could tell you the number of words that are needed in your answer.

Questions: Read the statements below. Can you predict the kinds of words that would probably fit in each blank?

1. Paper makes up about _____ of our trash.

2. _____ makes up about 1/3 of our trash.

3. _____ and _____ cannot be recycled, even though they are made from paper.

Answers: 1. 41% (*a percentage or fraction*) 2. packaging (*a general noun*) 3. juice cartons, pet-food bags (*specific nouns*)

REMEMBERING for Tests

Knowing how to take a test is important—remembering all the material you covered on the test is even more important. Luckily, there are some tricks you can use that will help you improve your memory. Here are a few you can begin using immediately!

Use Maps or Organizers ● A map is a drawing made up of circles, lines, and other shapes to help you organize your thoughts. (***SEE*** pages 296-297.)

Use Acronyms ● Acronyms are words made up of the first letters of a title or a group of words. NATO, for example, is an acronym for North Atlantic Treaty Organization. To help you remember things better, you can create your own acronyms.

> *HOMES . . . **H**uron, **O**ntario, **M**ichigan, **E**rie, **S**uperior*
> (the Great Lakes)
>
> *ROY G. BIV . . . **R**ed, **O**range, **Y**ellow, **G**reen, **B**lue, **I**ndigo, **V**iolet*
> (the colors of the rainbow)

Use Poems or Songs ● Sometimes a simple (even silly) song or poem can help you remember things. Using a familiar tune or poem, substitute information to be learned. Do you remember any of these?

A B C D   E F G H I

i before e, except after c, . . .
In 1492, Columbus sailed the ocean blue.

Talk to Others ● It may seem too simple to help much, but talking to others about things you need to remember can be very helpful. Here are some of the ways you can talk and learn.

- *Form a study group.*
- *Teach what you need to learn to someone else.*
- *Recite what you need to remember out loud.*
- *Ask questions.*

Draw or Visualize ● Use drawings or pictures in your mind to help you remember. Here's an example of a drawing used to help remember prepositions. (No matter where you put a balloon, you should be able to think of a preposition to tell you where it's located.)

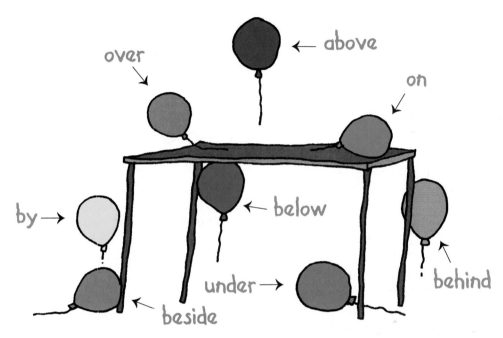

Rewrite It ● There are many different ways you can use writing to help you learn and remember. Here are just a few:

Write about it in a journal or learning log. (**SEE** pages 338-339 for more suggestions.)

Write down what you need to remember and hang it in front of you like a poster on the wall.

Note cards can be carried around and used like flash cards to drill yourself throughout the day.

Keeping Good Notes

A Plan of Action!

If you were told to get bagels, orange juice, a dozen eggs, a gallon of milk, and a bag of popcorn at the store, you *might* remember everything. If you had a list handed to you, remembering would be a lot easier. And, if *you* wrote the list, you might not even need to look at it once you got to the store. That's how powerful writing is as a learning tool.

Don't *Just* Write

Note taking is a very important writing and learning tool. But it's not just writing down everything you hear—it's listening carefully and writing down *just* the important ideas. That's what being a good note taker is all about.

To get started, all you need is a notebook and some helpful hints.

If you get the notebook, we'll provide the hints!

Being able to take good notes is a wonderful skill, one you'll use more and more throughout your school years.

Guidelines for Improving Note-taking Skills

The guidelines which follow will help you improve your note-taking skills. Read and follow each hint carefully. (**SEE** "Improving Listening Skills" on pages 292-293 for more suggestions.)

Pay attention!

1. Listen carefully.

2. Put the date and subject at the top of each page.

3. Write neatly and quickly!

Be brief!

1. Write down just the important ideas—**not** every single word.

2. Use abbreviations and symbols (#, $, &, =).

3. Summarize what is put on the board or overhead projector.

4. Draw pictures if they make the ideas clearer.

Be organized!

1. Use numbers or words to help organize your notes (1st, 2nd, before, after).

2. Circle words you have questions about.

3. Read over your notes; recopy those that are hard to read.

4. Use a **pen** or **marker** to highlight the main points.

Keeping a Learning Log

One kind of notebook is called a **learning log**. A learning log is a place for you to write down your thoughts and feelings about a subject. It is also a place to write questions you may have about a subject, to write reactions to reading assignments, to keep track of new vocabulary words, or to write whatever else you want.

The following guidelines will help you begin your own learning log. It will work best if you write freely and use your own words.

1 **Divide Your Notebook:** Divide your notebook into sections for each subject you would like to write about. Write the date each time you make an entry.

2 **Plan to Write:** Set aside a time for your writing. Plan to spend more time writing about a subject that is especially tough for you.

3 **Write Nonstop:** Write in short, nonstop bursts. See if you can "get it all down" without stopping. Some writings will take only 3-5 minutes to finish, but others will take longer. Don't stop until you've written down all your thoughts.

Sample Response to a Class Discussion

Jan. 6, 1994

What a crazy world! We want big factories to provide good jobs. We want lots of heat and light in our homes, and we love to ride around in our cars. But scientists say that the acid rain produced by factories, power plants, and cars may be wrecking our buildings and highways. And what's really bad is that this acid rain is also hurting our lakes, streams, and rivers. Many are just dead bodies of water. So should people give up jobs and cars? Should we . . .?

More Learning Log Activities

Here are some other ideas for keeping a learning log. Try them all! Then decide which ones work best for you.

First Thoughts ● Make a list of key words that come to mind after a lesson. These key words will help you focus on the most important ideas.

Nutshelling ● Have you ever heard the phrase "in a nutshell"? It means you say a lot in a few words. Try *nutshelling*: In one sentence, write the meaning of an important class discussion or a chapter you have read.

Stop 'n' Write ● Stop whatever you are studying and write about it. This is a quick way to be sure your mind is on your work.

Notes to the Teacher ● Jot down any questions you may have about the subject and give them to your teacher before or after class. Ask your teacher to react to your questions.

Clustering ● If you already use clustering, you know how valuable it can be to help you explore your thoughts about a subject. It is also a good activity to use in a learning log. (**SEE** page 26.)

Unsent Letters ● Write a letter to any person on a topic related to the subject. Writing a letter will help you think about the topic in a very personal way.

Draw ● You can even use your learning log to draw or illustrate something you learned or thought about in class.

Bright IDEA

You can also use your learning log to check your progress in your subjects. Are you doing well in all areas (reading and understanding, daily assignments, quizzes)? What needs improving? What can you do to improve?

Proofreader's Guide: Check It Out!

Writers Express

THESAURUS

Check It Out!

Marking Punctuation

Editing for Mechanics

Checking Your Spelling

Using the Right Word

Understanding Sentences

Understanding Our Language

"On your mark . . ."

Period ▶ 01

Ellipsis ▶ 07

Comma ▶ 11

Semicolon ▶ 24

Colon ▶ 27

Hyphen ▶ 32

Dash ▶ 38

Apostrophe ▶ 41

Quotation
Marks ▶ 48

Question Mark ▶ 53

Exclamation
Point ▶ 56

Italics ▶ 57

Parentheses ▶ 60

MARKING PUNCTUATION

Period

01 ▶ A **period** is used to end a sentence. It is also used after initials, after abbreviations, and as a decimal point.

02 ▶ **At the End of a Sentence**
A period is used at the end of sentences making statements or requests.

> My mother has a secret recipe for chocolate chip cookies. (statement)

> Please pass the cookies. (request)

CHECK IT OUT

03 ▶ After an Initial

Place a period after an initial in a person's name.

| Susan B. Anthony
| Booker T. Washington

04 ▶ As a Decimal

Use a period as a decimal point and to separate dollars and cents.

| **Robert is 99.9 percent sure that it costs $2.50 to get into the movies today.**

05 ▶ After Abbreviations

A period is placed after each part of an abbreviation.

| **Mr.   Mrs.   Ms.   Dr.   Ph.D.**

06 ▶ After Final Abbreviations

Only one period should be used at the end of the sentence when an abbreviation is the last word.

| **When Josie is nervous, she bites her nails, wiggles her thumbs, taps her toes, etc.**

Ellipsis

07 ▶

An **ellipsis** (three periods) may be used to show omitted words or sentences or to indicate a pause in dialogue.

Tip: When typing an ellipsis, leave one space before, after, and between each period.

08 ▶ To Show Omitted Words

An ellipsis is used to show that one or more words have been left out of a quotation.

| Complete Quote: **"All I know is that I saw something that hummed and glowed and looked like a giant sugar bowl with no handles, hovering above the water tower."**

| Shortened Quote: **"All I know is that I saw something that hummed and glowed . . . hovering above the water tower."**

09 ▶ At the End of a Sentence

If the words left out are at the end of a sentence, use a period followed by three dots.

| Complete Quote: **"That is the last thing I remember about my walk last night. Then I woke up here."**

| Shortened Quote: **"That is the last thing I remember. . . . Then I woke up here."**

10 ▶ Pause in Dialogue

An ellipsis is used to indicate a pause in dialogue.

| **"That's . . . incredible!" I cried.**

Comma

11 ▶ **Commas** are used to keep words and ideas from running together, making your writing easier to read. Commas tell the reader where to pause.

12 ▶ **Items in a Series**
Commas are used between words, phrases, or clauses in a series.

▎ I know someone who likes pepperoni, pineapple, and olives on her pizza. (words)

▎ In summer I like to go skateboarding, ride my bike, and play basketball. (phrases)

13 ▶ **In Dates and Addresses**
Commas are used to separate items in addresses and dates.

▎ We are having our next reunion on July 4, 1995, at Wells Park.

▎ His new address is 3344 South First Street, Atlanta, GA 30200.

Tip: Do not use a comma to separate the state from the ZIP code.

14 ▶ **To Keep Numbers Clear**
Commas are used in numbers of four digits or more to keep the numbers clear.

▎ Rodney's car has 200,000 miles on it. He's trying to sell it for $1,000.

Tip: Commas are not used in years: 1776, 1999, 2001.

15 ▶ **To Set Off Interruptions**
Commas are used to set off a word, phrase, or clause that interrupts the main thought of a sentence.

▎ As it turned out, however, Rodney sold the car for $250.

16 ▶ **Between Two Independent Clauses**
A comma may be used between two independent clauses which are joined by coordinating conjunctions such as the following: *and*, *but*, *or*, *nor*, *for*, *so*, and *yet*.

▎ My friend never does any homework, yet he hopes to get good grades.

▎ I always bring a lot of work home, and I expect to get good grades.

Tip: Do not connect two independent clauses with a comma unless you also use a conjunction. (See page 372 for more information about independent clauses.)

17 ▶ To Set Off Dialogue

Commas are used to set off the exact words of the speaker from the rest of the sentence.

> As Oscar the Grouch says, "One man's trash is another man's treasure."

No comma is needed when *reporting* rather than *repeating* what a speaker said.

> Carla said that the Frisbee just missed her nose.

18 ▶ In Direct Address

Commas are used to separate a noun of direct address (the person being spoken to) from the rest of the sentence.

> Carla, watch out!

19 ▶ In Letter Writing

Commas are used after the salutation, or greeting, in a friendly letter and after the closing in all letters.

> Dear Uncle Roberto, (greeting)

> Your niece, (closing)

20 ▶ To Separate Adjectives

Commas are used to separate two or more adjectives which equally modify the same noun.

> I like to wear old, moldy socks when I play basketball.

Tip: Use these tests to discover if adjectives modify equally:

➤ Switch the order of the adjectives; if the sentence is still clear, the adjectives modify equally.

➤ Insert *and* between the adjectives; if the sentence reads well, use a comma when *and* is omitted.

21 ▶ To Set Off Interjections

A comma is used to separate an interjection or weak exclamation from the rest of the sentence.

> Wow, you really did it this time!

> Hey, will you do me a favor?

22 ▶ To Set Off Appositives

An appositive is a word or phrase that renames the noun or pronoun before it.

> My father, a great cook, makes the best pizza in town. (an appositive phrase)

23 ▶ To Set Off Long Phrases and Clauses

Use a comma to separate a long modifying phrase or clause from the independent clause following it.

> After five long days in school, I am tired of sitting at a desk. (phrase)

> When you practice as much as I do, blade-skating is easy. (clause)

Semicolon

Colon

24 The **semicolon** is a cross between a period and a comma. It is sometimes used in place of a period; other times, it serves the same function as a comma.

25 Between Independent Clauses

A semicolon is used to join two or more independent clauses which are not connected with a coordinating conjunction. (This means that each clause could stand alone as a separate sentence.)

My uncle has a new motorcycle; I wish I were old enough to drive it.

He takes me for rides on it; however, I would still rather be driving it.

Tip: See page 372 for more information about independent clauses; see page 387 for an explanation of coordinating conjunctions.

26 To Separate Phrases

A semicolon is used to separate a series of phrases which already contain commas.

We should buy less processed food; grow some of our own fruits, vegetables, and grains; and drink more clean water, fresh juices, and low-fat milk.

Note: The second and third phrases above "already contain commas."

27 A **colon** is used in a sentence to introduce a list or draw attention to information that follows. Colons are also used between the numbers in time.

28 To Introduce a List

A colon is used to introduce a list.

Motorcycles are used for the following reasons: transportation, recreation, and racing events.

29 After a Salutation

A colon may be used after the salutation of a business letter.

Dear Ms. Davidson:

30 Between Numbers in Time

A colon is used between the parts of a number which indicate time.

The race begins at 1:30 p.m.

I'll meet you at 12:00 noon.

31 As a Formal Introduction

A colon may be used to introduce an important quotation in a serious report, essay, or news story.

President Lincoln concluded the Gettysburg Address with these famous words: " . . . a government of the people, by the people, and for the people, shall not perish from the earth."

Hyphen

32 A **hyphen** is used to divide or join words. Hyphens are also used to create new words.

To Divide a Word

33 A hyphen is used to divide a word when you run out of room at the end of a line. A word may be divided only between syllables. (The word *con-tri-bu-tion* can be divided in three places.)

> In 1883, Jan Matzeliger helped to make an important contri-bution to civilization.

Tip: Here are some other guidelines for hyphenating words:

➤ *Never* divide a one-syllable word: **helped, great**.

➤ *Never* divide a one-letter syllable from the rest of the word: **i-dentity**.

➤ *Never* divide contractions: **haven't, shouldn't**

In Compound Words

34 A hyphen is used to make some compound words.

> Matzeliger was not well-known, even though he invented a machine used to make shoes.

In Fractions

35 A hyphen is used between the numbers in a fraction.

> Matzeliger's machine shaped the upper one-half of the shoe and then attached it to the sole.

To Form an Adjective

36 The hyphen is used to join two or more words which work together to form a single adjective *before* a noun.

> Matzeliger's shoe-stitching machine revolutionized the process of making shoes.

To Create New Words

37 A hyphen is used to form new words beginning with the prefixes *self*, *ex*, *great*, *all*, and *half*. A hyphen is also used with suffixes such as *free* and *elect*.

> great-aunt, half-baked, all-purpose, self-esteem, sugar-free, president-elect

Dash

38 A **dash** may be used to show a change in thought or direction in a sentence, or to show that a speaker has been interrupted.

In a Sentence Break

39 A dash may be used to show a sudden break in a sentence.

> The skateboard—if you didn't notice—has a wheel missing.

In Interrupted Speech

40 A dash is used to show that someone's speech is being interrupted by another person.

> Well, hello—yes, I—that's right—yes, I—sure, I'd love to—eight o'clock is perfect!

Apostrophe

41 An apostrophe is used to form plurals, to show that a letter or letters have been left out of a word, or to show possession.

42 ▶ To Form Plurals

An apostrophe and *s* are used to form the plural of a letter, a number, or a sign.

A's (letter)

8's (number)

+'s (sign)

43 ▶ In Contractions

An apostrophe is used to show that one or more letters have been left out to form a contraction.

Contraction	*Short For*
don't	do not
it's	it is; it has
they'll	they will
he'd	he had
they're	they are
o'clock	of the clock

44 ▶ In Place of Numbers or Letters

An apostrophe is also used to show that one or more letters or numbers have been left out of numerals or words.

class of '99 (*19* is left out)

fixin' to go (*g* is left out)

45 ▶ In Singular Possessives

The possessive form of singular nouns is usually made by adding an apostrophe and *s*.

My sister's hobby is jazz dancing.

When a singular noun ends with an *s* or *z* sound, the possessive may be formed by adding just an apostrophe.

Lucas' hobby is collecting pencil stubs.

EXCEPT When a singular noun is a one-syllable word, add both an apostrophe and an *s*.

Gus's father took him fishing.

46 ▶ In Plural Possessives

The possessive form of plural nouns ending in *s* is usually made by adding just an apostrophe.

the girls' log-rolling team

For plural nouns not ending in *s*, an apostrophe and *s* must be added.

children's book

47 ▶ In Shared Possessives

When possession is shared by more than one noun, add an apostrophe and *s* to the last noun.

Jim, Joe, and Jerry's fish.

Quotation Marks

48 **Quotation marks** are used to enclose the exact words of the speaker, to show that words are used in a special way, and to punctuate titles.

49 **Direct Quotations**
Quotation marks are placed before and after the spoken words.

"Rosa Parks is a true American hero," the teacher reminded her students.

50 **Placement of Punctuation**
Periods and commas are always placed *inside* quotation marks.

The child said, "Tell me a story."

"I'm so tired," said the mom.

A question mark or an exclamation point is placed *inside* the quotation marks when it punctuates the quotation; it is placed *outside* when it punctuates the main sentence.

"Should I tell you a story?" asked the child.

"Please do!" answered the mom.

Did the dad say, "I want to listen, too"?

51 **Special Words**
Quotation marks may be used to set apart a word which is being discussed.

The word "got" is often used incorrectly.

52 **To Punctuate Titles**
Quotation marks are used to punctuate titles of songs, poems, short stories, essays, chapters of books, and articles found in magazines, newspapers, or encyclopedias. (See page 351 for other information about titles.)

"America the Beautiful" (song)

"The Toucan" (poem)

"McBroom Tells the Truth" (short story)

"Roses and Onions" (chapter)

Tip: When you write a title, capitalize the first word, last word, and every word in between except for articles (a, an, the), short prepositions (by, for, to), and short conjunctions (and, or).

Question Mark

53 A **question mark** is used after a direct question (an interrogative sentence) and to show doubt about the correctness of something.

54 **Direct Question**
A question mark is used at the end of a direct question.

Have you ever ridden on an airplane?

55 **Correctness**
A question mark is placed in parentheses to show that the writer isn't sure a fact is correct.

You'll see virtual reality TV shows by the year 2000 (?).

Exclamation Point

56 An **exclamation point** is used to express strong feeling. It may be placed after a word, a phrase, or a sentence.

Not! (word)

Happy birthday! (phrase)

I can't wait for Friday! (sentence)

Italics

57 **Italic** is a printer's term for a slightly slanted style of type. (The word *friend* is typed in italics.) **Italics** are used to indicate titles and special words.

Tip: In handwritten material each word or letter which should be in italics is *underlined*. If you use a computer, you may be able to print italics.

58 **For Titles**
Italics (or underlining) are used for titles of plays, books, newspapers, magazines, television programs, movies (videos), record albums (cassettes and CD's), and other complete works.

The Wiz OR The Wiz (play)

Talking Walls (book)

Ghostwriter (television program)

Home Alone (movie)

59 **For Specific Words**
Use italics (or underlining) to indicate names of aircraft and ships.

Columbia OR Columbia (spacecraft)

Merrimac (Civil War ship)

Use italics (or underlining) to indicate foreign words.

E pluribus unum, meaning "one out of many," is written on every U.S. nickel.

Use italics (or underlining) to indicate words discussed as words, rather than for their meaning.

The word *freedom* means different things to different people.

Parentheses

60 Parentheses are used around words included in a sentence to add information or to help make an idea clearer.

61 **To Add Information**
Parentheses are used to add information.

The map (figure 2) will help you understand the explorer's route.

62 **To Make an Idea Clearer**
Parentheses are used to make an idea clearer.

Five of the students provided background music (humming very quietly) for the singer.

Unsolved Mysteries

Do you know the difference between an *acronym* and an *aardvark?* No? Do you know when to capitalize *mother, father, aunt,* or *uncle?* Not sure? Do you know when to add *s* to a word and when to add *es?* Another unsolved mystery?

Well, this is your lucky day. We're about to take some of the mystery out of these and other questions about the mechanics of writing:

Capitalization ▶ **63**

Plurals ▶ **77**

Numbers ▶ **85**

Abbreviations ▶ **89**

EDITING FOR MECHANICS

Capitalization

63 ▶ **Proper Nouns and Proper Adjectives**

Capitalize all proper nouns and proper adjectives. A proper noun names a specific person, place, thing, or idea. A proper adjective is formed from a proper noun.

Proper Nouns:
Miami Dolphins
Beverly Cleary

Proper Adjectives:
Hawaiian pineapples
a **Philadelphia** museum

64 ▶ **Names of People**

Capitalize the names of people and also the initials or abbreviations that stand for those names.

John Steptoe, Harriet Tubman, C. S. Lewis, Pocahontas

65 ► Words Used as Names

Capitalize words such as *mother, father, aunt,* and *uncle* when these words are used as names.

Will you ask Mother what we're having for lunch? (*Mother* is used as a name; you could use her first name in its place.)

Will you ask my mother what we're having for lunch? (In this sentence, *mother* describes someone but is not used as a name.)

66 ► Titles Used with Names

Capitalize titles used with names of persons.

President Carter
Dr. Martin Luther King, Jr.
Mayor Sharon Sayles Belton
(Do not capitalize titles when they are used alone: the president, the doctor, the mayor.)

68 ► Historical Events

Capitalize the names of historical events, documents, and periods of time.

Emancipation Proclamation, Stamp Act, Stone Age

69 ► Abbreviations

Capitalize abbreviations of titles and organizations.

M.D. (Doctor of Medicine)

A.I.M. (American Indian Movement)

70 ► Organizations

Capitalize the name of an organization, association, or a team and its members.

Girl Scouts of America, the Democratic Party, Chicago Bulls, Republicans

67 ► Capitalizing Geographic Names

Planets and heavenly bodies	**Earth, Jupiter, Milky Way**
Continents	**Europe, Asia, South America, Australia, Africa**
Countries	**Morocco, Haiti, Greece, Chile, United Arab Emirates**
States	**New Mexico, Alabama, West Virginia, Delaware, Iowa**
Provinces	**Alberta, British Columbia, Quebec, Ontario**
Cities and counties	**Montreal, Portland, Wayne County, Dade County**
Bodies of water	**Delaware and Hudson Bays, Chickamunga Lake, Saskatchewan River, Indian Ocean, Gulf of Mexico**
Landforms	**Appalachian Mountains, Bitterroot Range, Capitol Reef**
Public areas	**Vietnam Memorial, Sequoia National Forest**
Roads and highways	**New Jersey Turnpike, Interstate 80, Central Avenue, Adam's Apple Road**
Buildings	**Pentagon, Te Paske Theatre, Empire State Building**

CHECK IT OUT

71

Capitalize	Do Not Capitalize
January, March	winter, spring
Mother (as a name)	my mother (describing her)
President Clinton	Bill Clinton, our president
Mayor Hefty	Ms. Hefty, the mayor
Lake Ontario	the lake area
the South (section of the country)	south (a direction)
planet Earth	the earth we live on

72 ▶ Titles

Capitalize the first word of a title, the last word, and every word in between except articles (a, an, the), short prepositions, and short conjunctions.

▌ *Sports Illustrated for Kids* (magazine)

▌ *Itsy Bitsy Teeny Weeny Yellow Polka Dot Bikini* (song)

▌ *Beauty and the Beast* (movie)

▌ *It's Not the End of the World* (book)

Tip: Don't lowercase every short word in a title. Even though *Not* and *End* are short, they are not articles, prepositions, or conjunctions.

73 ▶ First Words

Capitalize the first word of every sentence.

▌ **The first basketball game is on Monday after school.**

Capitalize the first word of a direct quotation.

▌ **Jamir shouted, "Keep that ball moving."**

74 ▶ Days and Months

Capitalize the names of days of the week, months of the year, and special holidays.

▌ **Wednesday, March, Arbor Day, Easter, Passover, Kwanzaa**

Tip: Do not capitalize the seasons.

▌ **winter, spring, summer, fall**

75 ▶ Names of Religions, Nationalities, Languages

Capitalize the names of religions, nationalities, and languages.

▌ **Christian, Hindu** (religion)

▌ **Australian, Somali** (nationality)

▌ **English, Spanish** (language)

76 ▶ Official Names

Capitalize the names of businesses and the official names of their products.

▌ **Burger King, Post Sugar Crisps, Popsicle, Crest toothpaste**

Tip: Do not capitalize a general descriptive word like *toothpaste* when it follows the product name.

Plurals

77 The **plurals** of most nouns are formed by adding *s*.

balloon → balloons
shoe → shoes

Nouns Ending in sh, ch, x, s, and z

78 The plurals of nouns ending in *sh*, *ch*, *x*, *s*, and *z* are made by adding *es* to the singular.

brush → brushes
bunch → bunches, box → boxes,
dress → dresses, buzz → buzzes

Nouns Ending in o

79 The plurals of most words ending in *o* are formed by adding *s*.

patio → patios, rodeo → rodeos

The plurals of most nouns ending in *o* (with a consonant letter just before the *o*) are formed by adding *es*.

echo → echoes, hero → heroes

EXCEPT Musical terms and words of Spanish origin always form plurals by adding *s*; consult a dictionary for other words of this type.

piano → pianos, solo → solos,
taco → tacos, burrito → burritos

Nouns Ending in ful

80 The plurals of nouns that end with *ful* are formed by adding an *s* at the end of the word.

two cupfuls, five platefuls

Nouns Ending in f or fe

81 The plurals of nouns that end in *f* or *fe* are formed in one of two ways.

1. If the final *f* is still heard in the plural form of the word, simply add *s*.

goof → goofs, chief → chiefs
safe → safes, fife → fifes

2. If the final *f* has the sound of *v* in the plural form, change the *f* to *v* and add *es*.

calf → calves, loaf → loaves
wife → wives, knife → knives

Nouns Ending in y

82 The plurals of common nouns which end in *y* (with a consonant letter just before the *y*) are formed by changing the *y* to *i* and adding *es*.

sky → skies, bunny → bunnies

The plurals of nouns which end in *y* (with a vowel before the *y*) are formed by adding only *s*.

monkey → monkeys
donkey → donkeys

Compound Nouns

83 The plurals of compound nouns are usually formed by adding *s* or *es* to the important word in the compound.

sisters-in-law

maids of honor

secretaries of state

Irregular Nouns

84 Some nouns form a plural by taking on an irregular spelling.

child → children, goose → geese
mouse → mice

Numbers

85 **Numbers** from one to nine are usually written as words; all numbers 10 and over are usually written as numerals.

▮ **one three 10 115 2,000**

EXCEPT Numbers being compared should be kept in the same style.

▮ **Students from 8 to 11 years old are invited.**

86 ▶ **Very Large Numbers**
You may use a combination of numbers and words for very large numbers.

▮ **15 million, 1.2 million**

87 ▶ **Sentence Beginnings**
Use words, not numerals, to begin a sentence.

▮ **Fourteen new students joined the jazz band.**

88 ▶ **Numerals Only**
Use numerals for any numbers in the following forms:

money **$3.00**
decimal **25.5**
percentage ....**6 percent**
chapter ....**chapter 8**
page............................**pages 17-20**
address.............. **445 E. Acorn Dr.**
date .... **July 4**
time ....**1:30 p.m.**
statistic ....**a vote of 5 to 2**

Abbreviations

89 ▶ An **abbreviation** is the shortened form of a word or phrase. Most abbreviations begin with a capital letter and end with a period.

Tip: The following abbreviations are always acceptable in both formal and informal writing:

▮ **Mr. Mrs. Ms. Dr.**
  a.m. p.m. B.C. A.D. M.D.

In formal writing, do not abbreviate the names of states, countries, months, days, or units of measure.

90 ▶ **Acronyms**
An acronym is a word formed from the first letter or letters of words in a phrase. Acronyms do not end with a period.

▮ **MADD (M**others **A**gainst **D**runk **D**riving)

▮ **CARE (C**ooperative for **A**merican **R**elief **E**verywhere)

▮ **radar (ra**dio **d**etecting **a**nd **r**anging)

91 ▶ **Initialism**
An initialism is like an acronym except the initials which form this abbreviation are not pronounced as a word.

▮ **TV** (television)
▮ **CD** (**C**ompact **D**isc)
▮ **MIA** (**M**issing **I**n **A**ction)
▮ **CIA** (**C**entral **I**ntelligence **A**gency)

STATE ABBREVIATIONS

Alabama	Ala.	AL	Kentucky	Ky.	KY	North Dakota	N.D.	ND
Alaska	Alaska	AK	Louisiana	La.	LA	Ohio	Ohio	OH
Arizona	Ariz.	AZ	Maine	Maine	ME	Oklahoma	Okla.	OK
Arkansas	Ark.	AR	Maryland	Md.	MD	Oregon	Ore.	OR
California	Calif.	CA	Massachusetts	Mass.	MA	Pennsylvania	Pa.	PA
Colorado	Colo.	CO	Michigan	Mich.	MI	Rhode Island	R.I.	RI
Connecticut	Conn.	CT	Minnesota	Minn.	MN	South Carolina	S.C.	SC
Delaware	Del.	DE	Mississippi	Miss.	MS	South Dakota	S.D.	SD
District of			Missouri	Mo.	MO	Tennessee	Tenn.	TN
Columbia	D.C.	DC	Montana	Mont.	MT	Texas	Tex.	TX
Florida	Fla.	FL	Nebraska	Neb.	NE	Utah	Utah	UT
Georgia	Ga.	GA	Nevada	Nev.	NV	Vermont	Vt.	VT
Hawaii	Hawaii	HI	New			Virginia	Va.	VA
Idaho	Idaho	ID	Hampshire	N.H.	NH	Washington	Wash.	WA
Illinois	Ill.	IL	New Jersey	N.J.	NJ	West Virginia	W. Va.	WV
Indiana	Ind.	IN	New Mexico	N.M.	NM	Wisconsin	Wis.	WI
Iowa	Iowa	IA	New York	N.Y.	NY	Wyoming	Wyo.	WY
Kansas	Kan.	KS	North Carolina	N.C.	NC			

ADDRESS ABBREVIATIONS

Avenue	Ave.	AVE	Lake	L.	LK	Rural	R.	R
Boulevard	Blvd.	BLVD	Lane	Ln.	LN	South	S.	S
Court	Ct.	CT	North	N.	N	Square	Sq.	SQ
Drive	Dr.	DR	Park	Pk.	PK	Station	Sta.	STA
East	E.	E	Parkway	Pky.	PKY	Street	St.	ST.
Expressway	Expy.	EXPY	Place	Pl.	PL	Terrace	Ter.	TER
Heights	Hts.	HTS	Plaza	Plaza	PLZ	Turnpike	Tpke.	TPKE
Highway	Hwy.	HWY	Road	Rd.	RD	West	W.	W

COMMON ABBREVIATIONS

AC alternating current
a.m. ante meridiem
ASAP as soon as
  possible
C.O.D. cash on delivery
D.A. district attorney
DC direct current
etc. and so forth

FM frequency modulation
kg kilogram
km kilometer
kw kilowatt
lb pound
M.D. Doctor of Medicine
mpg miles per gallon

mph miles per hour
oz ounce
pd. paid
pg. page (or **p.**)
p.m. post meridiem
qt. quart
R.S.V.P. please reply
vs. versus

CHECKING YOUR SPELLING

1 You'll need to be patient. **Learning to become a good speller takes time.**

2 **Check your spelling** by using a dictionary or list of commonly misspelled words (like the list which follows).

3 **Check a dictionary for the correct pronunciation** of each word you are trying to spell. Knowing how to pronounce a word will help you remember how to spell it.

4 Also **look up the meaning** of each word. (Knowing how to spell a word is of little use if you don't know what it means.)

5 **Practice seeing the word in your mind's eye**. Look away from the dictionary page and write the word on a piece of paper. Check the spelling in the dictionary. Repeat this process until you can spell the word correctly.

6 **Make a spelling dictionary.** Include any words you misspell in a special notebook. (**SEE** page 271.)

Just as you must watch and practice to become a better basketball player, you must read and write to become a better speller.

A

	afraid	angel	arrival
	after	angle	article
about	against	animal	artificial
above	agreement	anniversary	athlete
absent	allowance	anonymous	athletic
accept	all right	another	attention
accident	almost	answer	attitude
accompany	alone	anybody	attractive
accurate	along	apartment	audience
ache	a lot	apologize	August
achieve	already	application	aunt
across	although	appreciate	author
actual	always	April	automobile
address	American	aren't	autumn
adventure	among	argument	avenue
advertisement	amount	arithmetic	awful
advise	ancient	around	awhile

B

baggage
balloon
banana
bargain
basement
beautiful
because
become
been
before
beginning
behind
believe
belong
between
bicycle
birthday
biscuit
blanket
blizzard
bought
breakfast
brilliant
brother
brought
bruise
buckle
building
built
burglar
business
busy
button
buy

C

cafeteria
calendar
called
campaign
candidate
canoe
canyon

captain
careful
careless
casserole
caterpillar
caught
celebration
cemetery
century
certain
certificate
change
character
chief
children
chimney
chocolate
choir
choose
Christmas
church
city
civilization
classmates
classroom
climate
closet
cocoa
cocoon
color
come
coming
committee
community
company
complete
concert
congratulate
cooperate
cough
could
couldn't
country
courage
courteous
courtesy

cousin
criticize
cupboard
curious
customer

D

dairy
dangerous
daughter
day
dear
December
decorate
definition
delicious
describe
desert
dessert
developed
didn't
different
difficulty
disappear
disastrous
discover
discussion
distance
divide
division
doctor
does
done
doubt

E

early
earth
Easter
easy
edge
either
electricity
elephant

emergency
encourage
enormous
enough
entertain
environment
every
everybody
exactly
excellent
exercise
exhausted
expensive
experience
explain
expression
eyes

F

face
familiar
family
famous
fashion
faucet
favorite
February
fierce
fifty
finally
first
football
foreign
forty
forward
found
fountain
fourth
fragile
Friday
friend
from
front
fuel
full

G

gadget
generally
generous
genius
gentle
geography
getting
goes
gone
government
grade
graduation
grammar
grateful
great
grocery
group
guarantee
guard
guardian
guess
gymnasium

H

half
handkerchief
handsome
happened
happiness
haven't
having
hazardous
heard
heavy
height
history
holiday
honor
horrible
hospital
hour
humorous
hundreds

I

icicle
immediately
immigrant
impatient
important
impossible
individual
innocent
instead
intelligent
interested
island

J

January
jewelry
journal
journey
judgment
juicy
July
June

K

kitchen
knew
knife
knives
know
knowledge

L

language
laughed
league
leave
length
lesson
letter
light
lightning

likely
listen
literature
little
loose
lovable

M

magazine
making
manufacture
many
March
marriage
material
mathematics
May
maybe
mayor
might
millions
minute
mirror
Monday
money
morning

mountain
music
musician
mysterious

N

natural
necessary
neighborhood
neither
never
nice
noisy
none
no one
nothing
November
nuclear
number

O

obey
occasion
o'clock
October

office
often
once
operate
opposite
other
outside
own

P

package
paragraph
parallel
party
pasture
patience
peace
people
picture
piece
place
played
pleasant
please
pleasure
point
poison
practice
prejudice
preparation
present
president
pretty
principal
privilege
problem
products
psychology
pumpkin

Q

quarter
quickly
quiet

quit
quite
quotient

R

raise
ready
really
reason
receive
recognize
remember
responsibilities
restaurant
right
rough
route

S

safety
said
salad
salary
sandwich
Santa Claus
Saturday
says
scared
scene
school
sentence
September
several
shoes
should
since
skiing
something
sometimes
soon
special
started
store
straight

studying
suddenly
sugar
summer
Sunday
suppose
sure
surprise
surround
swimming
system

T

table
teacher
tear
temperature
terrible
Thanksgiving
their
there
they're
though
thought
thousands
through
Thursday
tired
together
tomorrow
tonight
toys
traveling
trouble
truly
Tuesday
turn

U

unconscious
unfortunately
until
unusual
upon

use
usually

V

vacation
vacuum
vegetable
vehicle
very
violence
visitor
voice
volume

W

wasn't
weather
Wednesday
weight
weird
welcome
welfare
were
we're
what
when
where
which
while
whole
whose
women
world
wouldn't
write
writing
wrote

Y

yellow
young
your
you're

CHECK IT OUT

USING THE RIGHT WORD

You will want to use "the right words" whenever you write. This section will help you do just that. Begin by looking over the commonly misused words on the next eight pages. Then, whenever you have a question about which word is the *right* word, come back to this section for help. P.S. Remember to look for your word in a dictionary if you don't find it here.

a, an	I played **a** joke on my dad.
	    (***A*** *is used before words beginning with a consonant sound.*)
	I placed **an** ugly rubber fish under his pillow.
	    (***An*** *is used before words beginning with a vowel sound.*)

accept, except	Please ***accept*** (receive) my apology. Everyone else has ***except*** (other than) you.
affect, effect	Jorge's funny face ***affected*** the whole class. (***Affect*** *is always a verb meaning "to influence."*) The ***effect*** (result) was a class full of giggling students.
allowed, aloud	We are ***allowed*** (permitted) to read to partners in class. But we may not read ***aloud*** in the library. (***Aloud*** *is an adverb meaning "clearly heard."*)
a lot	***A lot*** of my friends like jeans with holes in them. (***A lot*** *is always two words.*)

I **already** finished all of my homework.
    (**Already** is an adverb telling when.)
Now I'm **all ready** to play some buckets.
    (**All ready** is a phrase meaning "completely ready.")
	already, all ready

An **ant** is an insect. An **aunt** is a close relative.	**ant, aunt**
I **ate** a bowl of popcorn. He had **eight** pieces of licorice.	**ate, eight**
She put her **bare** feet into the cool stream. She didn't see the **bear** fishing on the other side.	**bare, bear**
I **blew** on my frozen fingers. The tip of my index finger looked almost **blue**.	**blew, blue**
A **board** is a piece of wood. When Tom is **bored**, he pounds nails into boards.	**board, bored**
Pump the **brake** to slow down. Otherwise, you or your bike may **break**.	**brake, break**

Please **bring** me my glasses.
    (**Bring** means "moving toward the speaker.")
Take your dishes to the kitchen.
    (**Take** means "to carry off.")
	bring, take

Did a Frisbee just fly **by** my window? I better **buy** some new glasses.	**by, buy**

Can I go off the high dive?
    (I am asking if I have the "ability" to do it.)
May I go off the high dive?
    (I am asking for "permission" to do something.)
	can, may

The **capital** city of Texas is Austin.
Be sure to begin Austin with a **capital** letter.
My uncle works in the **capitol** building.
    (**Capitol**, with an "ol," is used when talking
    about a building.)
	capital, capitol

Each flower costs 25 **cents**. The **scent** (smell) of the flowers was sweet. He **sent** her 75 **cents** worth of scented flowers.	**cent, scent, sent**

Ben **chose** to take drum lessons last year.
He will **choose** a different instrument this year.
    (**Chose** [chōz] is the past tense of the verb
    choose [chooz].)
	chose, choose

close, clothes	*Close* the window. Then put the *clothes* in the dryer.
coarse, course	A cat's tongue feels *coarse* to the touch. I took a *course* called "Caring for Cats."
creak, creek	Old houses *creak* when the wind blows through them. The water in the nearby *creek* is clear and cold.
dear, deer	Bambi is my *dear* friend. The *deer* enjoyed the corn in our garden.
desert, dessert	A cactus grows in the *desert* near our house. My favorite *dessert* is cactus pie.
dew, do, due	The *dew* on the grass was cool on my feet. I *do* my homework right after school. The report is *due* on Wednesday.
die, dye	The plant will *die* if it isn't watered. The red *dye* in the sweatshirt turned everything in the wash pink.
doesn't, don't	Mom *doesn't* dance. (*doesn't* = does not) I *don't* either. (*don't* = do not)
eye, I	For the play, Sam wore a patch over his left *eye*. *I* have a patch on my jeans.

fewer, less	There are *fewer* drums than drummers in the
	    school band.
	    (*Fewer* refers to something you can count.)
	So I get *less* and *less* time to practice.
	    (*Less* refers to something you can not count.)

find, fined	Did you *find* your book? Yes, but the librarian *fined* me because it was overdue.
fir, fur	*Fir* trees are evergreen trees. Would you ever wear a *fur* coat?
for, four	You can eat the caramel corn *for* a snack. The *four* of you can also share the chips.

good, well	Rosie looks *good* in that outfit.
	    (**Good** is an adjective describing Rosie.)
	It fits her *well*.
	    (**Well** is an adverb modifying "fits.")

A *hare* looks like a large rabbit. My *hair* looks like a wet rabbit.	**hare, hair**
It takes a long time for a blister to *heal*. Jose has a blister on his *heel*.	**heal, heel**
How could I *hear* you? I was over *here*, and you were over there.	**hear, here**
We *heard* the noise, all right! It sounded like a *herd* of charging elephants.	**heard, herd**
An *heir* is a person who inherits something. *Air* is what we breathe.	**heir, air**
Say *hi* to the pilot for me. How *high* is this plane flying?	**hi, high**
A donut has a *hole* in the middle of it. Michael ate a *whole* donut.	**hole, whole**
It takes one *hour* to get to school by bus. *Our* school has very slow buses.	**hour, our**
Our bus needs *its* heater repaired. *It's* not only cold but noisy. (*It's* is the contraction of "it is.")	**its, it's**
I finally *knew* everyone's name. Then two *new* kids were added to our class.	**knew, new**
The *knight* guarded the tower gates. Thursday is the knight's *night* off.	**knight, night**
I have a *knot* in my shoelaces. I am *not* able to get it untied.	**knot, not**
Do you *know* how to turn on the computer? *No*, we'll have to ask Robert.	**know, no**
Robert *knows* all about computers. His *nose* is always in a computer manual.	**knows, nose**
Please *lay* the sleeping bag on the floor. (*Lay* means "to place.") I must *lie* down for a while. (*Lie* means "to recline.")	**lay, lie**
Pencils have a small strip of *lead* in them. I have to *lead* my dog around the show ring. The drill team *led* the parade.	**lead, led**

CHECK IT OUT

learn, teach	I don't want to **learn** another fact about the moon. 　　(**Learn** *means "to get information."*) I know so much I could **teach** the class myself. 　　(**Teach** *means "to give information."*)
loose, lose	Joe's pet tarantula is **loose**! 　　(**Loose** *[loos] means "free or untied."*) No one but Joe could **lose** a big, fat spider. 　　(**Lose** *[looz] means to "misplace or fail to win."*)
made, maid	Yes, I have **made** a big mess. I need a **maid** to help me clean it up.
mail, male	Some people receive **mail** on their computers. Men are **male**; women are female.
main, Maine, mane	She does many things, but her **main** job is writing. The state of **Maine** has a rugged coastline. The hair on a horse's neck is called a **mane**.
meat, meet	I like **meat** and potatoes for breakfast. I'll **meet** you at the table.
metal, medal	Gold is a precious **metal**. So is the **medal** I won for finishing first.
miner, minor	Some coal **miners** suffer from black lung disease. **Minors** are individuals who are not legally adults.
oar, or, ore	You use an **oar** to row a boat. Kim **or** Rosa will do the rowing. Iron **ore** is a mineral containing metal.
one, won	He has **one** hot bike! He **won** it by guessing the number of beans in a jar.
pain, pane	A bee sting usually causes **pain**. A broken window **pane** can, too.

A *pair* (two) of pigeons roosted on our windowsill. To *pare* an apple means to peel it. A *pear* is a sweet, juicy fruit.	pair, pare, pear
The school bus *passed* a stalled truck. In the *past*, most children walked to school.	passed, past
Ms. Brown likes *peace* and quiet in her room. I like a *piece* of cake in my lunch.	peace, piece
Toni wanted a *plain* (basic) white dress. The coyote ran across the flat *plain*. A stunt *plane* can fly upside down.	plain, plane
A *pore* is an opening in the skin. Please *pour* me another glass of Gatorade. That store has a *poor* choice of books.	pore, pour, poor

My *principal* is a strong leader.
   (*Principal* as a noun is a school administrator;
   as an adjective, it means "most important.")
She asks students to follow this *principle*:
    Respect each other, and I'll respect you.
   (*Principle* means "idea" or "belief.")
	principal,
	principle

Libraries are supposed to be *quiet* places. *Quit* talking, or we will get in trouble. There is *quite* a bit of whispering going on.	quiet, quit, quite
The *rain* made the field very muddy. Deb will *reign* (rule) as queen of the fair. Pull the *reins* to stop the horse.	rain, reign, rein
Please don't *raise* (lift) the shades. The sun's *rays* are very bright this afternoon. To *raze* means "to tear something down."	raise, rays, raze
Have you *read* any books by Betsy Byars? Why do we always have *red* Jell-O?	read, red
Is this the *right* place to turn right? I'll *write* you a letter and let you know.	right, write
My house is one block from the main *road*. I *rode* my bike to the pond. Then I *rowed* the boat to my favorite fishing spot and threw in a line.	road, rode, rowed
The movie has a great chase *scene*. Have you *seen* it yet?	scene, seen

CHECK IT OUT

sea, see	A *sea* is a body of salty water. It's difficult to *see* any salt, though.
seam, seem	The *seam* in my jacket is ripped. I *seem* to remember catching it on the door handle.
sew, so, sow	Will you please *sew* my ripped jacket? I have time, *so* I will do it for you now. Good. Then I can go *sow* seeds in the garden.
sit, set	Can I *sit* in one of those folding chairs? Yes, if you help me *set* them up first.
some, sum	I have *some* math problems to do. What is the *sum* of 58 + 17?
son, sun	Joe Jackson is the *son* of Kate Jackson. The *sun* is the source of the earth's energy.
sore, soar	His feet were so *sore* he could hardly walk. His hopes *soared* when he heard a car coming.
stationery, stationary	I use my best *stationery* (paper) when I write to my pen pal. A *stationary* bike stays in place while you pedal it.
steal, steel	You can *steal* third base, but don't take it home! Many knives are made of *steel*.
tail, tale	A snake uses its *tail* to move its body. "Sammy the Spotted Snake" is my favorite tall *tale*.

than, then	Your dog is bigger *than* my dog.
	    (*Than* is used in a comparison.)
	Then my dog immediately ran the other way.
	    (*Then* tells when.)

their, there, they're	What should we do with *their* tickets? (*Their* shows ownership.) Put them over *there* for now. *They're* going to the game later. (*they're* = they are)

He **threw** the ball at the basket. It swished **through** the net.	**threw, through**
Josie threw the ball **to** Maria. Lea is **too** tired to guard her. (**Too** means "also" or "very.") Maria easily scored **two** points.	**to, too, two**

My little sister's **waist** is as small as one of my legs.
You look like you are going to **waste** away.
   (The verb *waste* means "to shrink"; the noun
   waste refers to useless material.)
	waist, waste

I can't **wait** for the field trip. My brother lifts **weights** to get strong.	**wait, weight**
There are many different **ways** to lose weight. I **weigh** more than he does.	**way, weigh**
How long have you had a **weak** back? I've had a weak back for about a **week**.	**weak, week**
The crossing guards **wear** yellow ponchos. **Where** do you think they got them?	**wear, where**
I like rainy **weather**. My dad goes golfing **whether** it's nice out or not.	**weather, whether**
Which book should I read? You'll like *The Lion, the **Witch**, and the Wardrobe*.	**which, witch**
The man **who** answered the door was my dad. The movie, **which** was very funny, ended too soon. The puppy **that** I really wanted was sold already.	**who, which, that**
Who ordered this pizza? The pizza was ordered by **whom**?	**who, whom**

Who's that knocking at the door?
   (**Who's** is the contraction for "who is.")
Whose door are you talking about?
   (**Whose** shows ownership.)
	who's, whose

Baseball bats are made of **wood**. **Would** you like to play baseball after school?	**wood, would**

You're talking to the right person!
   (**You're** is the contraction for "you are.")
You can pick up **your** pizzas after school.
   (**Your** shows ownership.)
	you're, your

Sentence Sense . . .

This section of your handbook covers all the basic information you need to understand and use sentences correctly.

Here's what you'll find inside:

Parts of a Sentence 371

Subject
Predicate
Modifier
Phrases
Clauses

Types of Sentences 373

Simple
Compound
Complex

Kinds of Sentences 373

Declarative
Interrogative
Imperative
Exclamatory

UNDERSTANDING SENTENCES

5 *Things You Should Know!*

1. A sentence is made up of one or more words which express a complete thought.

2. A sentence has two basic parts—a subject and a predicate (verb).

3. A sentence makes a statement, asks a question, gives a command, or shows strong emotion.

4. A sentence begins with a capital letter and ends with a period, a question mark, or an exclamation point.

5. More information on sentences is included on pages 50-53 and 85-89.

Parts of a Sentence

SUBJECT

Simple Subject

A **subject** is the part of a sentence which is doing something.

*Maria **baked a chocolate cake.***

A subject can also be the word that is talked about.

My** friend **is a marvelous cook.

Complete Subject

The **complete subject** is the simple subject and all the words which describe it.

***My best friend** baked a chocolate cake.*

(*My best friend* is the complete subject.)

Compound Subject

A **compound subject** is made up of two or more simple subjects.

*Maria **and her** sister **also baked some blue- berry muffins.***

PREDICATE

Simple Predicate

A **predicate** (verb) is the part of the sentence which says something about the subject.

*Maria **baked** the cake for my birthday.*

(*Baked* tells what the subject did.)

Complete Predicate

The **complete predicate** is the simple predicate with all the words which describe it.

*Maria **baked the cake yesterday.***

(The complete predicate is *baked the cake yesterday*.)

*My friend Maria **is a marvelous cook.***

(The complete predicate is *is a marvelous cook*.)

Compound Predicate

A **compound predicate** is made up of two or more simple predicates.

*Maria **frosted** and **decorated** the cake.*

MODIFIER

A Modifier

A **modifier** is a word or group of words which add details to the sentence. Modifiers are either adjectives or adverbs.

CLAUSES

A Clause	A clause is a group of related words that has both a subject and a predicate. *We ride **our bikes to school.*** (*We* is the subject and *ride* is the predicate in this clause.) ***when** the **weather is** nice* (*Weather* is the subject and *is* is the predicate in this clause.)
Independent	An independent clause expresses a complete thought and can stand alone as a sentence. *We ride our bikes to school.*
Dependent	A dependent clause does *not* express a complete thought and cannot stand alone as a sentence. *when the weather is nice* **NOTE:** A *dependent clause* can be combined with an **independent clause** to form a complex sentence. (See page 373 for more information.) *We ride our bikes to school when the weather is nice.*

PHRASES

A Phrase	A phrase is a group of related words that does not have a subject, or a predicate, or both. Phrases do not make a complete thought, so they are not sentences. *the fifth graders* (This is a noun phrase.) *wrote their reports* (This is a verb phrase.) *about George Washington* (This is a prepositional phrase. See page 386.) **NOTE:** If you put these three phrases together, they would form a complete sentence. *The fifth graders wrote their reports about George Washington.*
Kinds of Phrases	Phrases are named by how they are used in a sentence. **Noun:** *The fifth graders* **Verb:** *wrote their reports* **Prepositional:** *about George Washington*

TYPES OF SENTENCES

Simple

A simple sentence has just one independent clause (one complete thought). It may, however, have a compound subject or compound predicate, and even a phrase or two.

My knees ache. (A basic simple sentence)

My face and neck look red and feel hot. (This simple sentence has a *compound subject* and a *compound predicate*.)

I just skated for two hours. (This simple sentence includes a *prepositional phrase*.)

Compound

A compound sentence is made up of two or more simple sentences joined by a comma and a connecting word (*and, but, or, for, so, yet*), or by a semicolon.

I've skated in Los Angeles, but I have only seen a picture of New York.

Los Angeles is 30 miles from my home; New York is 3,000 miles away.

Complex

A complex sentence contains one **independent** clause and one or more *dependent* clauses.

Because it was raining, the race was called off.

KINDS OF SENTENCES

Declarative

Declarative sentences make statements.

The capital of Florida is Tallahassee.

Interrogative

Interrogative sentences ask questions.

Did you know that Florida's major industry is tourism?

Imperative

Imperative sentences give commands.

You must never swim alone.

NOTE: Imperative sentences sometimes use an understood subject [*you*].

Never swim alone. Stay here.

Exclamatory

Exclamatory sentences show emotion or surprise.

I just saw a dolphin!

The Parts of Speech

All the words in our language have been divided into eight groups. These word groups are called the *parts of speech*.

Each part of speech includes words that are used in the same way in a sentence. With this information in hand (**or in eight hands**), you should be ready to learn more about the words in our language.

UNDERSTANDING OUR LANGUAGE

8 *Things You Should Know!*

1. **Nouns** name a person, place, thing, or idea. (*Bill, billboard*)
2. **Pronouns** are used in place of nouns. (*I, me, you*)
3. **Verbs** express action or state of being. (*is, are, run, jump*)
4. **Adjectives** describe a noun or pronoun. (*tall, quiet, neat*)
5. **Adverbs** tell something about a verb, an adjective, or another adverb. (*gently, easily, fast*)
6. **Prepositions** show how a noun is related to some other word in the sentence. (*on, near, over*)
7. **Interjections** show emotion or surprise. (*Wow, Oh, Yikes!*)
8. **Conjunctions** connect words or groups of words. (*and, or, because*)

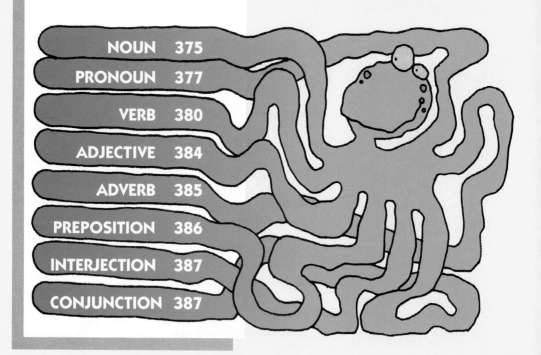

NOUN 375

PRONOUN 377

VERB 380

ADJECTIVE 384

ADVERB 385

PREPOSITION 386

INTERJECTION 387

CONJUNCTION 387

Noun

A **noun** is a word which names a person, place, thing, or idea.

Person	Maria, friend, Josh, parent
Place	home, Miami, city, backyard
Thing	baseball, homework, secret
Idea	happiness, trouble, friendship

KINDS OF NOUNS

Common and Proper Nouns

A **common noun** is the *general* name of a person, place, thing, or idea. (Common nouns are not capitalized.)
A **proper noun** is the *specific* name of a person, place, thing, or idea. (Proper nouns are always capitalized.)

Common Nouns	Proper Nouns
woman	Hillary Clinton
fort	the Alamo
mountains	the Rocky Mountains
team	the Boston Red Sox
park	Disneyland

Concrete and Abstract Nouns

Concrete nouns name things that *can* be touched or seen. **Abstract nouns** name things that *cannot* be touched or seen.

Concrete	magazine, cactus, Toyota
Abstract	love, happiness, democracy

Singular and Plural Nouns

A **singular noun** names one person, place, thing, or idea. A **plural noun** names more than one person, place, thing, or idea.

Singular	note, paper, pen pal, hope
Plural	notes, papers, pen pals, hopes

USES OF NOUNS

Subject Nouns	A **subject noun** is a noun that does something or is being talked about. ***Josh told Maria the secret.*** (The noun *Josh* did something: *told the secret.*)
Predicate Nouns	A **predicate noun** is a noun that renames the subject. It is linked to the subject by a linking verb. ***The note is a secret.*** (The noun *secret* renames the subject *note*; it is another name for the subject. *Secret* is linked to *note* by the verb *is.*)
Possessive Nouns	A **possessive noun** is a noun used to show possession or ownership. ***Josh told Maria the secret in Gloria's note.*** (The *'s* added to *Gloria* shows that the note belongs to her.)

NOUNS AS OBJECTS

Direct Objects	A noun is a **direct object** when it receives the action of the verb. ***Josh told the secret.*** (*Secret* is a direct object because it receives the action of the verb.)
Indirect Objects	A noun is an **indirect object** when it names the person to or for whom something is done. ***Josh told Maria the secret.*** (*Maria* is an indirect object because something has been done to her.)
Objects of a Preposition	A noun is an **object of a preposition** when it is part of a prepositional phrase. (See page 386.) ***Josh told Maria the secret in Gloria's note.*** (The noun *note* is the object of the preposition *in.*)

Pronoun

A pronoun is a word used in place of a noun.

Carlotta dropped her lunch tray.

She dropped her lunch tray. (*She* is a pronoun that replaces the noun *Carlotta*.)

NOTE: The most common pronouns are called personal pronouns. All of the personal pronouns are discussed and listed on this page.

USES OF PERSONAL PRONOUNS

Subject Pronouns

A subject pronoun is used as the subject of a sentence.

I can never remember jokes. (singular)

They really make people laugh. (plural)

Singular	I, you, he, she, it
Plural	we, you, they

Object Pronouns

An object pronoun is used after an action verb or in a prepositional phrase.

Mr. Otto teases me. (*Me* comes after the action verb *teases*.)

My friends made a funny card for him. (*Him* is the object in the prepositional phrase *for him*.)

Singular	me, you, him, her, it
Plural	us, you, them

Possessive Pronouns

A possessive pronoun shows ownership.

Jackie finished writing her story. (*Her* comes before the noun *story*.)

The idea for it was mine. (*Mine* can stand alone.)

Before a noun
my, your, his, her, its, our, their

Stand alone
mine, yours, his, hers, its, ours, theirs

Agreement of Pronouns

The pronouns in your sentences must *agree* with the words they replace.

> *Jack's skateboard works great now that it is oiled.* (The pronoun *it* and the word it replaces, *skateboard*, are both singular, so they agree.)

> *The other kids' boards look like they could use some oil, too.* (The pronoun *they* and the word it replaces, *boards*, are both plural, so they agree.)

An antecedent is the name for the noun that a pronoun replaces.

> *Jack practices whenever he can.* (*Jack* is the antecedent of the pronoun *he*.)

PERSON OF A PRONOUN

The *person* of a pronoun tells us whether the pronoun is speaking, listening, or being spoken about.

First-Person Pronoun

A first-person pronoun is used in place of a speaker.

> *I like blue-moon ice cream.* (*I* replaces the speaker's name.)

> *We like ice cream in waffle cones.* (*We* replaces the names of two or more speakers.)

Second-Person Pronoun

A second-person pronoun is used in place of a person (or thing) spoken to.

> *Todd, have you decided on a flavor?* (*You* replaces the name *Todd*, the person being spoken to.)

> *You guys do not need triple-dip cones.* (*You* replaces *guys*, the people being spoken to.)

Third-Person Pronoun

A third-person pronoun is used in place of the person (or thing) being spoken about.

> *Jonathan said that he was ordering pumpkin ice cream.* (*He* replaces *Jonathan*, the person being spoken about.)

> *The four guys said they needed some water.* (*They* replaces *guys*, the people being spoken about.)

TYPES OF PRONOUNS

Personal	A personal pronoun is the most common type of pronoun. (See a complete list on page 377.)
Relative	A relative pronoun connects one part of a sentence with a word in another part of the sentence.
	Any fifth grader who wants to join our music group should see Carlos.
	who, whose, which, what, that, whoever, whatever, whichever
Demonstrative	A demonstrative pronoun points out or identifies a noun without naming it.
	That sounds like a great idea!
	this, that, these, those
Interrogative	An interrogative pronoun asks a question.
	Who is going to play the keyboard?
	who, whose, whom, which, what
Intensive and Reflexive	An intensive pronoun stresses the word it refers to. A reflexive pronoun refers back to the subject.
	Carlos himself taught the group a new song. (intensive)
	The performers admired themselves in the mirror. (reflexive)
	myself, himself, herself, yourself, itself, themselves, ourselves
Indefinite	An indefinite pronoun does not name the word it replaces.
	Somebody needs to videotape the practice.
	all, another, any, anybody, anyone, anything, both, each, either, everybody, everyone, everything, few, many, most, much, neither, nobody, none, no one, nothing, one, other, several, some, somebody, someone, something

Verb

A **verb** shows action or links the subject to another word in the sentence. The verb is the main word in the predicate part of the sentence. (See page 371 for more about the predicate.)

> *The boys fight often.* (The verb shows action.)
>
> *I am sad about that.* (The verb links two words.)

TYPES OF VERBS

Action Verbs

An **action verb** tells what the subject is doing. Action verbs make writing clear and specific.

> *I watched the entire game.*
>
> *Janet left after the third quarter.*

Linking Verbs

A **linking verb** links a subject to a noun or an adjective in the predicate part of the sentence.

> *That car is a Dodge Neon.* (The verb *is* links the noun *Dodge Neon* to the subject *car*.)
>
> *A Dodge Neon looks funny.* (The verb *looks* links the adjective *funny* to the subject *Dodge Neon*.)

"Be" Verbs
is, are, was, were, am, been

Other Linking Verbs
smell, look, taste, remain, feel, appear, sound, seem, become, grow, stand, turn

Helping Verbs

Helping verbs come before the main verb, and they help state an action or show time.

> *Lee will write in his journal.* (The verb *will* helps state a future action, *will write*.)
>
> *Lee has been writing in his journal.* (The verbs *has been* help state a continuing action, *has been writing*.)

Helping Verbs
is, are, was, were, am, been, shall, will, could, would, should, must, can, may, might, have, had, has, do, did

FORMS OF VERBS

Singular and Plural Verbs

A singular verb must be used when the subject in a sentence is singular.

Ben** likes **peanut butter and olive sandwiches. (The subject *Ben* and the verb *likes* are both singular.)

A plural verb must be used when the subject is plural.

Black olives** taste **like wax. (The subject *olives* and the verb *taste* are both plural.)

NOTE: When a subject and verb are both singular or plural, they agree in number. (See page 88.)

Active and Passive Voice

A verb is active if the subject is doing the action in the sentence.

Gus** threw **a rotten tomato. (*Threw* is active because the subject *Gus* is doing the action.)

A verb is passive if the subject does not do the action.

A rotten tomato** was thrown **by Gus. (*Was thrown* is passive because the subject *tomato* is not doing the action.)

Regular Verbs

Most verbs in our language are regular. You add *ed* to regular verbs to state a past action or when you use a helping verb (*has, have, had*).

> **Regular Verbs**
> I play.   Earlier I played.   I have played.
> He walks. Earlier he walked. He has walked.

Irregular Verbs

Some verbs in our language are irregular. An irregular verb does not end in *ed* when you state a past action or when you use a helping verb. For most irregular verbs, the word changes.

> **Irregular Verbs**
> I ride.   Earlier I rode.   I have ridden.
> She eats. Earlier she ate.   She has eaten.

NOTE: The chart on the next page lists the common irregular verbs in our language.

Common Irregular Verbs

The **principal parts** of the common irregular verbs are listed below. The part used with the helping verbs *has, have,* or *had* is called the **past participle**.

REMEMBER: With most irregular verbs, the word changes when you state an action in the past or when you use a helping verb.

Present Tense	Past Tense	Past Participle
I hide.	Earlier I hid.	I have hidden.

Principal Parts of Irregular Verbs

Present Tense	Past Tense	Past Participle	Present Tense	Past Tense	Past Participle
am, be	was, were	been	lie (recline)	lay	lain
begin	began	begun	ride	rode	ridden
bite	bit	bitten	ring	rang	rung
blow	blew	blown	rise	rose	risen
break	broke	broken	run	ran	run
bring	brought	brought	see	saw	seen
burst	burst	burst	set	set	set
catch	caught	caught	shake	shook	shaken
come	came	come	shine (light)	shone	shone
dive	dove, dived	dived	shrink	shrank	shrunk
do	did	done	sing	sang, sung	sung
draw	drew	drawn	sink	sank, sunk	sunk
drink	drank	drunk	sit	sat	sat
drive	drove	driven	speak	spoke	spoken
eat	ate	eaten	spring	sprang, sprung	sprung
fall	fell	fallen	steal	stole	stolen
fight	fought	fought	swear	swore	sworn
fly	flew	flown	swim	swam	swum
freeze	froze	frozen	swing	swung	swung
give	gave	given	take	took	taken
go	went	gone	tear	tore	torn
grow	grew	grown	throw	threw	thrown
hang	hung	hung	wake	woke, waked	waked
hide	hid	hidden, hid	wear	wore	worn
know	knew	known	weave	wove	woven
lay (place)	laid	laid	write	wrote	written
lead	led	led			

THE TENSE OF A VERB

Tense	We call the time of a verb its tense. Tense is shown by endings (*talked*), by helping verbs (*will talk*), or by both (*have talked*). There are three common tenses: present, past, and future. There are also three special tenses: present perfect, past perfect, and future perfect.
Present Tense	The present tense of a verb states an action that is happening now, or that happens regularly. *I like soccer.* *We practice every day.*
Past Tense	The past tense of a verb states an action that happened at a specific time in the past. *She liked soccer.* *Beth was the goalie.*
Future Tense	The future tense of a verb states an action that will take place. The future tense is made by using the helping verbs *will* or *shall* before the main verb. *I will like soccer even better next year.* *We shall practice every day.*

SPECIAL TENSES

Present Perfect Tense	The present perfect tense of a verb states an action that is still going on. It is formed by using *has* or *have* before the main verb. *Roy has slept for two hours.*
Past Perfect Tense	The past perfect tense of a verb states an action that began and was completed in the past. It is formed by using *had* before the main verb. *Roxanne had slept for eight hours.*
Future Perfect Tense	The future perfect tense of a verb states an action that will begin in the future and end at a specific time in the future. It is formed by adding *will have* or *shall have* before the main verb. *Riley will have slept for 12 hours.*

Adjective

	An adjective is a word that describes a noun or pronoun.
	Male peacocks have beautiful feathers.
	The feathers are colorful. (An adjective after a linking verb is called a *predicate adjective*.)
Articles	The articles *a, an,* and *the* are adjectives.
	Owlet is the name for a baby owl.

FORMS OF ADJECTIVES

Positive	The positive form of an adjective describes a noun without comparing it to anyone or anything else.
	A hummingbird is small.
Comparative	The comparative form of an adjective compares two people, places, things, or ideas.
	A hummingbird is smaller than a sparrow. (The ending *er* is added to one-syllable adjectives.)
	A hummingbird is more graceful than a pelican. (*More* is added before most adjectives with two or more syllables.)
Superlative	The superlative form of an adjective compares three or more people, places, things, or ideas.
	A hummingbird is the smallest bird I've seen. (The ending *est* is added to one-syllable adjectives.)
	A swan is the most graceful bird in the zoo. (*Most* is added before most adjectives with two or more syllables.)
Special Forms	The adjectives listed in this chart use different words to make comparisons:

Positive	Comparative	Superlative
good	better	best
bad	worse	worst
many	more	most

Adverb

An adverb is a word that describes a verb, an adjective, or another adverb. Most adverbs tell **where**, **how**, or **when**.

> *The first pitch curved inside.* (tells *where*)
>
> *Roberto hit the next pitch hard.* (tells *how*)
>
> *Roberto ran immediately.* (tells *when*)

NOTE: Adverbs often end in *-ly*, but not always. Words like *not, never, very,* and *always* are common adverbs.

FORMS OF ADVERBS

Positive

In the positive form, an adverb does not make a comparison.

> *Roberto plays hard from the first pitch to the last out.*

Comparative

The comparative is formed by adding *er* to one-syllable adverbs or the word *more* or *less* before longer adverbs.

> *He plays harder than his cousin.*
>
> *He plays more often than his cousin.*

Superlative

The superlative is formed by adding *est* to one-syllable adverbs or the word *most* or *least* before longer adverbs.

> *Roberto plays hardest in close games.*
>
> *Roberto plays most often in center field.*

Special Forms

The adverbs below use different words to make comparisons:

Positive	Comparative	Superlative
well	better	best
badly	worse	worst

NOTE: Do not confuse *good* and *well*. *Good* is an adjective and *well* is usually an adverb.

> *He has a good swing.*
>
> *He runs bases well, too.*

Preposition

	A **preposition** is a word that relates a noun or pronoun to another word in the sentence. *One cat rested on the desk top.* *Another cat watched from a desk drawer.*
Object of the Preposition	The **object of the preposition** is the noun or pronoun that comes after the preposition. *One other cat lay under the desk.* (*Desk* is the object of the preposition *under*.)
Prepositional Phrase	A **prepositional phrase** includes a preposition, the object of the preposition, and any describing words that come in between. *A fourth cat sat beside the old oak desk.*

COMMON PREPOSITIONS

about	for	on	past	under
above	from	on top of	since	underneath
across	in	onto	through	until
after	in front of	out of	to	up
against	inside	outside	toward	upon
along	instead of	over		with
among	into			within
around	like			without
at	near			
before	of			
behind	off			
below				
beneath				
beside				
between				
by				
down				
during				
except				

Interjection

An **interjection** is a word or phrase used to express strong emotion or surprise. A comma or an exclamation point is used to separate an interjection from the rest of the sentence.

*Wow, **look at those mountains!***

*Hey! **Keep your eyes on the road!***

Conjunction

A **conjunction** connects individual words or groups of words.

*The river is wide **and** deep.*

*We can fish in the morning **or** in the evening.*

KINDS OF CONJUNCTIONS

Coordinate

A **coordinate conjunction** connects equal parts: two or more words, two or more phrases, and so on.

*The river winds down the valley **and** through the prairies.* (The conjunction *and* connects two prepositional phrases.)

> and, but, or, nor, for, so, yet

Correlative

A **correlative conjunction** is used in pairs.

*Either **snow** or **wind may delay the trip.*** (*Either* and *or* work as a pair in this sentence.)

> either, or; neither, nor; both, and; just, as

Subordinate

A **subordinate conjunction** connects two clauses to make a complex sentence.

*Our trip was delayed **when** the snowstorm hit.*

*We stayed in town **until** the snow stopped.*

> after, although, as if, because, before, if, in order that, since, so, that, though, unless, until, when, where, while

The Student Almanac

The Student Almanac

Useful Tables and Lists

Using Maps

Improving Math Skills

History in the Making

Useful Tables and Lists

The tables and lists in this section of your handbook should be both interesting and helpful. You can look through this section when you have "nothing better to do," when you need to find information to complete an assignment, or when you need to send a "signed" message across a noisy room.

SIGN LANGUAGE

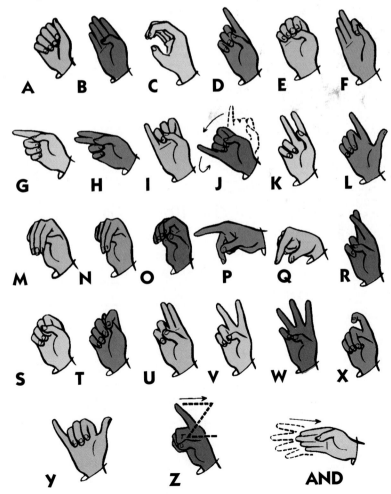

Foreign Words

There are more than 220 languages (spoken by at least a million people each) in the world today. And there are hundreds of dialects, or versions, of those languages! No wonder people sometimes have trouble communicating, especially when they travel. Here are some foreign words that may help you bridge the "communication gap."

LANGUAGE	HELLO OR GOOD DAY	GOOD-BYE
Chinese (Mandarin dialect)	dzău	dzàijyàn
Danish	hallo	farvel
French	bonjour	au revoir
German	Guten Tag	Auf Wiedersehen
Hawaiian	aloha	aloha
Hebrew	shalom	shalom
Italian	buon giorno	addio
Farsi (Iran)	salaam سلام	khoda hafez خدا حافظ
Polish	hallo	żegnam
Portuguese	alô	adeus
Russian pronunciation	Здравствуйте ZDRAHST-vooy-tyeh	до свидания daw svee-DA-nee-ya
Swahili	neno la kusalimu rafiki au mtani	kwa heri
Tagalog (Philippines)	kumusta	paalám
Spanish	holá	adiós
Swedish	god dag	adjö
Thai	sa wat dee ka	la kone na ka

THINK IT OVER You will see that several words for saying "hello" look or sound alike. The same thing is true for the "good-bye" words. Many languages of today began as the same language thousands of years ago. That's why there are so many similar words.

Animal Facts

Animal	Male	Female	Young	Group	Gestation (days)	Longevity (years)
Bear	He-bear	She-bear	Cub	Sleuth	180-240	18-20 (34)*
Cat	Tom	Queen	Kitten	Clutter/Clowder	52-65	10-17 (30)
Cattle	Bull	Cow	Calf	Drove/Herd	280	9-12 (25)
Chicken	Rooster	Hen	Chick	Brood/Flock	21	7-8 (14)
Deer	Buck	Doe	Fawn	Herd	180-250	10-15 (26)
Dog	Dog	Bitch	Pup	Pack/Kennel	55-70	10-12 (24)
Donkey	Jack	Jenny	Foal	Herd/Pace	340-385	18-20 (63)
Duck	Drake	Duck	Duckling	Brace/Herd	21-35	10 (15)
Elephant	Bull	Cow	Calf	Herd	515-760	30-60 (98)
Fox	Dog	Vixen	Cub/Kit	Skulk	51-60	8-10 (14)
Goat	Billy	Nanny	Kid	Tribe/Herd	135-163	12 (17)
Goose	Gander	Goose	Gosling	Flock/Gaggle	30	25-30
Horse	Stallion	Mare	Filly/Colt	Herd	304-419	20-30 (50+)
Lion	Lion	Lioness	Cub	Pride	105-111	10 (29)
Monkey	Male	Female	Boy/Girl	Band/Troop	149-179	12-15 (29)
Rabbit	Buck	Doe	Bunny	Nest/Warren	27-36	6-8 (15)
Sheep	Ram	Ewe	Lamb	Flock/Drove	121-180	10-15 (16)
Swan	Cob	Pen	Cygnet	Bevy/Flock	30	45-50
Swine	Boar	Sow	Piglet	Litter/Herd	101-130	10 (15)
Tiger	Tiger	Tigress	Cub		105	19
Whale	Bull	Cow	Calf	Gam/Pod/Herd	276-365	37
Wolf	Dog	Bitch	Pup	Pack	63	10-12 (16)

* ( ) Record for oldest animal of this type

THE METRIC SYSTEM

Even though the metric system is not the official system of measurement in the United States, it is used in science, medicine, and some other fields.

The metric system is a simple form of measurement. It is based on the decimal system (units of ten), so there are no fractions. The table below lists the basic measurements in the metric system.

Linear Measure

1 centimeter	= 10 millimeters	=	0.3937 inch
1 decimeter	= 10 centimeters	=	3.937 inches
1 meter	= 10 decimeters	=	39.37 inches or 3.28 feet
1 dekameter	= 10 meters	=	393.7 inches
1 kilometer	= 1,000 meters	=	0.621 mile

Square Measure

1 square centimeter	= 100 square millimeters	=	0.155 square inch
1 square decimeter	= 100 square centimeters	=	15.5 square inches
1 square meter	= 100 square decimeters	=	1,549.9 sq. inches or 1.196 sq. yards
1 square dekameter	= 100 square meters	=	119.6 square yards
1 square kilometer	= 100 square hectometers	=	0.386 square mile

Capacity Measure

1 centiliter	= 10 milliliters	=	0.338 fluid ounce
1 deciliter	= 10 centiliters	=	3.38 fluid ounces
1 liter	= 10 deciliters	=	1.057 liquid qts. or 0.908 dry qt.
1 kiloliter	= 1,000 liters	=	264.18 gallons or 35.315 cubic feet

Land Measure

1 centare	= 1 square meter	=	1,549.9 square inches
1 hectare	= 100 ares	=	2.471 acres
1 square kilometer	= 100 hectares	=	0.386 square mile

Volume Measure

1 cubic centimeter	= 1,000 cubic millimeters	=	0.061 cubic inch
1 cubic decimeter	= 1,000 cubic centimeters	=	61.023 cubic inches
1 cubic meter	= 1,000 cubic decimeters	=	35.314 cubic feet

Weights

1 centigram	= 10 milligrams	=	0.1543 grain
1 decigram	= 10 centigrams	=	1.5432 grains
1 gram	= 10 decigrams	=	15,432 grains
1 dekagram	= 10 grams	=	0.3527 ounce
1 kilogram	= 1,000 grams	=	2.2046 pounds

American to Metric Table

The following table shows you what the most common U.S. measurements are in the metric system. You probably already know that 1 inch equals 2.54 centimeters. But, did you know that 1 gallon equals 3.7853 liters?

Linear Measure (Length or Distance)

1 inch		=	2.54 centimeters
1 foot	= 12 inches	=	0.3048 meter
1 yard	= 3 feet	=	0.9144 meter
1 mile	= 1,760 yards or 5,280 feet	=	1,609.3 meters

Square Measure (Area)

1 square inch		=	6.452 square centimeters
1 square foot	= 144 square inches	=	929 square centimeters
1 square yard	= 9 square feet	=	0.8361 square meter
1 acre	= 4,840 sq. yards	=	0.4047 hectare
1 square mile	= 640 acres	=	259 hectares or 2.59 sq. kilometers

Cubic Measure

1 cubic inch		=	16.387 cubic centimeters
1 cubic foot	= 1,728 cubic inches	=	0.0283 cubic meter
1 cubic yard	= 27 cubic feet	=	0.7646 cubic meter
1 cord	= 8 cord feet	=	3.625 cubic meters

Dry Measure

1 pint		=	0.5505 liter
1 quart	= 2 pints	=	1.1012 liters
1 peck	= 8 quarts	=	8.8096 liters
1 bushel	= 4 pecks	=	35.2383 liters

Liquid Measure

4 fluid ounces	= 1 gill	=	0.1183 liter
1 pint	= 4 gills	=	0.4732 liter
1 quart	= 2 pints	=	0.9463 liter
1 gallon	= 4 quarts	=	3.7853 liters

Five Ways to Measure When You Don't Have a Ruler

1. Many floor tiles are 12-inch by 12-inch squares.
2. U.S. paper currency is 6-1/8 inches long by 2-5/8 inches wide.
3. A quarter is approximately 1 inch wide.
4. A penny is approximately 3/4 inch wide.
5. A standard sheet of paper is 8-1/2 inches by 11 inches.

CONVERSION TABLE

You can use the following table to change, or convert, metric measurements into American measurements (and vice versa).

To change	to	multiply by
acres	square miles	0.001562
Celsius	Fahrenheit	*1.8
	*(Multiply Celsius by 1.8; then add 32)	
cubic meters	cubic yards	1.3079
cubic yards	cubic meters	0.7646
Fahrenheit	Celsius	*0.55
	*(Multiply Fahrenheit by .55 after subtracting 32)	
feet	meters	0.3048
feet	miles	0.0001894
feet/sec.	miles/hr.	0.6818
grams	ounces	0.0353
grams	pounds	0.002205
hours	days	0.04167
inches	centimeters	2.5400
kilowatts	horsepower	1.341
liters	gallons (U.S.)	0.2642
liters	pints (dry)	1.8162
liters	pints (liquid)	2.1134
liters	quarts (dry)	0.9081
liters	quarts (liquid)	1.0567
meters	miles	0.0006214
meters	yards	1.0936
metric tons	tons	1.1023
miles	kilometers	1.6093
miles	feet	5,280
miles/hr.	feet/min.	88
millimeters	inches	0.0394
ounces	grams	28.3495
ounces	pounds	0.0625
pounds	kilograms	0.45359
pounds	ounces	16
quarts (dry)	liters	1.1012
square feet	square meters	0.0929
square kilometers	square miles	0.3861
square meters	square feet	10.7639
square miles	square kilometers	2.5900
square yards	square meters	0.8361
tons	metric tons	0.9072
tons	pounds	2,000
yards	meters	0.9144
yards	miles	0.0005682

Additional Units of Measure

Below are some additional units of measure that you may come across in or out of school. They are used to measure everything from boards to "light." The ones at the bottom of the page are used in shipbuilding, in the military, and with horses.

Astronomical Unit (A.U.) ● 93,000,000 miles, the average distance of the earth from the sun (Used in astronomy)

Board Foot (bd. ft.) ● 144 cubic inches (12 in. x 12 in. x 1 in.) (Used for lumber)

Bolt ● 40 yards (Used for measuring cloth)

Btu ● British thermal unit—amount of heat needed to increase the temperature of one pound of water by one degree Fahrenheit (252 calories)

Gross ● 12 dozen or 144

Knot ● Not a distance, but a rate of speed—one nautical mile per hour

Light, Speed of ● 186,281.7 miles per second

Light-year ● 5,878,000,000,000 miles—the distance light travels in a year

Pi (π) ● 3.14159265+—the ratio of the circumference of a circle to its diameter

Roentgen ● Dosage unit of radiation exposure produced by X rays

Score ● 20 units

Sound, Speed of ● Usually placed at 1,088 ft. per second at 32° F at sea level

MISCELLANEOUS MEASUREMENTS

3 inches	=	1 palm
4 inches	=	1 hand
6 inches	=	1 span
18 inches	=	1 cubit
21.8 inches	=	1 Bible cubit
2-1/2 feet	=	1 military pace

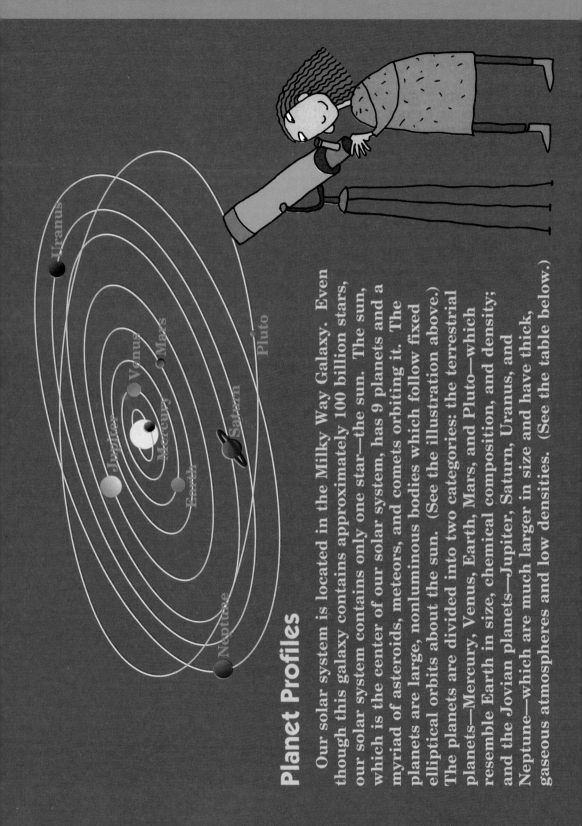

Planet Profiles

Our solar system is located in the Milky Way Galaxy. Even though this galaxy contains approximately 100 billion stars, our solar system contains only one star—the sun. The sun, which is the center of our solar system, has 9 planets and a myriad of asteroids, meteors, and comets orbiting it. The planets are large, nonluminous bodies which follow fixed elliptical orbits about the sun. (See the illustration above.) The planets are divided into two categories: the terrestrial planets—Mercury, Venus, Earth, Mars, and Pluto—which resemble Earth in size, chemical composition, and density; and the Jovian planets—Jupiter, Saturn, Uranus, and Neptune—which are much larger in size and have thick, gaseous atmospheres and low densities. (See the table below.)

	Sun	Moon	Mercury	Venus	Earth	Mars	Jupiter	Saturn	Uranus	Neptune	Pluto
Orbital Speed (in miles per second)		.6	29.8	21.8	18.5	15.0	8.1	6.0	4.1	3.4	2.9
Rotation on Axis	24 days 16 hrs. 48 min.	27 days 7 hrs. 38 min.	59 days	243 days	23 hrs. 56 min.	1 day 37 min.	9 hrs. 55 min.	10 hrs. 39 min.	16 to 28 hours	16 hrs.	6 days
Mean Surface Gravity (Earth = 1.00)		0.16	0.38	0.87	1.00	0.38	2.87	1.32	0.93	1.23	0.03
Density (times that of water)	100 (core)	3.3	5.4	5.3	5.5	3.9	1.3	0.7	1.2	1.6	1.0
Mass (times that of Earth)	333,000	0.012	0.055	0.82	6×10^{21} metric tons	0.11	318	95	14.6	17.2	0.0026
Approx. Weight of a Human (in pounds)		25	57	135	150	57	431	198	140	185	4.5
Number of Satellites	9 planets	0	0	0	1	2	16	23	15	8	1
Mean Distance to Sun (in millions of miles)		93.0	36.0	67.23	92.96	141.7	483.7	886.2	1,781	2,793	3,660
Revolution Around Sun		365.25 days	88.0 days	224.7 days	365.25 days	686.99 days	11.86 years	29.46 years	84.0 years	164.8 years	247.6 years
Approximate Surface Temperature (degrees Fahrenheit)	10,000° (surface) 27,000,000° (center)	lighted side 200° dark side -230°	-315° to 648°	850°	-126.9° to 136°	-191° to -24°	-236°	-285°	-357°	-400°	-342° to -369°
Diameter (in miles)	867,000	2,155	3,031	7,520	7,926	4,200	88,700	74,600	31,570	30,800	1,420

Using Maps

All About Maps

As you know, the world has changed a lot in the past several years. As "global citizens," it is up to each of us to stay on top of those changes. We should try to understand something about each of the countries in the world as well as our own. The section which follows will give you the map skills you need to begin your work.

Reading Maps

Maps have many uses. There are different kinds of maps for each of the different uses. Your handbook uses one kind of map, the *political map.* Political maps show how the earth is divided into countries and states. They also show the capitals and major cities. The different sizes and styles of type used for names on the maps are also important. Usually, the most important names are typed in the largest print.

Map Symbols

Mapmakers use special marks and symbols to show direction (north, south, east, and west). On most maps, north is at the top. But you should always check the *directional finder* to make sure you know where north is. If there is no symbol, you can assume that north is at the top of the page.

The Legend

Other important marks and symbols are explained in a box printed on each map. This box is called the *legend,* or *key*. It is included to help you understand and use the map. This map legend, which goes with the United States map, also includes symbols for state capitals and state boundaries.

The Map Scale

Legends also explain the map scale. The map scale shows you how far it really is between places. For example, a scale might show that one inch on the map equals 100 miles on the earth. If two cities are shown five inches apart, then they are really 500 miles apart. A ruler makes using a scale easy, but even an index card or a piece of paper will work. Here is the scale from the map of the United States.

Line up an index card or a piece of paper under it. Put a dot on the card at "0." Now put another dot on your card at the 100, 200, 300, and 400 marks. Use the card to judge the distance between points on the map. Don't forget that scales differ from map to map. Always refer to the scale on the map you are using.

Latitude and Longitude

Latitude and *longitude* lines are another feature of most maps and can be very useful. Latitude and longitude refer to imaginary lines that mapmakers use. When used together, these lines can be used to locate any point on the earth.

Latitude ● The imaginary lines that go from east to west around the earth are called lines of **latitude**. The line of latitude that goes around the earth exactly halfway between the North Pole and the South Pole is called the *equator*. Latitude is measured in degrees, with the equator being 0 degrees (0°).

Above the equator, the lines are called *north latitude* and measure from 0° to 90° north (the North Pole). Below the equator, the lines are called *south latitude* and measure from 0° to 90° south (the South Pole). On a map, latitude numbers are printed along the sides.

Longitude ● The imaginary lines that run from the North Pole to the South Pole are lines of **longitude**. Longitude is also measured in degrees, beginning with 0 degrees. The north-south line measuring 0° passes through Greenwich, England. This line is called the *prime meridian*.

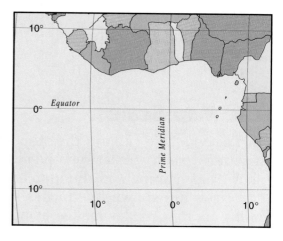

Lines east of the prime meridian are called *east longitude*. Lines west of the prime meridian are called *west longitude*. On a map, longitude numbers are printed at the top and bottom.

Coordinates ● The latitude and longitude numbers of a country or other place are called its **coordinates**. In each set of coordinates, latitude is given first, then longitude. To locate a place on a map using its coordinates, find the point where the two lines cross. (On the map above, Guinea is located at 10° N, 10° W. Can you find it? Check the map on page 409 to be sure.)

THE WORLD
MERCATOR PROJECTION

International Date Line

Longitude East of Greenwich

Longitude West of Greenwich

Oceans and Seas:
EAST SIBERIAN SEA, BERING SEA, ALEUTIAN IS., NORTH PACIFIC OCEAN, TASMAN SEA, NEW ZEALAND, NEW CALEDONIA (Fr.), VANUATU, FIJI, SOLOMON IS., CORAL SEA, LAPTEV SEA, SEA OF OKHOTSK, Sakhalin Island, Kuril Is., Sea of Japan, Yellow Sea, East China Sea, TAIWAN, South China Sea, PHILIPPINES, PAPUA NEW GUINEA, INDONESIA, AUSTRALIA, KARA SEA, NOVAYA ZEMLYA, BARENTS SEA, SVALBARD (Nor.), GREENLAND SEA, NORWEGIAN SEA, ICELAND, Str. of Denmark, GREENLAND (Den.), BAFFIN BAY, Baffin Island, Foxe Basin, HUDSON BAY

RUSSIA, ASIA, MONGOLIA, CHINA, KAZAKHSTAN, UZB., KYR., TURKM., AFGH., PAK., NEPAL, BANG., MYANMAR, THAI., LAOS, VIETNAM, CAMBODIA, MALAYSIA, SINGAPORE, INDIA, SRI LANKA, B. of Bengal, INDIAN OCEAN, Kerguelen (Fr.), MAURITIUS, Mozambique Chan., MADAGASCAR, ARABIAN SEA, OMAN, SAUDI ARABIA, G. of Aden, SOMALIA, IRAN, IRAQ, TURKEY, SYRIA, Caspian Sea, Black Sea, UKRAINE, Nile, EGYPT, SUDAN, DJIBOUTI, ETHIOPIA, UGANDA, KENYA, TANZANIA, MOZAMBIQUE, ZIM., SWAZILAND, LESOTHO, SOUTH AFRICA, C. of Good Hope

EUROPE, FINLAND, SWEDEN, NORWAY, North Cape, Baltic Sea, POL., LITH., BEL., GER., North Sea, UNITED KINGDOM, IRELAND, FRANCE, SPAIN, PORTUGAL, ITALY, Mediterranean Sea, TUNISIA, ALGERIA, MOROCCO, W. SAHARA, MAURITANIA, SENEGAL, CAPE VERDE, Canary Is., Azores (Port.), Madeira, SAHARA, LIBYA, CHAD, NIGER, NIGERIA, MALI, BURKINA, GHANA, IVORY COAST, LIBERIA, SIERRA LEONE, GUINEA, CAM., CONGO, GABON, ANGOLA, ZAIRE, ZAMBIA, NAMIBIA, BOTS., CENT. AFR. REP., ERITREA

AFRICA, SOUTH ATLANTIC OCEAN, NORTH ATLANTIC OCEAN, SCOTIA SEA, ANTARCTICA

C. Farewell, Newfoundland, C. Race, Bermuda (Br.), BAHAMAS, WEST INDIES, PUERTO RICO (U.S.), CUBA, Caribbean Sea, G. of Mexico, MEXICO, CENTRAL AMERICA, SOUTH AMERICA, BRAZIL, GUYANA, SURINAME, VEN., COL., ECU., PERU, BOLIVIA, PAR., CHILE, ARGENTINA, URU., Cape Horn

NORTH AMERICA, UNITED STATES, CANADA, QUEEN ELIZABETH IS., Pr. Patrick I., Banks I., Victoria I., Melville I., McClure Str., Devon I., Amundsen G., Gt. Bear L., Gt. Slave L., Mackenzie, BEAUFORT SEA, Pt. Barrow, G. of Alaska, Alaska, UNITED STATES, U.S. Hawaii, BERING SEA, Bering Str., Yukon, NORTH PACIFIC OCEAN, SOUTH PACIFIC OCEAN, Galapagos Is. (Ec.)

Arctic Circle, Tropic of Cancer, Equator, Tropic of Capricorn

C. Chelyuskin, Lena, Miss.

N

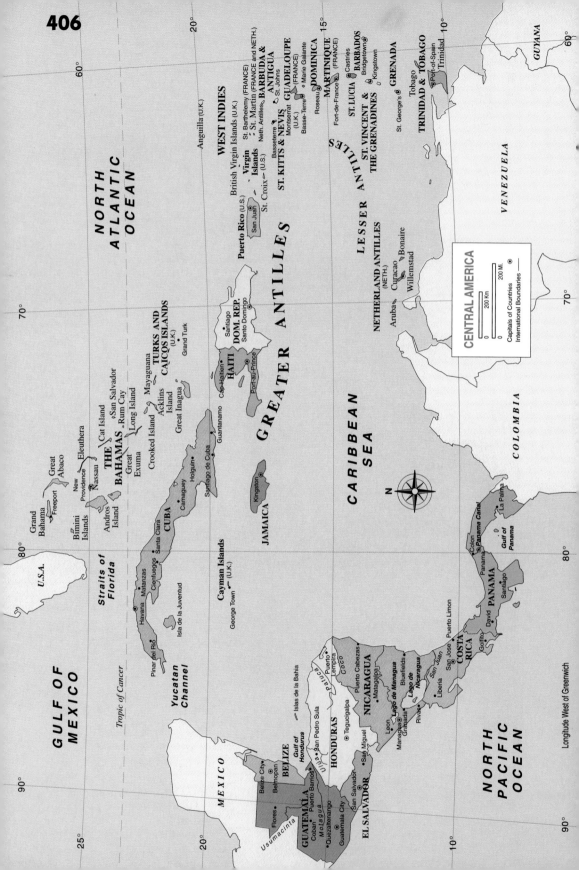

Caribbean Sea

West Indies

Pt. Gallinas

G. de Venezuela

Port of Spain

TRINIDAD & TOBAGO

Barranquilla

Maracaibo

Cumana

Caracas

Monteria

Cucuta

Ciudad Guayana

VENEZUELA

Orinoco

Georgetown

NORTH ATLANTIC OCEAN

PANAMA

G. of Panama

Medellin

San Cristobal

Paramaribo

GUYANA

SURINAME

FR. GUIANA

Cayenne

Buenaventura

COLOMBIA

Bogota

Orinoco

Boa Vista

Oyapock

Cali

Pasto

Putumayo

Negro

Branco

Macapa

I. de Marajo

Equator

Quito

ECUADOR

Japurá

Belém

Abaetetuba

Sao Luis

Guayaquil

G. of Guayaquil

Iquitos

Benjamin Constant

Amazon

Manaus

Amazon

Santarem

Tapajos

Xingu

Fortaleza

Teresina

Sullana

Maranon

Javari

Jurua

Purus

Madeira

Araguaia

Tocantins

Parnaiba

Natal

Chiclayo

Roosevelt

Juazeiro do Norte

Trujillo

Rio Branco

Porto Velho

B R A Z I L

Porto Nacional

Recife

PERU

Guapore

Aracaju

Lima

Ica

Trinidad

Lake Titicaca

BOLIVIA

Cuiaba

Brasilia

Sao Francisco

Salvador

Ilhéus

Arequipa

La Paz (de facto)

Cochabamba

Santa Cruz

Sucre (legal)

Goiania

Arica

Paraguay

Belo Horizonte

Tocopilla

Mariscal Estigarribia

Campo Grande

Vitória

Tropic of Capricorn

PARAGUAY

Parana

Sao Paulo

Santos

Rio de Janeiro

Antofagasta

San Salvador de Jujuy

Picomayo

Asuncion

Curitiba

Paranaguá

Copiapó

San Miguel de Tucuman

Resistencia

Parana

Uruguay

Florianopolis

La Serena

Cordoba

Salado

Santana do Livramento

Porto Alegre

Ovalle

Rosario

Salto

I. dos Patos

Valparaiso

Santiago

Mendoza

Melo

URUGUAY

Montevideo

Concepcion

Buenos Aires

La Plata

Rio de la Plata

Santa Rosa

C. San Antonio

Mar del Plata

Valdivia

Negro

Colorado

Bahia Blanca

Puerto Montt

Ancud

San Carlos de Bariloche

Pto. Madryn

G. San Matias

I. Grande de Chiloé

Chubut

ARCHIPIELAGO de los CHONOS

Comodoro Rivadavia

G. San Jorge

Puerto Aisen

C. Tres Puntas

ARGENTINA

CHILE

ANDES MOUNTAINS

San Julián

Bahia Grande

FALKLAND ISLANDS
(Br. - claimed by Arg.)

Rio Gallegos

Stanley

I. Santa Inés

Punta Arenas

I. de los Estados

Cape Horn

SOUTH GEORGIA ISLAND
(U.K.)

PACIFIC OCEAN

ATLANTIC OCEAN

N

SOUTH AMERICA

0   600 Km

0   600 Mi.

Capitals of Countries ⊙

International Boundaries ——

80° 70° 60° 50° 40°

10° 10°

0° 0°

10° 10°

20° 20°

30° 30°

40° 40°

50° 50°

90° 80° 70° Longitude West of Greenwich 50° 40° 30° 20°

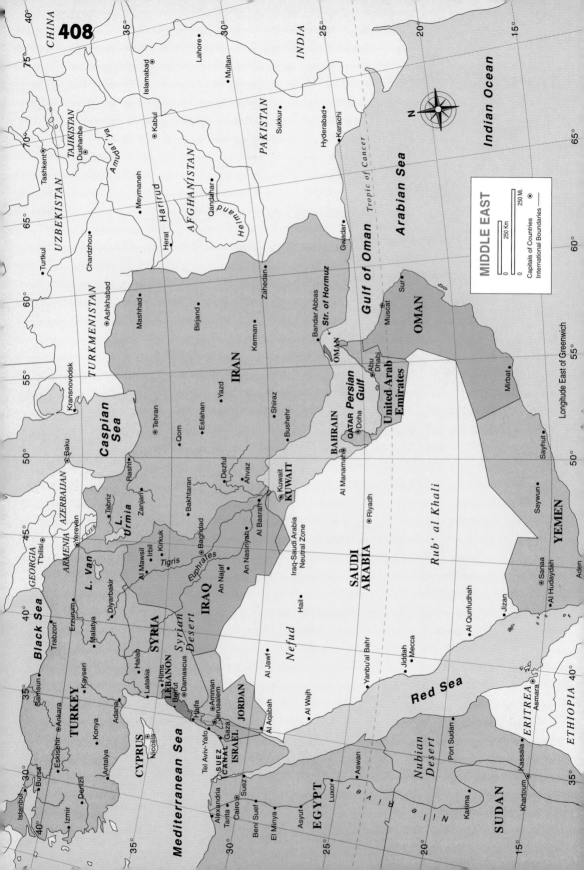

MIDDLE EAST

408

CHINA
INDIA
Indian Ocean
Lahore
Multan
PAKISTAN
Islamabad
Kabul
AFGHANISTAN
Sukkur
Hyderabad
Karachi
TAJIKISTAN
Dushanbe
Tashkent
UZBEKISTAN
Turkul
Meymaneh
Herat
Qandahar
Arabian Sea
Gwadar
Gulf of Oman
Tropic of Cancer
TURKMENISTAN
Chardzhou
Ashkhabad
Krasnovodsk
Mashhad
Birjand
Zahedan
Str. of Hormuz
Sur
Muscat
OMAN
IRAN
Kerman
Bandar Abbas
OMAN
Abu
Dhabi
Mirbat
Caspian
Sea
Baku
Tehran
Yazd
Shiraz
United Arab
Emirates
Persian
Gulf
QATAR
Doha
Sayhut
GEORGIA
T'bilisi
AZERBAIJAN
Yerevan
Rasht
Qom
Esfahan
Bushehr
BAHRAIN
Al Manamah
YEMEN
ARMENIA
AZER
L.
Urmia
Tabriz
Zanjan
Bakhtaran
Deztul
Ahvaz
Kuwait
KUWAIT
Riyadh
Saywun
Sanaa
L. Van
Kirkuk
Al Mawsil
Irbil
Baghdad
Al Basrah
Iraq-Saudi Arabia
Neutral Zone
Rub' al Khali
Aden
Al Hudaydah
Turkul
Black Sea
Trabzon
Erzurum
Diyarbakir
Tigris
Euphrates
An Najaf
An Nasiriyah
SAUDI
ARABIA
Jizan
Sanaa
Samsun
Malatya
Kayseri
SYRIA
Halab
IRAQ
Hail
Al Qunfudhah
ERITREA
Asmara
TURKEY
Ankara
Latakia
Hims
Syrian
Desert
Al Jawf
Nefud
ETHIOPIA
Eskisehir
Konya
LEBANON
Damascus
Beirut
Amman
JORDAN
Kassala
Bursa
Denizli
Antalya
Adana
CYPRUS
Nicosia
Tel Aviv-Yafo
Jerusalem
Gaza
ISRAEL
Al Wajh
Yanbu'al Bahr
Jiddah
Mecca
Red Sea
Port Sudan
Khartoum
Istanbul
Izmir
Mediterranean Sea
SUEZ
CANAL
Suez
Al Aqabah
Nubian
Desert
SUDAN
Alexandria
Cairo
Tanta
Beni Suef
El Minya
Asyut
EGYPT
Luxor
Aswan
Katima

MIDDLE EAST
0   250 Km
0   250 Mi.
● Capitals of Countries
─── International Boundaries
Longitude East of Greenwich

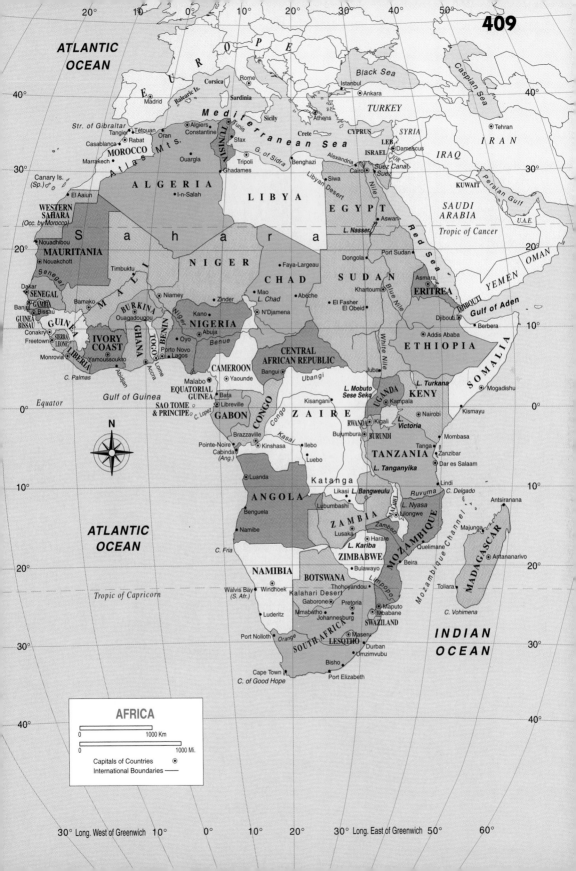

EUROPE

Capitals of Countries ◉
International Boundaries ―――

600 Km.
600 Mi.

ATLANTIC OCEAN

ICELAND

Reykjavik

Faeroe Is.
(Den.)

Shetland Is.

Orkney Is.

GREAT
BRITAIN

SCOTLAND
Aberdeen
Edinburgh

HEBRIDES

NORTHERN
IRELAND
Belfast

IRELAND
Dublin
Cork

UNITED
KINGDOM
Newcastle
Liverpool

WALES
Cardiff

ENGLAND
London

IRISH
SEA

St. George's Channel
Land's End
English Channel

NORWEGIAN
SEA

Norwegian
Sea

North Cape
Tromso
Narvik
Lofoten Is.

N O R W A Y

Trondheim
Bergen
Stavanger
Oslo

S W E D E N
Gavle
Stockholm
Goteborg
Norrkoping

Gotland

Baltic
Sea

DENMARK
Copenhagen
Kattegat
Skagerrak

North
Sea

NETH.
Amsterdam
The Hague
BELGIUM
Brussels

GERMANY
Hamburg
Berlin
Leipzig
Bonn
Cologne
Frankfurt
Munich

Murmansk
Kola Pen.

F I N L A N D
Oulu
Tampere
Vaasa
Helsinki

Gulf of Finland
ESTONIA
Tallinn

Gulf of Bothnia
Lulea

Barents
Sea

White Sea

Kolguyev I.

Nar'yan-Mar
Pechora

L. Onega
Petrozavodsk

L. Ladoga
St. Petersburg
(Leningrad)

RUSSIA

LATVIA
Riga

LITHUANIA
Vilnius
Kaliningrad (RUSSIA)

POLAND
Gdansk (Danzig)
Poznan
Warsaw
Krakow

CZECH
REPUBLIC
Prague

SLOVAKIA
Bratislava

AUSTRIA
Vienna
Graz

SWITZ.
Bern

LIECHT.
Munich

Strasbourg

Rhine

FRANCE
Le Havre
Rouen
Paris
Nantes
Lyon
Bordeaux
Toulouse
Marseille
Nice

Seine
Loire
Rhone

Bay of
Biscay

PORTUGAL
Oporto
Lisbon

C. Finisterre
C. St. Vincent

SPAIN
Madrid
Bilbao
Barcelona
Valencia
Sevilla
Malaga

ANDORRA
Pyrenees
Ebro
Tagus

BALEARIC IS.
Minorca
Majorca
Mallorca

Corsica
(French)
Ajaccio

Sardinia
(Italian)
Cagliari

GIBRALTAR
(U.K.)
Str. of Gibraltar
Tangier

Mediterranean Sea

A F R I C A

Longitude West of Greenwich

Yekaterinburg
Chelyabinsk
Magnitogorsk

U R A L   M O U N T A I N S

Syktyvkar
Perm
Izhevsk
Ufa
Orenburg
Samara
Kama
Kuybyshev Res.

Arkhangel'sk
Northern Dvina

R U S S I A

Kirov
Nizhniy Novgorod
Volga
Penza
Saratov
Voronezh

Andropov
Rybinsk Res.
Yaroslavl'
Tver'
Moscow
Smolensk
Kursk

Don

Volgograd
(Stalingrad)
Rostov

Astrakhan

Caspian
Sea

Baku
AZERBAIJAN
ARMENIA
Yerevan
GEORGIA
Tbilisi
Caucasus Mts.
Grozny
Krasnodar

Donets'k
Sea of
Azov
Sevastopol'
Crimea
Black Sea

BELARUS
Minsk
Gomel

UKRAINE
Kiev
Dnipro
Kharkiv
Krivoy Rog
Dnipropetrovsk
Odessa
Lviv

MOLDOVA
Chisinau

ROMANIA
Cluj-Napoca
Bucharest

BULGARIA
Varna
Sofia

Danube

HUNGARY
Budapest

YUGOSLAVIA
Belgrade
Serbia
Montenegro

BOSNIA-
HERZ.
Sarajevo

CROATIA
Zagreb
SLOVENIA
Ljubljana

MACED.
Skopje

ALBANIA
Tirana

GREECE
Thessaloniki
Larisa
Athens
Patrai

Ionian
Sea

Adriatic Sea

Venice
Milan
Florence
Rome
VATICAN
CITY
SAN
MARINO
MONACO
Naples
Tyrrhenian
Sea
Palermo
Sicily
Catania

I T A L Y

Elba

T U R K E Y
Istanbul
Sea of Marmara
Izmir
Ankara

CYPRUS

Aegean Sea

CRETE
Irakleion

Black Sea

Longitude East of Greenwich

Arctic Circle

N

60° 50° 40° 30° 20° 10° 0° 10° 20° 30° 40° 50° 60°

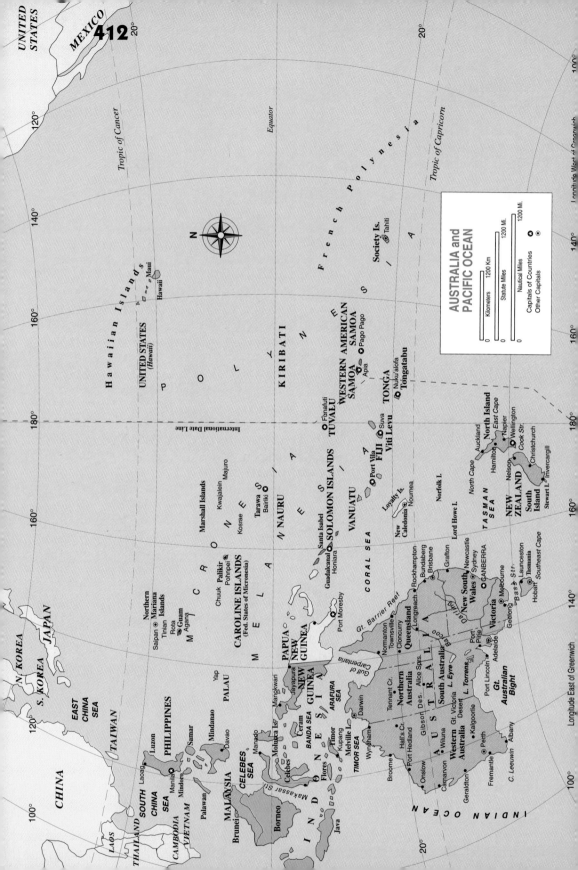

AUSTRALIA and
PACIFIC OCEAN

Index to World Maps

Country	Latitude	Longitude	Country	Latitude	Longitude
Afghanistan	33° N	65° E	Costa Rica	10° N	84° W
Albania	41° N	20° E	Croatia	45° N	16° E
Algeria	28° N	3° E	Cuba	21° N	80° W
Andorra	42° N	1° E	Cyprus	35° N	33° E
Angola	12° S	18° E	Czech Republic	50° N	15° E
Antigua and			Denmark	56° N	10° E
Barbuda	17° N	61° W	Djibouti	11° N	43° E
Argentina	34° S	64° W	Dominica	15° N	61° W
Armenia	41° N	45° E	Dominican Republic	19° N	70° W
Australia	25° S	135° E	Ecuador	2° S	77° W
Austria	47° N	13° E	Egypt	27° N	30° E
Azerbaijan	41° N	47° E	El Salvador	14° N	89° W
Bahamas	24° N	76° W	Equatorial Guinea	2° N	9° E
Bahrain	26° N	50° E	Eritrea	17° N	38° E
Bangladesh	24° N	90° E	Estonia	59° N	26° E
Barbados	13° N	59° W	Ethiopia	8° N	38° E
Belarus	54° N	25° E	Fiji	19° S	174° E
Belgium	50° N	4° E	Finland	64° N	26° E
Belize	17° N	88° W	France	46° N	2° E
Benin	9° N	2° E	Gabon	1° S	11° E
Bhutan	27° N	90° E	The Gambia	13° N	16° W
Bolivia	17° S	65° W	Georgia	43° N	45° E
Bosnia-			Germany	51° N	10° E
Herzegovina	44° N	18° E	Ghana	8° N	2° W
Botswana	22° S	24° E	Greece	39° N	22° E
Brazil	10° S	55° W	Greenland	70° N	40° W
Brunei	4° N	114° E	Grenada	12° N	61° W
Bulgaria	43° N	25° E	Guatemala	15° N	90° W
Burkina Faso	13° N	2° W	Guinea	11° N	10° W
Burundi	3° S	30° E	Guinea-Bissau	12° N	15° W
Cambodia	13° N	105° E	Guyana	5° N	59° W
Cameroon	6° N	12° E	Haiti	19° N	72° W
Canada	60° N	95° W	Honduras	15° N	86° W
Cape Verde	16° N	24° W	Hungary	47° N	20° E
Central African			Iceland	65° N	18° W
Republic	7° N	21° E	India	20° N	77° E
Chad	15° N	19° E	Indonesia	5° S	120° E
Chile	30° S	71° W	Iran	32° N	53° E
China	35° N	105° E	Iraq	33° N	44° E
Colombia	4° N	72° W	Ireland	53° N	8° W
Comoros	12° S	44° E	Israel	31° N	35° E
Congo	1° S	15° E	Italy	42° N	12° E

Country	Latitude	Longitude	Country	Latitude	Longitude
Ivory Coast	8° N	5° W	Nigeria	10° N	8° E
Jamaica	18° N	77° W	Northern Ireland	55° N	7° W
Japan	36° N	138° E	Norway	62° N	10° E
Jordan	31° N	36° E	Oman	22° N	58° E
Kazakhstan	45° N	70° E	Pakistan	30° N	70° E
Kenya	1° N	38° E	Panama	9° N	80° W
Kiribati	0° N	175° E	Papua New Guinea	6° S	147° E
North Korea	40° N	127° E	Paraguay	23° S	58° W
South Korea	36° N	128° E	Peru	10° S	76° W
Kuwait	29° N	47° E	Philippines	13° N	122° E
Kyrgyzstan	42° N	75° E	Poland	52° N	19° E
Laos	18° N	105° E	Portugal	39° N	8° W
Latvia	57° N	25° E	Qatar	25° N	51° E
Lebanon	34° N	36° E	Romania	46° N	25° E
Lesotho	29° S	28° E	Russia	60° N	80° E
Liberia	6° N	10° W	Rwanda	2° S	30° E
Libya	27° N	17° E	St. Kitts & Nevis	17° N	62° W
Liechtenstein	47° N	9° E	Saint Lucia	14° N	61° W
Lithuania	56° N	24° E	Saint Vincent and		
Luxembourg	49° N	6° E	the Grenadines	13° N	61° W
Macedonia	43° N	22° E	San Marino	44° N	12° E
Madagascar	19° S	46° E	Sao Tome and		
Malawi	13° S	34° E	Principe	1° N	7° E
Malaysia	2° N	112° E	Saudi Arabia	25° N	45° E
Maldives	2° N	70° E	Scotland	57° N	5° W
Mali	17° N	4° W	Senegal	14° N	14° W
Malta	36° N	14° E	Serbia	45° N	21° E
Mauritania	20° N	12° W	Seychelles	5° S	55° E
Mauritius	20° S	57° E	Sierra Leone	8° N	11° W
Mexico	23° N	102° W	Singapore	1° N	103° E
Moldova	47° N	28° E	Slovakia	49° N	19° E
Monaco	43° N	7° E	Slovenia	46° N	15° E
Mongolia	46° N	105° E	Solomon Islands	8° S	159° E
Montenegro	43° N	19° E	Somalia	10° N	49° E
Morocco	32° N	5° W	South Africa	30° S	26° E
Mozambique	18° S	35° E	Spain	40° N	4° W
Myanmar	22° N	98° E	Sri Lanka	7° N	81° E
Namibia	22° S	17° E	Sudan	15° N	30° E
Nauru	1° S	166° E	Suriname	4° N	56° W
Nepal	28° N	84° E	Swaziland	26° S	31° E
Netherlands	52° N	5° E	Sweden	62° N	15° E
New Zealand	41° S	174° E	Switzerland	47° N	8° E
Nicaragua	13° N	85° W	Syria	35° N	38° E
Niger	16° N	8° E	Taiwan	23° N	121° E

Country	Latitude	Longitude	Country	Latitude	Longitude
Tajikistan	39° N	71° E	United Kingdom	54° N	2° W
Tanzania	6° S	35° E	United States	38° N	97° W
Thailand	15° N	100° E	Uruguay	33° S	56° W
Togo	8° N	1° E	Uzbekistan	40° N	68° E
Tonga	20° S	173° W	Vanuatu	17° S	170° E
Trinidad/Tobago	11° N	61° W	Venezuela	8° N	66° W
Tunisia	34° N	9° E	Vietnam	17° N	106° E
Turkey	39° N	35° E	Wales	53° N	3° W
Turkmenistan	40° N	55° E	Western Samoa	10° S	173° W
Tuvalu	8° S	179° E	Yemen	15° N	44° E
Uganda	1° N	32° E	Yugoslavia	44° N	19° E
Ukraine	50° N	30° E	Zaire	4° S	25° E
United Arab			Zambia	15° S	30° E
Emirates	24° N	54° E	Zimbabwe	20° S	30° E

TOPOGRAPHIC TALLY TABLE

THE CONTINENTS

	Area (Sq Km)	Percent of Earth's Land
Asia	44,026,000	29.7
Africa	30,271,000	20.4
North America	24,258,000	16.3
South America	17,823,000	12.0
Antarctica	13,209,000	8.9
Europe	10,404,000	7.0
Australia	7,682,000	5.2

LONGEST RIVERS

	Length (Km)
Nile, *Africa*	6,671
Amazon, *South America*	6,437
Chang Jiang (Yangtze), *Asia*	6,380
Mississippi-Missouri, *North America*	5,971
Ob-Irtysk, *Asia*	5,410
Huang (Yellow), *Asia*	4,672
Congo, *Africa*	4,667
Amur, *Asia*	4,416
Lena, *Asia*	4,400
Mackenzie-Peace, *North America*	4,241

MAJOR ISLANDS

	Area (Sq Km)
Greenland	2,175,600
New Guinea	792,500
Borneo	725,500
Madagascar	587,000
Baffin	507,500
Sumatra	427,300
Honshu	227,400
Great Britain	218,100
Victoria	217,300
Ellesmere	196,200
Celebes	178,700
South (New Zealand)	151,000
Java	126,700

THE OCEANS

	Area (Sq Km)	Percent of Earth's Water Area
Pacific	166,241,000	46.0
Atlantic	86,557,000	23.9
Indian	73,427,000	20.3
Arctic	9,485,000	2.6

Improving Math Skills

I Love/Hate Math!

What's your favorite subject? Your least favorite? Chances are you answered "Math" to one of these questions. Most students either like math a lot or *not at all!* One of the reasons is that math has its own language. Some students pick up this language (which is mostly signs and symbols) very easily; other students don't pick it up so easily. Either way, the following chapter should help you.

In this chapter, you will find a list of the most common math symbols, a table for converting fractions to decimals, and step-by-step guidelines for solving word problems. You'll even find a sample computer keyboard with a picture of which fingers go where so you can practice "keyboarding."

Solving Word Problems

You might be able to take the easy way out in some of your school work (ever skip over parts of a reading assignment?) or in your work at home (ever stuff dirty clothes under your bed?).

But when it comes to solving word problems, you should follow all of the steps in the process. It's just too easy to miss important details if you try to take shortcuts. Suppose you were asked to complete the following job:

An Everyday Problem

Your class is making pictures of the Big Dipper in science, and it's your job to cut out enough stars for everyone.

At first, this seems like an easy enough task. But how will you carry out your work? You won't know until you turn it into a word problem. You can do this by *filling in the numbers* and then *identifying the problem:*

- First, filling in the numbers: You would have to know how many stars there are in the Big Dipper (7), and how many students there are in your classroom (let's say, 29).

- Second, identifying the problem: How many stars do I need to cut out altogether so that every student has seven? (29 x 7)

THINK IT OVER

You are faced with problems like this day in and day out, in school and at home. So in a sense, word problems are everyday problems. You just have to be able to recognize them, and know how to solve them.

The Steps in the Process

1 **Read the problem carefully.** It's important that you understand all the parts. Pay special attention to the key words and phrases—such as "in all" or "how many." For example, in our constellation problem, we have the phrases "how many" and "altogether."

2 **Collect the information.** Gather together all the information you will need to solve the problem. In our constellation problem, the information we need includes the numbers 7 and 29. (Don't forget: sometimes numbers are written as words.)

 Study any maps, charts, or graphs which go along with the problem. They often contain important information, too.

3 **Set up the problem.** This means you need to decide how to solve the problem (add, subtract, multiply, divide). Pay attention to the key words and phrases.

■ The following words tell you to add or multiply: *in all, in total, altogether.*

■ The following phrases tell you to subtract: *how many more than, how many less than, find the difference, how many are left, how much younger than.*

■ Each of these phrases tell you to divide: *how much . . . each, how many . . . each.*

4 **Solve the problem.** Follow the order of the problem. Show all of your work so you can check it later. Here's our constellation problem again:

$$
\begin{array}{r}
29 \\
\times\ 7 \\
\hline
203
\end{array}
\begin{array}{l}
\text{students} \\
\text{stars for each student} \\
\text{stars altogether}
\end{array}
$$

5 **Check your answer.** Here are several ways: Do the problem again, do it a different way, use a calculator, or start with your answer and work backward. For example, in our constellation problem, our answer (product) was 203. If we divide 203 by 7, we should get 29. Or if we divide 203 by 29, we should get 7.

Sample Word Problem

1 **Read the problem carefully.** The soccer team parents bought 48 cans of cola, 36 cans of root beer, and 36 cans of lemonade to sell at the soccer match. Only 42 cans of soda were sold. How many cans were left?

2 **Collect the information.** After you read the problem, you know how many cans of soda were purchased: 48, 36, and 36. You also know how many cans are left over: 42.

3 **Set up the problem.**

```
   2
  48
  36
 +36
 ───
 120
```

Discussion: This is really a two-step problem. Before you can find out how many cans of soda were left, you have to find out how many cans there were to begin with. So you add 48, 36, and 36 for a total of 120.

4 **Solve the problem.**

```
  1 10
  120
 - 42
 ───
   78
```

Discussion: Then subtract the 42 cans sold in order to find out the number of cans remaining.

5 **Check your answer.**

```
   1
  78
 +42
 ───
 120
```

Discussion: Check your work. You can check a subtraction problem by adding your answer to the second number in the subtraction problem. Also, make sure that your answer makes sense.

(**Answer:** 78 cans of soda were left.)

Symbols, Numbers, and Tables

You can use the following two pages whenever you need help with your basic math work. The first list includes common symbols and their meanings; the second list includes more advanced symbols. The other "tables" include prime numbers, multiplication facts, decimal equivalents, and Roman numerals.

Common Math Symbols

+ plus (addition)
− minus (subtraction)
× multiplied by
÷ divided by
= is equal to
≠ is not equal to
% percent
¢ cents
$ dollars
° degree
′ minute (also foot)
″ second (also inch)

Advanced Math Symbols

< is less than
> is greater than
± plus or minus
: is to (ratio)
π pi
$\sqrt[2]{}$ or $\sqrt{}$ square root
≥ is greater than or equal to
≤ is less than or equal to
∠ angle
⊥ is perpendicular to
‖ is parallel to
∴ therefore

A Chart of Prime Numbers Less than 500

2,	3,	5,	7,	11,	13,	17,	19,	23,	29,
31,	37,	41,	43,	47,	53,	59,	61,	67,	71,
73,	79,	83,	89,	97,	101,	103,	107,	109,	113,
127,	131,	137,	139,	149,	151,	157,	163,	167,	173,
179,	181,	191,	193,	197,	199,	211,	223,	227,	229,
233,	239,	241,	251,	257,	263,	269,	271,	277,	281,
283,	293,	307,	311,	313,	317,	331,	337,	347,	349,
353,	359,	367,	373,	379,	383,	389,	397,	401,	409,
419,	421,	431,	433,	439,	443,	449,	457,	461,	463,
467,	479,	487,	491,	499					

Table of Basic Multiplication Facts

X	0	1	2	3	4	5	6	7	8	9	10
0	0	0	0	0	0	0	0	0	0	0	0
1	0	1	2	3	4	5	6	7	8	9	10
2	0	2	4	6	8	10	12	14	16	18	20
3	0	3	6	9	12	15	18	21	24	27	30
4	0	4	8	12	16	20	24	28	32	36	40
5	0	5	10	15	20	25	30	35	40	45	50
6	0	6	12	18	24	30	36	42	48	54	60
7	0	7	14	21	28	35	42	49	56	63	70
8	0	8	16	24	32	40	48	56	64	72	80
9	0	9	18	27	36	45	54	63	72	81	90
10	0	10	20	30	40	50	60	70	80	90	100

Decimal Equivalents of Common Fractions

1/2	.5000	1/32	.0313	3/11	.2727	6/11	.5455
1/3	.3333	1/64	.0156	4/5	.8000	7/8	.8750
1/4	.2500	2/3	.6667	4/7	.5714	7/9	.7778
1/5	.2000	2/5	.4000	4/9	.4444	7/10	.7000
1/6	.1667	2/7	.2857	4/11	.3636	7/11	.6364
1/7	.1429	2/9	.2222	5/6	.8333	7/12	.5833
1/8	.1250	2/11	.1818	5/7	.7143	8/9	.8889
1/9	.1111	3/4	.7500	5/8	.6250	8/11	.7273
1/10	.1000	3/5	.6000	5/9	.5556	9/10	.9000
1/11	.0909	3/7	.4286	5/11	.4545	9/11	.8182
1/12	.0833	3/8	.3750	5/12	.4167	10/11	.9091
1/16	.0625	3/10	.3000	6/7	.8571	11/12	.9167

Roman Numerals

I	1	VII	7	XL	40	C	100	$\overline{\text{C}}$	100,000
II	2	VIII	8	L	50	D	500	$\overline{\text{D}}$	500,000
III	3	IX	9	LX	60	M	1,000	$\overline{\text{M}}$	1,000,000
IV	4	X	10	LXX	70	$\overline{\text{V}}$	5,000		
V	5	XX	20	LXXX	80	$\overline{\text{X}}$	10,000		
VI	6	XXX	30	XC	90	$\overline{\text{L}}$	50,000		

Computer Keyboard

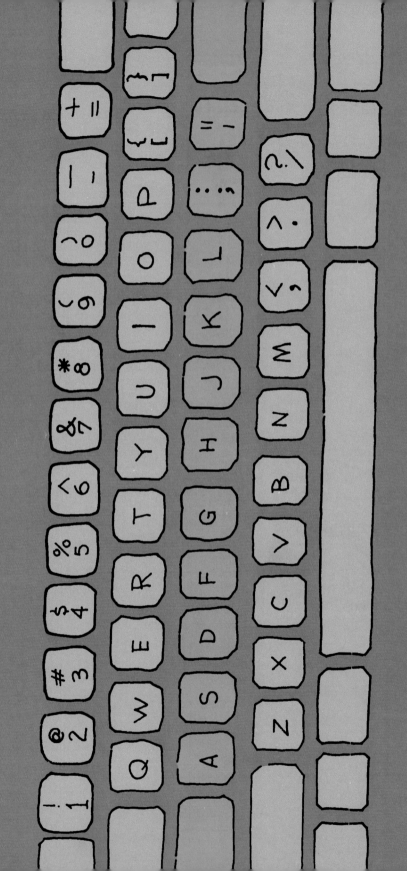

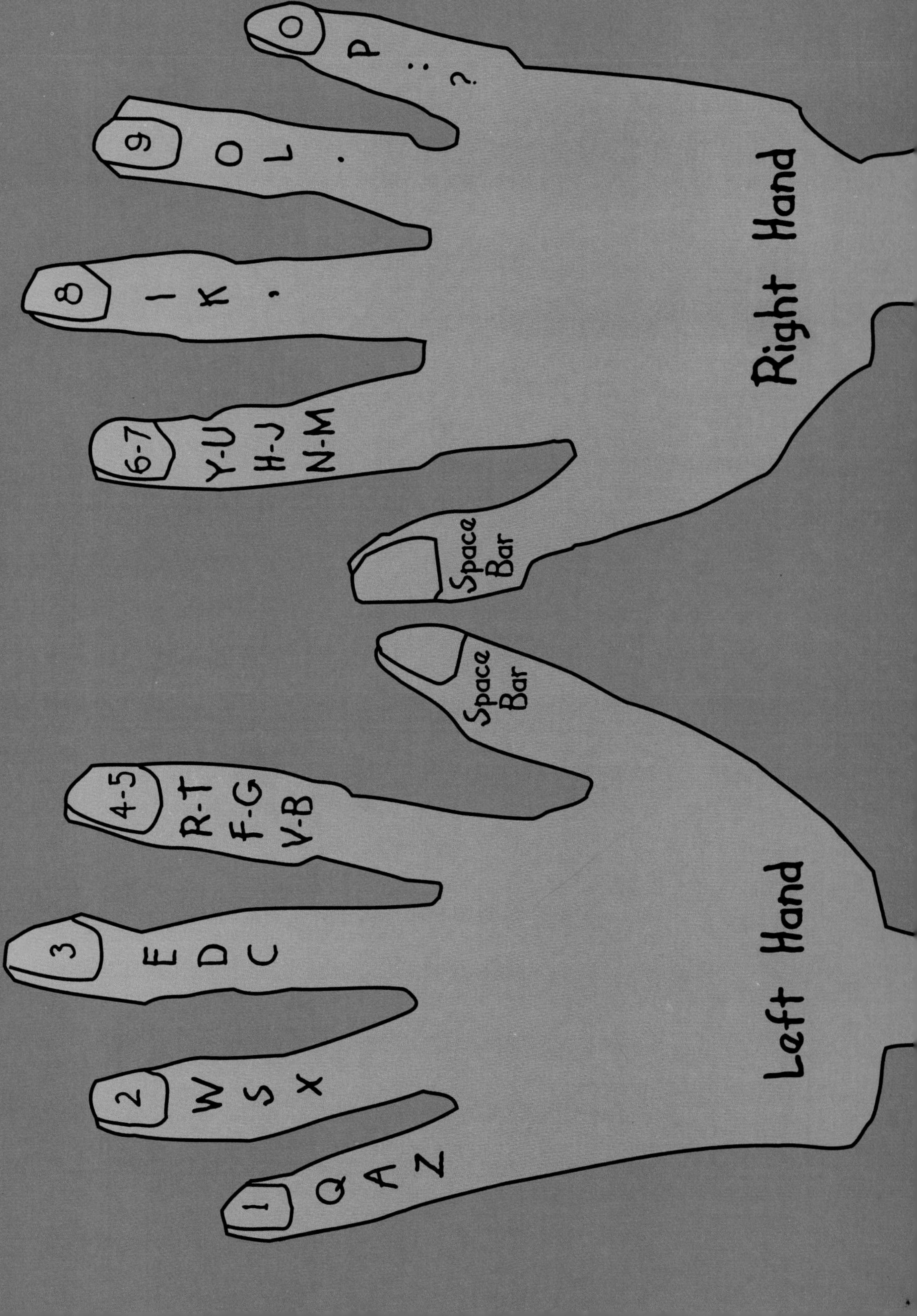
1
Q
A
Z
2
W
S
X
3
E
D
C
4-5
R-T
F-G
V-B
Space
Bar
Left Hand
Space
Bar
6-7
Y-U
H-J
N-M
8
I
K
,
9
O
L
.
0
P
;
?
Right Hand

History in the Making

This section of your handbook includes a close look at the U.S. Constitution, a chart of presidents and vice presidents, and a complete historical time line.

The U.S. Constitution

Of the many history-making events in United States history, none is more important than the convention held in Philadelphia in 1787. It was held to revise the Articles of Confederation. Instead, the delegates decided to write a new plan of government.

By the time the convention ended five months later, George Washington and the other delegates had passed the United States Constitution.

Through the years this Constitution has been changed (amended) several times, but it is still the "law of the land," just as it was 200 years ago.

The Parts of the Constitution

The Constitution is made up of three main parts: a **preamble**, 7 **articles**, and 27 **amendments**. The *preamble* states the purpose of the Constitution, the *articles* explain how the government works, and the *amendments* list the basic rights guaranteed to all American citizens. Together, these parts contain the laws and guidelines necessary to set up and run a successful national government.

But the Constitution doesn't give power just to the national government. It also gives some power to the states and some to the people. Remember this when you study the Constitution.

The Preamble

We the people of the United States, in order to form a more perfect Union, establish justice, insure domestic tranquility, provide for the common defense, promote the general welfare, and secure the blessings of liberty to ourselves and our posterity, do ordain and establish this Constitution for the United States of America.

The Articles of the Constitution

The articles of the Constitution explain how each branch of government works and what each can and cannot do. The articles also explain how the federal and state governments must work together, and how the Constitution can be amended or changed.

ARTICLE 1 explains the legislative branch, how laws are made, and how Congress works.

ARTICLE 2 explains the executive branch, the offices of the President and Vice President, and the powers of the executive branch.

ARTICLE 3 explains the judicial branch, the Supreme Court and other courts, and warns people about trying to overthrow the government.

ARTICLE 4 describes how the United States federal government and the individual state governments work together.

ARTICLE 5 tells how the Constitution can be amended, or changed.

ARTICLE 6 states that the United States federal government and the Constitution are the law of the land.

ARTICLE 7 outlines how the Constitution must be adopted to become official.

The Bill of Rights

To get the necessary votes to approve the Constitution, a number of changes (amendments) had to be made. These 10 original amendments are called the Bill of Rights. They guarantee all Americans some very basic rights, including the right to worship and speak freely, and to have a jury trial.

AMENDMENT 1   People have the right to worship, to speak freely, to gather together, and to question the government.

AMENDMENT 2   People have the right to own guns.

AMENDMENT 3   The government cannot have soldiers stay in people's houses without their permission.

AMENDMENT 4   People and their property cannot be searched without the written permission of a judge.

AMENDMENT 5   People cannot be tried for a serious crime without a jury. They cannot be tried twice for the same crime or be forced to testify against themselves. Also, they cannot have property taken away while they are on trial. Any property taken for public use must receive a fair price.

AMENDMENT 6   In criminal cases people have a right to a trial, to be told what they are accused of, to hear witnesses against them, to get witnesses in their favor, and to have a lawyer.

AMENDMENT 7   In cases involving more than $20, people have the right to a jury trial.

AMENDMENT 8   People have a right to fair bail (money given as a promise the person will return for trial), fines, and punishments.

AMENDMENT 9   People have rights that are not listed in the Constitution.

AMENDMENT 10   Powers not given to the federal government are given to the states or to the people.

The Other Amendments

The Constitution and the Bill of Rights were ratified in 1791. Since that time, over 7,000 amendments to the Constitution have been proposed. Because three-fourths of the states must approve an amendment before it becomes law, just 27 amendments have been passed. The first 10 are listed under the Bill of Rights; the other 17 are listed below. (The date each amendment became law is given in parentheses.)

AMENDMENT 11   A person cannot sue a state in federal court. (1795)

AMENDMENT 12   President and Vice President are elected separately. (1804)

AMENDMENT 13   Slavery is abolished, done away with. (1865)

AMENDMENT 14   All persons born in the United States or those who have become citizens enjoy full citizenship rights. (1868)

AMENDMENT 15   Voting rights are given to all citizens regardless of race, creed, or color. (1870)

AMENDMENT 16   Congress has the power to collect income taxes. (1913)

AMENDMENT 17   United States Senators are elected directly by the people. (1913)

AMENDMENT 18   Making, buying, and selling alcoholic beverages is no longer allowed. (1919)

AMENDMENT 19   Women gain the right to vote. (1920)

AMENDMENT 20   The President's term begins January 20; Senators' and Representatives' terms begin January 3. (1933)

AMENDMENT 21   (Repeals Amendment 18) Alcoholic beverages can be made, bought, and sold again. (1933)

AMENDMENT 22   The President is limited to two elected terms. (1951)

AMENDMENT 23   District of Columbia residents gain the right to vote. (1961)

AMENDMENT 24   All voter poll taxes are forbidden. (1964)

AMENDMENT 25   If the Presidency is vacant, the Vice President takes over. If the Vice Presidency is vacant, the President names someone and the Congress votes on the choice. (1967)

AMENDMENT 26   Citizens 18 years old gain the right to vote. (1971)

AMENDMENT 27   No law changing the pay for members of Congress will take effect until after an election of Representatives. (1992)

U.S. Presidents and Vice Presidents

(*Did not finish term)

1 George Washington	Apr. 30, 1789 - Mar. 3, 1797	John Adams 1
2 John Adams	Mar. 4, 1797 - Mar. 3, 1801	Thomas Jefferson 2
3 Thomas Jefferson	Mar. 4, 1801 - Mar. 3, 1805	Aaron Burr 3
Thomas Jefferson	Mar. 4, 1805 - Mar. 3, 1809	George Clinton 4
4 James Madison	Mar. 4, 1809 - Mar. 3, 1813	George Clinton
James Madison	Mar. 4, 1813 - Mar. 3, 1817	Elbridge Gerry 5
5 James Monroe	Mar. 4, 1817 - Mar. 3, 1825	Daniel D. Tompkins 6
6 John Quincy Adams	Mar. 4, 1825 - Mar. 3, 1829	John C. Calhoun 7
7 Andrew Jackson	Mar. 4, 1829 - Mar. 3, 1833	John C. Calhoun
Andrew Jackson	Mar. 4, 1833 - Mar. 3, 1837	Martin Van Buren 8
8 Martin Van Buren	Mar. 4, 1837 - Mar. 3, 1841	Richard M. Johnson 9
9 William H. Harrison*	Mar. 4, 1841 - April 4, 1841	John Tyler 10
10 John Tyler	Apr. 6, 1841 - Mar. 3, 1845	
11 James K. Polk	Mar. 4, 1845 - Mar. 3, 1849	George M. Dallas 11
12 Zachary Taylor*	Mar. 5, 1849 - July 9, 1850	Millard Fillmore 12
13 Millard Fillmore	July 10, 1850 - Mar. 3, 1853	
14 Franklin Pierce	Mar. 4, 1853 - Mar. 3, 1857	William R. King 13
15 James Buchanan	Mar. 4, 1857 - Mar. 3, 1861	John C. Breckinridge 14
16 Abraham Lincoln	Mar. 4, 1861 - Mar. 3, 1865	Hannibal Hamlin 15
Abraham Lincoln*	Mar. 4, 1865 - Apr. 15, 1865	Andrew Johnson 16
17 Andrew Johnson	Apr. 15, 1865 - Mar. 3, 1869	
18 Ulysses S. Grant	Mar. 4, 1869 - Mar. 3, 1873	Schuyler Colfax 17
Ulysses S. Grant	Mar. 4, 1873 - Mar. 3, 1877	Henry Wilson 18
19 Rutherford B. Hayes	Mar. 4, 1877 - Mar. 3, 1881	William A. Wheeler 19
20 James A. Garfield*	Mar. 4, 1881 - Sept. 19, 1881	Chester A. Arthur 20
21 Chester A. Arthur	Sept. 20, 1881 - Mar. 3, 1885	
22 Grover Cleveland	Mar. 4, 1885 - Mar. 3, 1889	Thomas A. Hendricks 21
23 Benjamin Harrison	Mar. 4, 1889 - Mar. 3, 1893	Levi P. Morton 22
24 Grover Cleveland	Mar. 4, 1893 - Mar. 3, 1897	Adlai E. Stevenson 23
25 William McKinley	Mar. 4, 1897 - Mar. 3, 1901	Garret A. Hobart 24
William McKinley*	Mar. 4, 1901 - Sept. 14, 1901	Theodore Roosevelt 25
26 Theodore Roosevelt	Sept. 14, 1901 - Mar. 3, 1905	
Theodore Roosevelt	Mar. 4, 1905 - Mar. 3, 1909	Charles W. Fairbanks 26
27 William H. Taft	Mar. 4, 1909 - Mar. 3, 1913	James S. Sherman 27
28 Woodrow Wilson	Mar. 4, 1913 - Mar. 3, 1921	Thomas R. Marshall 28
29 Warren G. Harding*	Mar. 4, 1921 - Aug. 2, 1923	Calvin Coolidge 29
30 Calvin Coolidge	Aug. 3, 1923 - Mar. 3, 1925	
Calvin Coolidge	Mar. 4, 1925 - Mar. 3, 1929	Charles G. Dawes 30

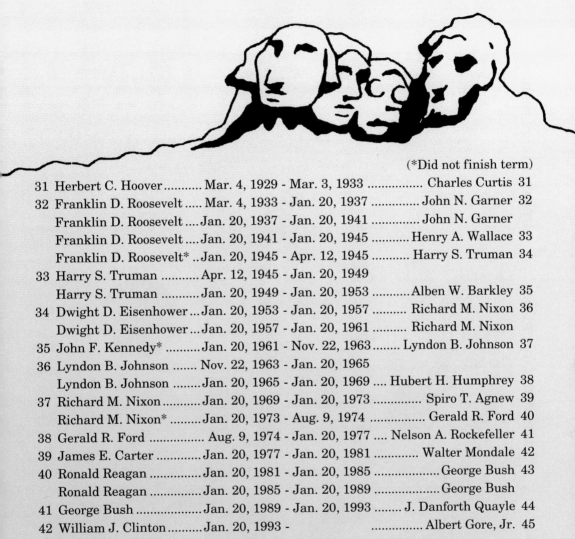

(*Did not finish term)

31 Herbert C. Hoover .... Mar. 4, 1929 - Mar. 3, 1933 .... Charles Curtis 31
32 Franklin D. Roosevelt ..... Mar. 4, 1933 - Jan. 20, 1937 .... John N. Garner 32
   Franklin D. Roosevelt ....Jan. 20, 1937 - Jan. 20, 1941 .... John N. Garner
   Franklin D. Roosevelt ....Jan. 20, 1941 - Jan. 20, 1945 .... Henry A. Wallace 33
   Franklin D. Roosevelt* ..Jan. 20, 1945 - Apr. 12, 1945 .... Harry S. Truman 34
33 Harry S. Truman .... Apr. 12, 1945 - Jan. 20, 1949
   Harry S. Truman .... Jan. 20, 1949 - Jan. 20, 1953 .... Alben W. Barkley 35
34 Dwight D. Eisenhower ...Jan. 20, 1953 - Jan. 20, 1957 .... Richard M. Nixon 36
   Dwight D. Eisenhower ...Jan. 20, 1957 - Jan. 20, 1961 .... Richard M. Nixon
35 John F. Kennedy* ....Jan. 20, 1961 - Nov. 22, 1963 .... Lyndon B. Johnson 37
36 Lyndon B. Johnson .... Nov. 22, 1963 - Jan. 20, 1965
   Lyndon B. Johnson ....Jan. 20, 1965 - Jan. 20, 1969 .... Hubert H. Humphrey 38
37 Richard M. Nixon ....Jan. 20, 1969 - Jan. 20, 1973 .... Spiro T. Agnew 39
   Richard M. Nixon* ....Jan. 20, 1973 - Aug. 9, 1974 .... Gerald R. Ford 40
38 Gerald R. Ford .... Aug. 9, 1974 - Jan. 20, 1977 .... Nelson A. Rockefeller 41
39 James E. Carter ....Jan. 20, 1977 - Jan. 20, 1981 .... Walter Mondale 42
40 Ronald Reagan ....Jan. 20, 1981 - Jan. 20, 1985 .... George Bush 43
   Ronald Reagan ....Jan. 20, 1985 - Jan. 20, 1989 .... George Bush
41 George Bush ....Jan. 20, 1989 - Jan. 20, 1993 .... J. Danforth Quayle 44
42 William J. Clinton..........Jan. 20, 1993 -   .... Albert Gore, Jr. 45

Order of Presidential Succession

1. Vice president
2. Speaker of the House
3. President pro tempore of the Senate
4. Secretary of state
5. Secretary of the treasury
6. Secretary of defense
7. Attorney general
8. Secretary of the interior
9. Secretary of agriculture
10. Secretary of commerce
11. Secretary of labor
12. Secretary of health and human services
13. Secretary of housing and urban development
14. Secretary of transportation
15. Secretary of energy
16. Secretary of education
17. Secretary of veterans affairs

1500	1520	1540	1560	1580

United States History

1492
Columbus discovers the West Indies.

1519
Magellan begins three-year voyage around the world.

1565
Spain settles St. Augustine, Florida, first permanent European city.

1588
England defeats the Spanish Armada and rules the seas.

1513
Ponce de León explores Florida.

1521
Cortez defeats Aztecs and claims Mexico for Spain.

1559
Spanish colony of Pensacola, Florida, lasts two years.

1519
Aztec empire dominates Mexico.

1570
League of the Iroquois Nations formed.

1590
English colony of Roanoke vanishes.

Science and Inventions

1507
Book on surgery is developed.

1530
Bottle corks are invented.

1543
Copernicus challenges beliefs by claiming sun-centered universe.

1585
Decimals introduced by Dutch mathematicians.

1531
Unknown comet, later named Halley's Comet, appears and causes panic.

1558
Magnetic compass invented by John Dee.

1590
First paper mill is used in England.

1509
Watches are invented.

1545
French printer Garamond sets first type.

1596
Thermometer is invented.

Literature and Life

1500
Game of bingo developed.

1536
First songbook used in Spain.

1564
First horse-drawn coach used in England.

1580
First water closet designed in Bath, England.

1507
Glass mirrors are greatly improved.

1541
Michelangelo completes largest painting, "The Last Judgement."

1582
Pope Gregory XIII introduces the calendar still in use today.

1518
Forks are first used.

1503
Pocket handkerchiefs are first used.

1538
Mercator draws map with America on it.

1599
Copper coins made.

U.S. Population: (Native American)   **(Spanish)**

approximately 1,100,000   1,021

| 1600 | 1620 | 1640 | 1660 | 1680 | 1700 |

1607
England establishes Jamestown, Virginia, first English settlement.

1620
Pilgrims found Plymouth Colony.

1629
Massachusetts Bay Colony is established.

1664
The Dutch colony of New Netherlands becomes the English colony of New York.

1673
Marquette and Joliet explore Mississippi River for France.

1609
Henry Hudson explores the Hudson River.

1619
House of Burgesses in Virginia establishes first representative government in colonies.

1634
Colony of Maryland is founded.

1682
William Penn founds Pennsylvania.

1608
Telescope is invented.

1629
Human temperature measured by physician in Italy.

1668
Reflecting telescope invented by Sir Isaac Newton.

1687
Newton describes gravity.

1641
First cotton factories begin operating in England.

1682
Halley's Comet is studied by Edmund Halley and named for him.

1609
Galileo makes first observations with telescope.

1643
Torricelli invents the barometer.

1671
First calculation machine invented.

1600
William Shakespeare's plays are performed at Globe Theatre in London.

1630
Popcorn is introduced to Pilgrims by Quadequina.

1685
First drinking fountain used in England.

1653
First postage stamps used in Paris.

1622
January 1 accepted as beginning of the year (instead of March 25).

1697
Tales of Mother Goose written by Charles Perrault.

1609
"Three Blind Mice" is written.

1658
First illustrated book for children, *World of Visible Objects in Pictures*, written by John Comenius.

(English)

| 350 | 2,302 | 26,634 | 75,058 | 151,507 |

1700	1710	1720	1730	1740

United States History

1700
France builds forts at Mackinac and Detroit and controls fur trade.

1705
Virginia Act establishes public education.

1707
England (English) and Scotland (Scots) unite and become Great Britain (British).

Scotland

England

1718
New Orleans founded by France.

1733
James Oglethorpe founds Georgia.

1733
British Molasses Act places taxes on sugar and molasses.

1735
Freedom of the press established during trial of John Peter Zenger.

1747
Ohio Company formed to settle Ohio River Valley.

Science and Inventions

1701
Seed drill that plants seeds in a row is invented by Jethro Tull.

1712
Thomas Newcomen develops first practical steam engine.

1709
The pianoforte (first piano) is invented by Christofori Bartolommeo.

1728
First dental drill is used by Pierre Fauchard.

1732
Sedatives for operations discovered by Thomas Dover.

1735
Rubber found in South America.

1742
Benjamin Franklin invents efficient Franklin stove.

1738
First cuckoo clocks invented in Germany.

Literature and Life

1700
The Selling of Joseph by Samuel Sewall is first protest of slavery.

1716
First hot-water home heating system developed.

1704
First successful newspaper in colonies, *Boston News-Letter*, is published.

1719
Robinson Crusoe written by Daniel Defoe.

1726
Gulliver's Travels written by Jonathan Swift.

1731
Ben Franklin begins first subscription library.

1736
First American cookbook is written by Mrs. E. Smith.

1744
John Newbery publishes children's book, *A Little Pretty Pocket-Book*

U.S. Population (English Colonies)

250,888	331,711	466,185	629,445	905,563

1750	1760	1770	1780	1790	1800

1750
The French
and Indian
War begins.

1763
Britain defeats France in
French and Indian War.

1781
British surrender at
Yorktown October 19.

1765
Stamp Act
tax imposed
on colonies
by Britain.

1776
Declaration of
Independence
signed at Second
Continental
Congress on July 4.

1787
The United States
Constitution is signed.

1789
George Washington
elected first president
of the United States.

1750
Flatbed
boats and
Conestoga
wagons begin
moving
settlers west.

1775
First battles
of the Revolu-
tionary War
are fought.

1781
United colonies
adopt Articles
of Confederation
as first government.

1752
Benjamin Franklin
discovers lightning
is a form of electricity.

1770
First steam
carriage is invented
by French engineer
Nicholas Cugnot.

1793
Eli Whitney
invents cotton
gin that takes
seeds out
of cotton.

1764
"Spinning Jenny"
for cotton is invented
by James Hargreaves.

1783
First balloon is flown
by Frenchmen Joseph
and Jacques Montgolfier.

1758
Sextant for
navigation
is invented by
John Bird.

1781
Uranus, first planet
not known to ancient
world, is discovered.

1798
Eli Whitney
invents
mass
production.

1752
First general
hospital is established
in Philadelphia.

1769
Venetian blinds
are first used.

1786
First ice-cream
company in America
begins production.

1764
Mozart writes
first symphony.

1782
The American
Bald Eagle
is first used
as symbol
of the United States.

1795
Food
canning is
introduced.

1757
Streetlights
are installed
in Philadelphia.

1780
The waltz
becomes
popular dance.

1790
Official U.S.
census begins.

1,170,760	1,593,625	2,148,076	2,780,369	3,929,157

| **1800** | **1810** | **1820** | **1830** | **1840** |

United States History

1800
Washington, D.C., becomes U.S. capital.

1803
Louisiana Purchase from France doubles U.S. size.

1804
Lewis & Clark explore Louisiana & Northwest Territories.

1812-1814
War of 1812 fought between U.S. and Britain.

1819
U.S. acquires Florida from Spain.

1830
Indian Removal Act forces Native Americans west of Mississippi River.

1836
Texans defend the Alamo.

1838
Cherokee Nation forced west on "Trail of Tears."

1846
Mexican War gives U.S. Southwestern territories.

1846
Britain cedes Oregon Country to U.S.

1848
Gold discovered in California

Science and Inventions

1800
The battery is invented by Count Volta.

1802
Steamboat is built by Robert Fulton.

1808
Chemical symbols are developed by Jöns Berzelius.

1816
Stethoscope invented by René Laënnec.

1819
Electromagnetism discovered by Hans Christian Oestad.

1836
Samuel Morse invents telegraph.

1839
Bicycle is invented by Kirkpatrick Macmillan.

1841
Stapler is developed.

1844
Safety match produced.

1846
Elias Howe invents sewing machine.

Literature and Life

1804
First book of children's poems is published.

1806
Gas lighting used in homes.

1812
Army meat inspector, "Uncle Sam" Wilson, inspires U.S. symbol.

1814
Francis Scott Key writes "The Star-Spangled Banner."

1816
Niepce takes first photograph.

1820
Rip Van Winkle is written by Washington Irving.

1823
A Visit from St. Nicholas written by Clement Clark Moore.

1828
Webster's Dictionary is published.

1834
Louis Braille perfects a letter system for the blind.

1835
Hans Christian Anderson publishes *Tales Told to Children.*

1849
Safety pin is invented.

U.S. Population

| 5,308,080 | 7,240,102 | 9,638,453 | 12,860,702 | 17,063,353 |

| 1850 | 1860 | 1870 | 1880 | 1890 | 1900 |

1853
National Council of Colored People is founded.

1860
Abraham Lincoln elected 16th president of the U.S.

1876
Custer defeated at Battle of Little Big Horn.

1898
U.S. defeats Spain in Spanish-American War.

1861
Civil War begins when Confederates fire on Fort Sumter.

1876
U.S. Centennial

1889
Jane Addams founds Hull House in Chicago to help immigrants.

1862
Lincoln proclaims abolition of slavery in U.S.

1869
Coast-to-coast railroad is finished in Utah.

1857
Atlantic cable is completed.

1874
Barbed wire introduced by Joseph Glidden.

1887
Radio waves produced by Hertz.

1851
Isaac Singer produces sewing machine.

1860
Internal combustion engine built by Jean Lenoir.

1876
Alexander Graham Bell invents telephone.

1893
Charles and Frank Duryea build first successful U.S. gasoline automobile.

1877
Thomas Edison invents phonograph.

1852
Elisha Otis invents first elevator with a safety brake.

1865
Antiseptic practices are introduced by Joseph Lister.

1879
Edison makes incandescent light bulb.

1896
Marconi invents wireless radio.

1851
First World's Fair is held in London, England.

1864
Red Cross is established.

1876
National Baseball League established.

1888
Pneumatic bicycle tires invented by John Dunlop.

1855
Alexander Parks produces first synthetic plastic.

1866
Root beer introduced by Elmer Hires.

1882
Malted milk produced by William Horlick.

1889
Roll film produced by George Eastman.

1852
Uncle Tom's Cabin by Harriet Beecher Stowe strengthens anti-slavery movement.

1873
Zipper invented by Whitcomb Judson.

1883
Four U.S. time zones are established.

1892
"Pledge of Allegiance" is written by F. Bellamy.

| 23,191,876 | 31,443,321 | 38,558,371 | 50,189,209 | 62,979,766 |

1900	**1905**	**1910**	**1915**	**1920**

United States History

1900
First Olympics involving women held in Paris.

1903
Orville and Wilber Wright fly first successful airplane.

1909
National Association for the Advancement of Colored People (NAACP) is founded.

1913
Income Tax Amendment establishes a tax on wages people make.

1914
Panama Canal opens.

1914
World War I in Europe begins.

1918
World War I ends in Europe.

1917
United States enters World War I.

1920
Prohibition of alcoholic beverages begins.

1920
Women given right to vote.

Science and Inventions

1901
Walter Reed discovers yellow fever comes from mosquitos.

1904
New York City develops subway system.

1905
Albert Einstein announces theory of relativity ($E=mc^2$) of time and space.

$E=mc^2$

1913
Henry Ford establishes assembly line for automobiles.

1915
Coast-to-coast telephone system established.

1922
Philo T. Farnsworth develops electron scanner for television.

1921
Vaccine for tuberculosis is discovered.

Literature and Life

1900
American Baseball League established.

1900
Hot-dog sausages created in New York City.

1903
First World Series played.

1905
First nickelodeon movie theater established in Pittsburgh.

1907
Artists Picasso and Braque create cubism.

1903
Call of the Wild written by Jack London.

1913
Boy's Life magazine published by Boy Scouts.

1917
Doughnuts created for the soldier "doughboys" fighting in World War I.

1917
American Girl magazine published by Girl Scouts.

1920
First radio station, KDKA, founded in Pittsburgh.

U.S. Population

76,212,168	92,228,496	106,021,537

| 1925 | 1930 | 1935 | 1940 | 1945 | 1950 |

1927
Charles Lindbergh flies solo across the Atlantic Ocean.

1933
President Franklin Roosevelt inaugurated and begins New Deal to end Great Depression.

1939
Germany invades Poland to begin World War II.

1945
World War II ends.

1945
United States becomes a member of the United Nations.

1931
The 102-story Empire State Building completed as tallest in the world.

1933
Prohibition of alcoholic beverages repealed.

1941
Japanese bomb Pearl Harbor Dec. 7, and U.S. enters World War II.

1947
Jackie Robinson becomes the first black major league baseball player.

1926
John Baird demonstrates his television system.

1938
Modern-type ballpoint pens developed.

1947
Edwin Land invents Polaroid camera.

1929
Clarence Birdseye introduces frozen foods.

1938
First photocopy machine produced.

1947
Bell Lab scientists invent transistor.

1930
First analog computer invented by Vannevar Bush.

1935
Radar is invented.

1926
Alexander Fleming develops penicillin.

1940
Enrico Fermi develops nuclear reactor.

1925
Potato chips are produced in New York City.

1931
"Star-Spangled Banner" becomes U.S. national anthem.

1937
First full-length animated film, *Snow White and the Seven Dwarfs,* made.

1946
Highlights for Children magazine published.

1927
Wings wins first Academy Award for motion pictures.

1927
First "talking movie," *The Jazz Singer,* made.

1938
Superman "Action Comics" created by Harry Donefield.

1947
Anne Frank's Diary of life under Nazi control is published.

1928
My Weekly Reader magazine is founded.

1939
Nestles chocolate chips are produced.

123,202,624

132,164,569

1950	1955	1960	1965	1970

United States History

1950
United States enters Korean War.

1954
Korean War ends.

1955
Rosa Parks refuses to follow segregation rules on Montgomery bus.

1955
Martin Luther King, Jr., begins organizing protests against black discrimination.

1959
Alaska becomes 49th state.

1959
Hawaii becomes 50th state.

1961
Alan Shepard becomes first U.S. astronaut in space.

1963
President John F. Kennedy assassinated in Dallas, TX.

1965
U.S. combat troops sent to Vietnam to stop communism.

1968
Martin Luther King, Jr., is assassinated.

1969
Neil Armstrong and Buzz Aldrin are first men to walk on moon.

1971
Eighteen-year-olds are given right to vote.

Science and Inventions

1951
Fluoridated water discovered to prevent tooth decay.

1953
Watson and Crick map the DNA molecule.

1954
Jonas Salk discovers polio vaccine.

1957
Russia launches first satellite, Sputnik 1, beginning Space Age.

1958
Stereo long-playing records produced.

1960
First laser invented by Theodor Maiman.

1963
Cassette music tapes developed.

1967
Cholesterol discovered as cause of heart disease.

1968
First U.S. heart transplant is performed by surgeon Norman Shumway.

1971
Space probe Mariner maps surface of Mars

Literature and Life

1950
Peanuts comic strip produced by Charles Schulz.

1951
Fifteen million American homes have television.

1952
Humpty Dumpty magazine published.

1955
Cat in the Hat produced by Theodor "Dr. Seuss" Geisel.

1957
Elvis Presley is the most popular rock 'n' roll musician in U.S.

1961
Peace Corps is established, helping others around the world.

1964
The Beatles appear on *The Ed Sullivan Show* and change American music.

1970
First Earth Day beg a focus on protectir the environment.

1970
Sounder by William Armstrong wins Newbery Award for children's literature.

1970
Sesame Street television show with Jim Henson's Muppets begins.

U.S. Population

151,325,798	179,323,175	203,302,031

1975   1980   1985   1990   1995   2000

1975
Vietnam War ends.

1979
Iran seizes U.S. hostages.

1983
Sally Ride becomes first U.S. woman in space.

1989
Berlin Wall separating East and West Germany is torn down.

1994
U.S. expands NATO (North Atlantic Trade Organization) to Eastern European nations.

1974
President Richard Nixon resigns.

1981
Sandra Day O'Connor becomes first woman on Supreme Court.

1986
Challenger spacecraft explodes, killing entire crew.

1994
Earthquake rocks California, killing more than 50 people.

1981
U.S. hostages returned from Iran after 444 days.

1991
Persian Gulf War "Operation Desert Storm" begins.

1976
Concorde becomes world's first supersonic passenger jet.

1981
Scientists identify AIDS (acquired immune deficiency syndrome).

1988
NASA reports greenhouse effect of Earth's atmosphere is caused by destruction of forests.

1974
Sears Tower (110 stories) built in Chicago.

1984
Compact disk (CDs) music players developed.

1993
Apple's Newton Writing-Pad computer introduced.

1977
Apple Computers produce first personal computer.

1983
Pioneer 10 space probe passes Neptune and leaves solar system.

1991
Environmental Protection Agency cites growing danger of hole in Earth's ozone layer.

1976
Alex Haley's African-American saga *Roots* published.

1983
Martin Luther King, Jr., Day proclaimed national holiday.

1988
Thirty million U.S. school children have access to computers.

1993
Connie Chung is named first woman to co-anchor an evening news team.

CBS

1976
United States celebrates Bicentennial.

1979
Yellow ribbons displayed in support of return of U.S. hostages in Iran.

1993
Jurassic Park features new computer film-making techniques.

1977
Star Wars becomes largest money-making movie of all time.

1987
The Whipping Boy by Sid Fleischman wins Newbery Award.

226,542,203   248,709,873

Your Handbook Index

The **index** is your personal guide to using the *Writers Express* handbook. It will help you find specific information. For example, if you want to find a list of state abbreviations so you can address a letter, you can look under *abbreviations* or under *state*. Both entries will tell you where to turn in your handbook to find the information. (See if you can find the correct page for state abbreviations using the index.)

A

A/an, 362
A lot, 362
Abbreviations, 356
    Address, 357
    Common, chart, 357
    State, 357
Abstract,
    Noun, 375
Accept/except, 362
Acronym, 334, 356
Action, 244
Active voice, 381
Address,
    Abbreviations, 357
    Punctuation of, 119, 146, 345
Adjective, 384
    Colorful, 52
    Forms, 384
Adverb, 385
    Forms, 385
Affect/effect, 362
Agreement,
    Antecedent/pronoun, 89, 378
    Subject/verb, 88, 381
Air/heir, 365
All ready/already, 363
Alliteration, 183

Allowed/aloud, 362
Alphabet,
    Manual (Sign language), 391
Alphabet poetry, 186
Amendments,
    Constitutional, 426-427
Analyzing information, 304, 307
Anecdote, 35, 98
Animal facts, 393
Ant/aunt, 363
Antagonist, 244
Antecedent, 89
Antonym, 256, 257, 258
Aphorism, 35
Apostrophe, 349
Applying information, 303, 307
Appositives,
    Punctuating, 346
Arrangement, 98
    Of sentences, 68
Articles,
    Adjectives, 384
    Constitution, 425
Assignments, completing, 318-321
Assonance, 183
Ate/eight, 363
Audience, 98
Autobiography, 244

B

Ballad, 184
Bar graph, 249
Bare/bear, 363
Beginning, 33, 41
  Of an essay, 75, 76
Bibliography, 214
  Model entries, 231
Bill of Rights, 426
Biography, 244
Bio-poem, 35
Birth stories, 203
Blew/blue, 363
Board/bored, 363
Body, 61, 98, 116, 120, 128, 144, 214
Book,
  Capitalization of titles, 354
  Making your own, 57
  Parts of, 214
  Punctuation of titles, 351
Book review (report), 132-137
  Group sharing, 327
  Models, 133, 136
Brainstorming, 98
Brake/break, 363
Bring/take, 363
Business letter, 142-147
  Addressing the envelope, 146
  Model, 145
  Parts of a, 144
  Types, 142-143
By/buy, 363

C

Call number, 210
Can/may, 363
Capital/capitol, 363
Capitalization, 352-354, 258-259
  Abbreviations, 353
  Days, months, 354
  Geographic names, 353
  Historical events, 353
Card catalog, 208-209
  On-line computer, 211
Case study, 35
Cause and effect,
  Model paragraph, 304
Cent/sent/scent, 363
Character, 244
Character sketch, 35
Checklist,
  Basics of life, 27
  Editing and proofreading, 53
  Listener, 293
  Response Sheets, 45
  Revising, 39
Children's Magazine Guide, 215
Chose/choose, 363
Chronological order, 68
Cinquain, 184
Citing sources, 231
Clarifying skills, 325
Classroom report, 220-233
  Bibliography, 231
  Giving credit, 231
  Model, 221
Classroom skills, 318-339
Clause,
  Dependent, 372
  Independent, 372
  Punctuating, 345-347
Cliche, 98
Climax, 245
Clincher sentence, 61
Close/clothes, 364
Closing, letter, 116, 120
Closing sentence, 61, 98
Clustering, 26, 30, 222-223, 243, 339
Coarse/course, 364
Collecting details, 30-31
Collection sheet, 31, 167, 173, 194, 226
Colon, 347
Combining sentences, 90-93
Comedy, 244
Comma, 345-346

Commentary, 35
Common abbreviations, 357
Common noun, 375
Comparative form, adjectives, 384
Compare, 297, 330
Complaint, letter of, 142, 143
Complete sentence, 86, 371
Completing assignments, 318-321
Complex sentence, 93, 373
Composition, 98
Compound,
    Adjective, 348
    Predicate, 86, 92, 371
    Sentence, 86, 93, 373
    Subject, 86, 92, 371
    Verb, 86, 92, 371
Computers,
    Keyboard, 422-423
    Writing with, 16-17
Concrete noun, 375
Concrete poetry, 186
Conference guidelines, 44
    Response sheets, 45
Conferencing, 42-45, 98, 326
Conflict, 244
Conjunction, 387
Consonance, 183
Constitution, U.S., 424-427
    Amendments, 426-427
    Bill of Rights, 426
    Parts of, 425
    Preamble, 425
Context clues, 256
Continents, 415
Contractions, 349
Contrast, 297, 330
Conversion tables, 253, 394-397
Cooperating skills, 44, 322-327
Coordinate conjunctions, 387
Correction symbols,
    (inside back cover)
Correlative conjunction, 387
Couplet, 184
Course/coarse, 364

Crack-up riddles, 199
Creak/creek, 364
Creative writing, 153-205

D

Dash, 348
Dates,
    Punctuation of, 345
Dear/deer, 364
Decimal,
    Fraction table, 421
    In money, 344
Decision-making guidelines, 312
Declarative sentences, 373
Define, 330
Definition poetry, 186
Demonstration speech, 276-277
Demonstrative pronoun, 379
Dependent clause, 372
Description, 62, 98
Descriptive paragraph, 62
Desert/dessert, 364
Details, 99
    Arranging, 68
    Collecting, 30-31
    Kinds of, 67
Dew/do/due, 364
Diagrams,
    Sample line, 248
    Sample picture, 248
Dialogue, 244
    Journal, 108, 109
    Punctuation, 344, 346, 350
    Writing, 196
    Writing to learn, 243
Diary, 108
Diction, 99
Dictionary, using, 258-259
    Prefixes, 260, 261-262
    Roots, 260, 264-269
    Suffixes, 260, 263
Dictionary poems, 205

Die/dye, 364
Direct address, 346
Direct object, 376
Direct quotation,
    Punctuation of, 350
Directions, giving, 138-141
Do/dew/due, 364
Documentation,
    In classroom report, 231
Doesn't/don't, 364
Double,
    Negative, 89
    Subject, 89
Drama, 244
    Writing, 192-197
Dramatic monologue, 35

E

Editing, 99
    And proofreading, 5, 7, 50-53
    Checklist, 53
    Model, 11
Editor, letter to, 143
Effect/affect, 362
Eight/ate, 363
Elements of literature, 244-245
Ellipsis, 344
Encyclopedia, using the, 212
    Sample index entry, 212
End rhyme, 183
Ending, 41,
    Of an essay, 75-76
Essay, 72-83
    Comparison and contrast, 297
    Outlining, 77
    Samples, 76, 78-83
    Types, 73
Essay test, 330
Evaluate, 299
Evaluating,
    Group work, 326
    Writing, 15, 45

Event, writing about, 81
Evidence, using, 309
Exaggeration, 99
Except/accept, 362
Exclamation point, 351
Exclamatory sentence, 373
Experiences, writing about, 63,
    110-115
Explain, 330
Explanation writing, 138-141
Exposition, 99, 245
Expository paragraph, 65
Eye/I, 364

F

Fact vs. opinion, 309
Facts about animals, 393
Falling action, 245
Family stories, writing, 46-49, 203
Fantasy, writing, 153-159
Fewer/less, 364
Figure of speech, 99, 182
Fill in the blanks test, 333
Find/fined, 364
Fir/fur, 364
First draft editing, 14, 33, 37-41, 99
First person, 245
First thoughts, 243, 339
Five W's, 30
    Poetry, 186
Focus, 99
    Finding a, 13, 31-32
    Topic sentence, 60
Foreign words,
    Greetings, 392
    Punctuation of, 351, 392
Form, 99
Forming an opinion, 309
Forms of writing, 34-35
Found poems, 204
Four/for, 364

Fraction,
Decimal table, 421
Punctuation using a hyphen, 348
Fragment sentence, 87
Free verse, 180-182, 185
Model, 181
Free writing, 27, 28, 29, 30, 99
Friendly letter, 116-121
Envelope address, 119
Form, 116-117
Model, 117
Parts of a, 116
Social notes, 120-121
Fur/fir, 364
Future perfect tense, 383
Future tense, 383

G

Gathering grid, 225-226, 296
Generalization, 99
Giving credit, 231
Goals, setting guidelines, 319
Good/well, 364
Grammar, definition, 99
Graphic organizers, 296-297
Graphs, 249-251
Greetings, foreign words, 392
Grid, gathering, 225-226, 296
Group skills, 322-327
Clarifying, 325
Cooperating, 325
Deciding, 326
Evaluating your work, 326
Listening skills, 324
Sharing, 327
Writing, 42-45
Guidelines,
Completing assignments, 321
Conferencing, 44
Good decisions, 326
Listening skills, 293, 324

Note-taking skills, 336-337
Reading to learn, 238-242
Selecting a topic, 26-27
Setting goals, 319
Test-taking skills, 328-335
Thinking and writing, 307
TV-viewing, 291

H

Haiku, 185
Hair/hare, 365
Hand signs, 391
Handwriting, *(inside back cover)*
Hare/hair, 365
Heading, letter, 116-117, 144-145
Headline, 128
Heal/heel, 365
Heard/herd, 365
Heir/air, 365
Heirloom stories, 203
Helping verbs, 380
Here/hear, 365
Hi, high, 365
Historical story, 170-175
Time line, 430-439
Hole/whole, 365
Holiday stories, 203
Hour/our, 365
Hyphen, 348

I

I/eye, 364
Ideas for writing, 24-25
Imperative sentence, 373
Importance,
Arrangement by, 68
Indefinite pronoun, 379
Independent clause, 372
Punctuation of, 345, 347
Indirect object, 376
Information speech, 277

Informative paragraph, 65
Initial, punctuation of, 344
Initialism, 356
Inside address, 144-145
Intensive pronoun, 379
Interjection, 387
    Punctuation of, 346
Internal rhyme, 183
Interrogative,
    Pronoun, 379
    Sentence, 373
Interviewing, 125
    Model, 125
Introduction, speech, 278
Invitations, 120-121
Irony, 99
Irregular verb, 381, *see chart*, 382
Italics, 351
Its/it's, 365

J

Journal, 99
    Dialogue, 108-109
    Learning log, 338-339
    Personal, 106
    Reader response, 137
    Special event, 108
Journal writing, 105-109

K

Key words,
    For test taking, 330
    On-line computer, 211
Knew/new, 365
Knight/night, 365
Knot/not, 365
Know/no, 365
Knows/nose, 365
KWL, reading strategy, 242

L

Language, sign, 391
Languages, foreign, 392
Latitude, 402
Lay/lie, 365
Lead/led, 365
Lead, writing a, 128, 130
Learn/teach, 366
Learning log, 108, 338-339
Less/fewer, 364
Letter, punctuation of plurals, 349
Letters,
    Addressing the envelope, 146
    Business letters, 142-147
    Friendly letters, 116-121
    Letter of complaint, 142, 143
    Letter of request, 142, 143, 145
    Letter to an editor, 127, 131, 142
    Punctuation of, 144, 346, 347
Levels of thinking, 300-305, 307
Library, 207-215
    Card catalog, 208-209
    Children's Magazine Guide, 215
    Computer catalog, 211
    Reference section, 212-214
Lie/lay, 365
Life map, 25
Lifelong poems, 205
Limerick, 185
Limiting the subject, 99
Line graph, 249, 250
Linking verb, 380
List, in essay tests, 330
List poetry, 187
Listening skills, 292-293, 324
    Checklist, 293
Listing, 27
Lists, punctuating, 347
Literary terms, 244-245
Location, arrangement by, 68
Longitude, 402
Loose/lose, 366
Lyric, 185

M

Made/maid, 366
Mail/male, 366
Main/Maine/mane, 366
Managing time, 320
Mapping reading strategy, 241
Maps, 403-412
   Africa, 409
   Asia, 411
   Europe, 410
   South America, 407
   United States, 408
Matching test, 332
Math skills,
   Decimals, 421
   Fractions, 421
   Metric system, 394-396
   Multiplication table, 421
   Prime numbers, 420
   Symbols, 420
   Tables of weights/measures,
      394-396
   Word problems, 416-419
May/can, 363
Meat/meet, 366
Medal/metal, 366
Memory,
   Aids, 334-335
   Details, 67
Metaphor, 100
   In riddles, 200
Methods of arrangement, 68
Metric system, 394-396
Middle, 41
   Of an essay, 75, 76
Miner/minor, 366
Modeling the masters, 96-97
Modifier, 100, 384-385
Mood, 244
Moral, 244
Multiple choice test, 333
Multiplication facts table, 421
Myth, 244

N

Name
   Poetry, 187
   Stories, 203
Narration, 100
Narrative paragraph, 63
Narrator, 244
New/knew, 365
News release, 35
News story,
   Television, 288-293
   Types of, 127
   Writing a, 123-131
Night/knight, 365
No/know, 365
Nose/knows, 365
Not/knot, 365
Note cards, 227
Notes, social, 120-121
Note-taking skills, 336-339
Noun,
   Kinds of, 375
   Uses of, 376
Novel, 245
Number,
   Of nouns, 375
   Of pronouns, 377-378
   Of verbs, 381
Numbers, 345, 356
Numerals, Roman, 421
Nutshelling, 339

O

Oar/or/ore, 366
Object, describing an, 82
Object of preposition, 376, 386
Object pronoun, 377
Objective, 100
Objective tests, 332
Observation report, 35, 148-151
   Models, 150, 151

Observe, 299
One/won, 366
On-line catalog, 211
Onomatopoeia, 183
Opinion, letter of, 127, 143
    Model, 131
Opinion statement,
    In group work, 325
    Supporting and writing, 309-311
Or/oar/ore, 366
Oral history, 35
Organize, 299
Our/hour, 365
Outline,
    Essay, 77
    Speech, 279

P

Pain/pane, 366
Pair/pare/pear, 367
Paragraph, 59-71
    Basic parts, 60-61
    Detail, 67
    Model paragraphs, 62-65
    Organizing, 66, 68
    Topic sentence, 60
    Transition and linking words, 69
    Types, 62-65
Parallelism, 100
Parentheses, 351
Parody, 35
Parts of speech, 258, 259, 374-387
Passive voice, 381
Past/passed, 367
Past perfect tense, 383
Past tense, 383
Patterns, purpose, 239
Peace/piece, 367
Pear/pare/pair, 367
Performing poems, 282-287
Period, 343-344
Person, describing a, 79

Person,
    Of pronoun, 378
Personal narrative, 100, 110-115
    Model, 111, 115
Personal portfolio, 18-19
Personal pronouns, 379
Personal writing, 105-121
    Friendly letters, 116-121
    Journal writing, 105-109
    Narratives, 110-115
Personification, 100
    In riddles, 200
Persuasion, 100
Persuasive paragraph, 64
    Speech, 277
Pet peeve, 35
Petition, 35
Phrase, 92, 372
    Appositive, 92, 346
    Combining with, 92, 372
    Kinds of, 372
    Prepositional, 92, 386
    Punctuation of, 346
Phrase poetry, 187
Picture diagram, 248
Pie graph, 249, 251
Piece/peace, 367
Place, describing a, 80
Plain/plane, 367
Planet profiles, 398-399
Planning
    Your portfolio, 18-21
    Your writing, 32-33
Plays, writing, 192-197
Plot, 245
Plot line, 245
Plurals, 349, 355

Poetic devices, 183
Poetry,
  Dictionary, 205
  Five W's, 186
  Found, 204
  Free verse, 180-182
  Invented, 186-187
  Lifelong, 205
  Performing, 282-287
  Reading and appreciating, 177-179
  Sounds of, 183
  Telephone number, 205
  Traditional forms, 184-185
  Writing, 177-187
Point of view, 245
Pointed questions, 243
Pore/pour/poor, 367
Portfolio,
  Classroom, 20-21
  Personal, 18-19
Possessive pronoun, 377
Possessives, forming, 349
Preamble, U.S. Constitution, 425
Predicate adjective, 380, 384
Predicate noun, 376, 380
Predicate of a sentence, 371
  Compound, 371
Prefix, 260, list of, 261-262
  Numerical (chart), 262
Preparing for tests, 329
Preposition, 386
Prepositional phrase, 386
Present perfect tense, 383
Present tense, 383
Presidents, United States, 428-429
  Succession to, 429
Prewriting, 5, 6, 8, 23-32, 101
Prime meridian, 402
Prime numbers, 420
Principal/principle, 367
Problem-solving guidelines, 313
Process, 101
Profile, 35
Prompts for writing, 28-29

Pronoun,
  Agreement, 378
  Antecedent, 89, 378
  Number, 378
  Person, 378
  Personal, 379
    Uses of, 377
  Types, 379
Pronunciation, 258-259
Proofreading, 5, 7, 11, 15,
  50-53, 101
    Checklist, 53
    For spelling, 272
Proper adjective, 352
Proper noun, 352, 375
Prose, 101
Protagonist, 245
Prove, 330
Publishing, 5, 54-57
Pun, 101
Punctuation marks, 343-351
Purpose, 101
Purpose patterns, 239

Q

Quatrain, 185
Question, 299, 373
Question mark, 350
Quiet/quit/quite, 367
Quotation marks, 350
  For special words, 350
  Punctuating titles, 350
  Quote, 128, 230

R

RSVP, 120
Rain/reign/rein, 367
Raise/rays/raze, 367
Rambling sentences, 87
Reader response journal, 137

Reading,
  Context clues, 256
  Pictures, 246-253
  Prefix, suffix, root, 260-269
  Reviewing, 239
  Strategies, 237-245
  Vocabulary, 255-260
Realistic stories, 164-169
  Model, 165
Recalling information, 301, 307
Recipe stories, 203
Red/read, 367
Reference books, 213
  Parts of, 214
Reflexive pronoun, 379
Refrain, 189
Reign/rain/rein, 367
Relative pronoun, 379
Repetition, 183
Report, classroom, 220-233
  Bibliography, 231
  Gathering grid, 225-226
  Model report, 221
  Sample note cards, 227
Report, observation, 148-151
Reporter, parts of a, 124
Request, letter of, 142, 143, 145
Resolution, 245
Response journal, 108, 137
Response sheets, 45
Review,
  Book, 132-137
  Models, 133, 136
Revising, 5, 7, 10, 37-41, 101
  Checklist, 39
Rewording questions, 331
Rhyme, 183, 184-185
Rhyming dictionary, 191
Rhythm, 183
Riddles, writing, 198-201
Right/write, 367
Rising action, 245
Road/rode/rowed, 367
Roman numerals, 421

Romance, 245
Roots, 260, list of, 264-269
Run-on sentence, 87

S

Salutation, 116, 117, 144
Sarcasm, 101
Scent/cent/sent, 363
Scheduling work, 320
Science report,
  Model observation report, 151
Scoring a poem, 285
Scripting a poem, 284, 287
Sea/see, 368
Seam/seem, 368
Seen/scene, 367
Selecting subjects, 26-27
Semicolon, 347
Sensory
  Detail, 101
  Poetry, 187
Sent/scent/cent, 363
Sentence, 85-97, 371
  Arrangement, 68
  Beginnings, 51
  Combining, 51, 90-93
  Completion, 27
  Errors, 87-89
  Fragments, 87
  Kinds of, 373
    Complex, 373
    Compound, 373
    Simple, 373
  Modeling, 96-97
  Parts of, 86
  Styling, 94-95
Series, words in a, 345
Set/sit, 368
Setting, 245
Setting goals, 319
Sew/so/sow, 368
Sharing in groups, 322-327

Show don't tell, 40
Sign language, 391
Signature, 116, 120, 144
Signs,
    And symbols, 247
    Plural of, 349
Simile, 101
Simple sentence, 373
Simple subject, 371
Skills,
    Listening, 324
    Test-taking, 328
    Thinking, 295-299
    Viewing, 288-291
Slang, 101
So/sew/sow, 368
Soar/sore, 368
Social notes, 120
    Models, 121
Solving problems, 313
Some/sum, 368
Son/sun, 368
Songwriting, 188-191
Special-event journal, 108
Speech,
    Model, 281
    Skills, 275-281
Spelling, 270-273
    Commonly misspelled words,
      358-361
    Dictionary, 271
    Proofreading for, 272
    Rules, 273
    Self-help guide, 270
Spontaneous writing, 26-27
SRN, 240
State abbreviations, 357
Stationery/stationary, 368
Steal/steel, 368
Stop 'n' write, 243, 339
Stories, writing,
    Family, 46-49, 203
    Fantasies, 153-159
    History, 170-175

    Realistic, 164-169
    Tall tales, 160-163
Storyboards, 204
Study-reading,
    Guidelines, 238-243
Study skills, 318-321, 329, 334-339
Style, writing with, 94-95, 101
Subject,
    Complete, 371
    Compound, 371
    Of a sentence, 371
Subject card, 208-209
Subject noun, 376
Subject pronoun, 377
Subject-verb agreement, 88, 381
Subjective, 101
Subordinate conjunction, 387
Suffix, 260, list of, 263
Sum/some, 368
Summarize, 219
Summary, writing a, 216-219
Sun/son, 368
Superlative form adjectives, 384
Supporting details, 101
Syllabication, 258-259
    Use of hyphen, 348
Symbols, 247
    Correction, (*inside back cover*)
    Math, 420
Synonym, 256-259
Synthesizing information, 305, 307

T

Tables, 252
    Of weights and measures, 394-396
Tail/tale, 368
Take/bring, 363
Tall tales, writing, 160-163
Teach/learn, 366
Telephone number poems, 205
Television viewing, 288-291
Tense of verbs, 383

Terse verse, 187
Test,
Essay, 330-331
Objective, 332-333
Test-taking skills, 328-335
Than/then, 368
Thank-you notes, 120-121
Their/there/they're, 368
Theme, 101, 245
Thesaurus, 257
In songwriting, 191
Thinking,
Better, 295-299
Clearly, 308-313
Creatively, 313
Graphic organizers, 296-297
Logically, 308-313
Moves, 299
Thinking and writing, 300-307
Guidelines, 307
Levels of thinking, 300
Third person, 245
This is my life list, 24
Threw/through, 369
Time,
Management, 320
Punctuation of, 347
Time capsule, 35
Time line, historical, 430-439
Title card, 208-209
Title-down paragraph, 305
Titles,
Adding, 41
Capitalization, 354
Punctuation of, 350-351
To/too/two, 369
Tone, 245
Topic sentence, 60, 101
Topic web, 222-223
Topics,
Guidelines for selecting, 26-27,
222-224
Sample, 28-29
Total effect, 245

Traditional poetry, 184-185
Tragedy, 245
Transitions, 69, 101
Travelogue, 35
True/false test, 332
Two/to/too, 369
Types of sentences, 373

U

Underlining, as italics, 351
Understanding information, 302, 307
United States,
Constitution, 424-427
Map, 405
Presidents, 428-429
Unsent letters, 339
Usage and commonly misused words,
362-369
Using maps, 400-402

V

Venn diagram, 297
Verb, 371, 380
Action, 380
Helping, 380
Irregular, 381, *see chart*, 382
Linking, 380
Number, 381
Passive/active, 381
Tense, 383
Vivid, 52
Verse, 177-191
Viewing skills, 288-291
Visualizing, 335
Vivid details, 40-41, 95
Verbs, 52
Vocabulary,
Building skills, 255-269
Context clues, 256
Notebook, 256
Voice, writer's, 101

W

Waist/waste, 369
Wait/weight, 369
Way/weigh, 369
Wear/where, 369
Weather/whether, 369
Web, 222-223
Week/weak, 369
Weekly planner, 320
Weight/wait, 369
Weights and measures, 394-397
Well/good, 364
What am I riddle, 200-201
Where/wear, 369
Whether/weather, 369
Which/witch, 369
Who/which/that, 369
Who/whom, 369
Whole/hole, 365
Who's/whose, 369
Won/one, 366
Word choice,
    Specific, 52
Word history, 258, 259
Word pictures, studying, 246-253
Word problems, 416-419
Wordy sentence, 87
World maps, 403-412
Would/wood, 369
Write/right, 367
Writing,
    A lead, 130
    About a condition, 83
    About a person, 79
    About a place, 80
    About an event, 81
    About an object, 82
    About experiences, 81, 105-106,
        110-115
    An explanation, 138-141
    As a learning tool, 315-317
    Forms, 34-35
    Portfolio, 18-21

Prompts, 28-29
Terms, 98-101
To learn, 243, 315-317, 338-339
To persuade, 64, 127, 131, 277
With a computer, 16-17
With style, 94-95
Writing assignments,
    Correction symbols,
        (inside back cover)
    Guidelines, 12-15
Writing process, 3-11
    Editing and proofreading, 5, 7, 11,
        15, 50-53
    First draft, 5, 6, 9, 14, 33
    Guidelines, 12-15
    Plan, a basic, 32
    Prewriting, 5, 6, 8, 12-13, 23-32
    Revising, 5, 7, 10, 14, 37-41
    Terms, 98-101
    Topics, 29

Y

Your/you're, 369